MW00617991

Rewriting the Old Testament in Anglo-Saxon Verse

NEW DIRECTIONS IN RELIGION AND LITERATURE

This series aims to showcase new work at the forefront of religion and literature through short studies written by leading and rising scholars in the field. Books will pursue a variety of theoretical approaches as they engage with writing from different religious and literary traditions. Collectively, the series will offer a timely critical intervention to the interdisciplinary crossover between religion and literature, speaking to wider contemporary interests and mapping out new directions for the field in the early twenty-first century.

ALSO AVAILABLE FROM BLOOMSBURY:

Blake. Wordsworth. Religion, Jonathan Roberts
Do the Gods Wear Capes? Ben Saunders
England's Secular Scripture, Jo Carruthers
Glyph and the Gramophone, Luke Ferretter
John Cage and Buddhist Ecopoetics, Peter Jaeger
Late Walter Benjamin, John Schad
The New Atheist Novel, Arthur Bradley and Andrew Tate
Victorian Parables, Susan E. Colón

FORTHCOMING:

Faithful Reading, Mark Knight and Emma Mason

Rewriting the Old Testament in Anglo-Saxon Verse

Becoming the Chosen People

SAMANTHA ZACHER

B L O O M S B U R Y

LONDON · NEW DELHI · NEW YORK · SYDNEY

Bloomsbury Academic

An imprint of Bloomsbury Publishing Plc

50 Bedford Square   175 Fifth Avenue
London   New York
WC1B 3DP   NY 10010
UK   USA

www.bloomsbury.com

Bloomsbury is a registered trade mark of Bloomsbury Publishing Plc

First published 2013

© Samantha Zacher, 2013

British Library Cataloging-in-Publication Data
A catalogue record for this book is available from the British Library.

ISBN: PB: 978-1-4411-8560-0
HB: 978-1-4411-3477-6
ePub: 978-1-4411-2110-3
PDF: 978-1-4411-5093-6

Library of Congress Cataloging-in-Publication Data
A catalog record for this book is available from the Library of Congress

Typeset by Integra Software Services Pvt. Ltd.
Printed and bound in India

For Morris Zacher
zichrono l'vrachah

Contents

List of Figures

Preface: Becoming the Chosen People

*Wee shall find that the God of Israell is among us,
when ten of us shall be able to resist a thousand of
our enemies, when hee shall make us a prayse and
glory, that men shall say of succeeding plantacions:
the lord make it like that of new England.*

— JOHN WINTHROP, "A MODELL OF CHRISTIAN CHARITY,"
WRITTEN ON BOARDE THE ARRABELLA,
ON THE ATTLANTIK OCEAN. ANNO 1630[1]

*The Lord of Angels wishes to fulfill now what
He had promised long ago in days of old to our forefathers
with a covenant; if you will hold his holy teachings,
you may hereafter overcome every enemy, and conquer
every powerful court and every beer-hall of warriors
between the two seas. May your glory be great!*

—EXODUS, LINES 558–64, CA. 1000[2]

When the Puritans came to the New World, they envisioned their sojourn as a second Exodus, and the formation of their nation as an act of divine destiny. They used this scriptural analogy to identify themselves as the New Israel. In the words of Conrad Cherry, "Ecclesiastical and civic leaders in New England conceived of America as a place where a protestant reformation of church and society could be completed—a task that had not been carried out in England and Europe."[3] The sojourning pilgrims "envisioned their journey to these shores less as an escape from religious persecution than as a positive mission for the construction of a model Christian society."[4] Like the Israelites of old, they perceived themselves to be on an "errand in the wilderness"; their purpose was to build a holy commonwealth in which the people were covenanted with God by their pledge to erect a Christian society. For Puritan writers, preachers, and legislators, the biblical Exodus provided a template for their own migration myth and a model for religious and political freedom.

In the wake of independence from Britain, this self-comparison continued to provide a powerful paradigm for the construction of an American national identity. The New Israel was "transformed into a republic; a colonial destiny became a national destiny."[5] Preachers such as John Winthrop, Nicholas Street, and Samuel Langdon compared the constitution to the laws of Moses, and the social contract supporting these laws to a new covenant.[6] The comparison to ancient Israel was no mere allegory. This biblical paradigm was used in the service of the ideals of exceptionalism, separatism, and ultimately liberation from Britain, all of which were performed under the banner of enlightenment. The basic analogy was pervasive not only in the religious sphere, but also in the rhetoric and political language of the Founding Fathers. In their hands, the story of ancient Israel came to serve as an avatar for American nationalism itself.[7]

One Founding Father—Thomas Jefferson—saw Anglo-Saxon England as an important way station in the transmission of this status of "chosenness" to England and then to America.[8] Jefferson mapped this transmission from the Britons to the Anglo-Saxons, and then eventually to Protestant America. By asserting an ancestry that pre-dated the schisms in the English church, Jefferson could position Americans as the true descendants of the earliest English Germanic settlers. Old Testament narratives played a central and defining ideological role in transmission. In 1776, when the First Committee was established to design a Great Seal for the United States, two of its members—Benjamin Franklin and Thomas Jefferson—turned to the story of Exodus for inspiration. Franklin proposed the image of "Moses lifting his hand and the Red Sea dividing, with Pharaoh in his chariot being overwhelmed by the waters." This image was to be accompanied by the motto "Rebellion to tyrants is obedience to God," a slogan that deliberately conflated political and religious liberation as just causes for revolt.[9] Jefferson proposed a close variation. He wanted the front side of the seal to represent "the children of Israel in the wilderness, led by a cloud by day and pillar of fire by night"; and the reverse to contain an image of "Hengest and Horsa, the [fifth-century] Saxon chiefs from whom we claim the honor of being descended, and whose political principles and form of government we have assumed."[10] Jefferson's two-sided seal established a striking genealogy. For him, the Exodus narrative was most productively filtered and understood through the historical and mythical lens of the Germanic migration to, and conquest of, Britain.[11]

Jefferson, to be sure, had a unique stake in comparing the respective nationalist mythologies of ancient Israel, Anglo-Saxon England, and colonial America.[12] He was committed to establishing Anglo-Saxon law and political institutions, including Old English language, as models for contemporary American governance and its own distinctive vernacular.[13] Jefferson had tried (and generally failed) to establish a widespread educational reform in schools that would teach "Anglo-Saxon" grammar and literature alongside other ancient and modern languages as the true linguistic ancestor of present-day English. He had also been deeply invested in linking American Constitutionalism to Anglo-Saxon law. In his letter to Major John Cartwright (dated June 5, 1824), Jefferson enthusiastically endorsed the genealogy proposed by his correspondent (in his 1823 book *The English Constitution Produced and Illustrated*), which claimed that Anglo-Saxon law was the direct ancestor of English law.[14]

The imaginative lineage linking colonial and constitutional America back to the Anglo-Saxon period provides us with a powerful starting point for analysing the parallel development of the ethnogenetic myth of chosenness in the earliest English literature. In a broader study of Anglo-Saxon "migration and mythmaking," Nicholas Howe devoted a chapter to the analysis of the Old English poem, *Exodus*, in which he argued that the eponymous biblical text formed a framing analogy for the fifth-century Germanic migration to Britain. Howe's thesis was that "the journey of the Israelites across the Red Sea offered the poet of the Old English *Exodus* a model for reconciling the remembered pagan past of the Anglo-Saxons with their enduring Christian present."[15] He argued that this "biblical narrative of a dispossessed people's journey to a new homeland was particularly resonant for the Anglo-Saxons because of their ancestral migration from continent to island[;] the narrative became exemplary because the record of conversion—and thus of the pagan past—was celebrated in the cultural memory."[16]

According to Howe, the Hebrews of the biblical Exodus doubled for the pagan Germanic conquerors coming to Britain. He saw the analogy as applying solely to the past foundational moment of the Germanic transmarine migration. Anglo-Saxon writers recast their own conquest and migration as "a biblical event that predated the coming of Christ" because they were "neither able nor willing to discard their continental history."[17] For Howe, the basis for comparison between ancient Israel and Anglo-Saxon England collapsed once the Anglo-Saxons converted to Christianity. From this point, as the argument goes, the pre-Christian "English" were relegated to the rank of the formerly chosen people, and the new Christian *genus* assumed the position of rightful inheritor.

Important and groundbreaking as Howe's observations are, his analysis of the trope of migration in *Exodus* misjudges and, to a degree, distorts the purpose and performative force of the poem (namely, what the poem *does* as well as *what it communicates*). Reading the primary historical operation of the poem as nostalgia, he sees in it a regressive rather than a progressive utopian force at work. In this book, I hope to demonstrate that nostalgia is by no means the sole motivation for the use of this trope, either in *Exodus* or, indeed, in Old English Old Testament poetry in general. Rather, Old Testament poets used the central biblical theme of divine election as a contemporary instantiation of a political theology that is already worked out in scripture itself. Anglo-Saxon writers in different generations consciously constructed their own *gens* as the New Israel. In other words, far from merely serving as nostalgic reminders of former greatness, the Anglo-Saxon poets adopted the Old Testament narratives in order to make sense of their own political and religious situation. Bede used the trope of chosenness in his (eighth century) *Historia Ecclesiastica* to establish his own *gens Anglorum* as the New Israel, united under one church. From the age of Alfred onward (ninth century), West-Saxon kings used Old Testament iconography to assert divinely mandated rule and concretize the conception of a united "English nation." And, by the tenth century, biblical poets used the scriptural theme of chosenness in order to symbolize the ongoing covenant between the English people and God. The Old Testament trope of chosenness offered a powerful expression of religious community building and political self-understanding in Anglo-Saxon texts.

Three Old English poems form the centerpiece of this book— *Exodus*, *Daniel*, and *Judith*. I have chosen these poems in particular because they provide a range of artistic and cultural responses to these canonical and deuterocanonical books of the Old Testament, as well as to the Jewish laws, practices, and beliefs that are depicted and invariably distorted in them.[18] The authors of these anonymous texts draw on a wide variety of biblical media, including different versions of the bible, liturgical readings, intervening patristic commentaries, and oral legend. Each poem represents a unique instantiation of political theology. On the surface, the aim of these texts is the conservation and recuperation of the cultural and religious world of the Israelites as depicted in the biblical texts. The poets valorize the faith, observance, and laws of the Hebrews and uniformly present a positive view of righteous Old Testament Hebrews, and of their rituals and practices. They also accentuate and exaggerate the ethnogenetic myths that lie at the heart of the Pentateuch to support their own politico-theological perspectives. Yet in each case the project of recuperation is balanced by opposing tensions. The poems invariably present the Israelites in paradoxical terms—on the one hand, as the chosen people of God, and on the other hand, as a nation to be superseded by Christians. Thus, the *Exodus*-poet both celebrates God's covenant with the Israelites and, at the same time, regards it as being of transitory status. Similarly, the *Daniel*-poet exalts the chosenness of the faithful Israelites while arguing that their privileged status has been transferred to a new community of believers in Christ. Finally, the *Judith*-poet both lauds and represses aspects of Judith's physical and religious "otherness," in order to present her as a resplendent paradigm of faith and military prowess. In sum, the Anglo-Saxon biblical poems establish and at the same time contest the exemplary status of the Israelites, marking their chosenness as a model for imitation, as well as a temporary status to be awarded *in translatio* to the poems' Christian readers. By absorbing and reapplying the ethnogenetic myths of the Old Testament, Old English rewritings of biblical narratives represent a vital source of Anglo-Saxon religious identity and the constitution of community.

Scholars have noted for a long time this dependence on biblical narratives (after all, *Judith* was one of the first Old English poems to be edited). But there has been no satisfactory treatment of the peculiar methods by which biblical poets reproduced and reconstituted Old Testament texts under new conditions of interpretation. This book therefore begins with a seemingly simple premise—that Old English Old Testament poems should be studied first and foremost as *literature*. They do not, as is sometimes supposed, represent straightforward or simple channels for the transmission of wholesale biblical texts and narratives or patristic exegesis.[19] Rather, the poems both announce their status as derivative texts, by replicating and filtering biblical, liturgical, and exegetical sources, and claim a novel status as original and independent *works* that stand in need of exegesis. *Exodus*, *Daniel*, and *Judith* are all "strong translations" of a type, even though the precise aesthetic, religious, theological, and political mechanisms that make them "strong" vary widely. The qualifier "strong" here is to be taken in Harold Bloom's sense when he uses it to distinguish between "strong poets," who perform "strong misreadings" of their precursors, and "weak poets," who merely reproduce ideas as though following "a kind of doctrine."[20] The poems all retell and adapt biblical materials derived from, and associated with, the Old Testament texts, but at the same time they radically reframe, change, and embellish them in order to give expression to new ideas. They also transmit and update biblical materials for their own historical situation, participating in what is considered the ongoing project of *translatio studii*, which marks the transfer of culture, knowledge, and learning from one era, set of authors, or center of learning to another.

Read in this way, the Old Testament poems of the Anglo-Saxon era present a significant, if often overlooked, chapter in the history of the vernacularization and interpretation of the bible in the Middle

Ages. They offer creative and entirely original poetic responses to the bible and its political theologies, and present an important bridge between the celebrated biblical verse epics of Late Antiquity and the vibrant tradition of Latin biblical paraphrase that extended well into the late Middle Ages.[21] The poems also inaugurate a long tradition of scriptural paraphrase, translation, and epic rewriting in English—an enterprise that may be seen to culminate in Milton's *Paradise Lost*. When read in the context of this continuing tradition, one might detect in Anglo-Saxon Old Testament poetry the seeds of an early English national epic, since the poems transplant and transform portions of the epic account of the Old Testament into English idiom and imagination. Such "epic" status has sometimes been conferred upon *Beowulf*, the longest and most widely read poem in Old English. But while *Beowulf* is set in a glorified, heroic Scandinavian past, without a single reference to England, the Old Testament poetry looks Janus-like back to the past of ancient Israel as its own ancestral history, and at the same time, to the future of its own "chosen" people, as the poems exhort their audiences to "hear," "celebrate," and "experience" its living message. The poets ensured that the original covenant forged between God and the Israelites is not only remembered, but also carried forward in Anglo-Saxon England.

Notes

1 Quoted from Cherry (1971: 40).
2 Translation mine, from *Exodus*, ed. Lucas (1994).
3 Cherry (1971: 26).
4 Cherry (1971: 26).
5 Cherry (1971: 61).
6 Hoberman (2011) contextualizes the ideologies that shaped America as a "New Israel" by comparing them with actual interactions between Protestants and Jews in the colonies.
7 The claim to represent the "New Israel" was hardly unique to the founding mythology of colonial America. Indeed, writers going back all the way to antiquity had utilized similar claims of chosenness in

the service of constructing centralized political, religious, and cultural ideologies. See further Hughes (2003: 19–44). In England, William Tyndale, the biblical translator, played an especially important role in the dissemination of this textual trope. Tyndale's first edition had been suppressed by Henry VIII. In his revised preface to the second edition of his translation of the New Testament (1534), Tyndale identified the single central theme of all Holy Scripture as God's covenant with his chosen people. He envisioned the covenant as applicable not only to the ancient Israelites, but also, by extension, to Protestant English of his day. He urged that "if we meek ourselves to God, to keep all his laws, after the example of Christ [...] then God hath bound himself unto us to keep and make good all the mercies promised in Christ, throughout all scripture." Tyndale gave credit to his medieval literary sources. In his preface to the book of Jonah, for example, he quoted the sixth-century British historian Gildas who had employed the trope of Old Testament election first to establish the Britons (i.e. indigenous Celtic peoples) as the chosen nation of God, and then to explain the Germanic conquest of Britain in the fifth century as a consequence of God's wrath upon formerly chosen people. Tyndale cited the sinfulness of the fifth-century Britons as a warning to present-day English to repent and to accept the new truth of Protestantism. Gildas's analogy, as we shall see, provided a basic template for English writers (such as Bede, Alcuin, and Wulfstan) who sought to define their own *gens Anglorum* as the New Israel.

8   For Puritan writers, the most important point of origin, and the basis for conscious imitation, had undoubtedly been the Reformation in England, which established Protestantism as a return to the Truth of scripture.

9   Cherry (1971: 65).

10   Howe (1989: 1) and Frantzen (1990: 15–18) both discuss Jefferson's design for the seal and its cultural ancestry going back to Anglo-Saxon England. See also Cherry (1971: 65).

11   Neither seal by Jefferson or Franklin was adopted. The winning design was submitted by Charles Thomson (depicting the familiar rising eagle with a scroll in its beak containing the motto *E Pluribus Unum*. For images and descriptions of the seals, see http://www. greatseal.com/committees/firstcomm/.

12   Related claims have persisted in many different forms to the present day. The anti-Semitic terrorist group Christian Identity Movement has been described as "an anti-Semitic group who would see Anglo-Saxons as the special chosen people of the Old

Testament, not the Jews" (Dillinger 2008: 58). They espouse Anglo-Israelism: this is belief that the Anglo-Saxons (and their descendants to present-day Britain, Canada, and the United States) are the true descendants of the ten lost tribes of Israel.

13   Jefferson was a scholar of Anglo-Saxon language, literature, and history. He campaigned for Anglo-Saxon language and law to be taught in universities. For Jefferson's political and linguistic views (and the important intersections between them), and an account of his early English book collection, see Hauer's excellent article (1983: 879–98).

14   Jefferson wrote, "Your derivation of [the English Constitution] from the Anglo-Saxons, seems to be made on legitimate principles. Having driven out the former inhabitants of that part of the island called England, they became aborigines as to you, and your lineal ancestors. They doubtless had a constitution; and although they have not left it in a written formula, to the precise text of which you may always appeal, yet they have left fragments of their history and laws, from which it may be inferred with considerable certainty.... And although this constitution was violated and set at naught by Norman force, yet force cannot change right. A perpetual claim was kept up by the nation, by their perpetual demand of a restoration of their Saxon laws; which shews they were never relinquished by the will of the nation."

15   Howe (1989: 72).

16   Howe (1989: 72). Howe admits to the limitations of his own analogy: "the correspondence between Anglo-Saxon and Old Testament histories was by no means exact; the Germanic tribes that came to Britain were more dispossessors than dispossessed. And the lands they left could not easily be construed as Egypt. This looseness, however, gave the correspondence its imaginative power, for it could be used by the Anglo-Saxons to record their migration and thus locate its place in Christian history. *Exodus* is the densest of Old English biblical poems because it expresses the parallel between the first Exodus and the tribal migration across the North Sea.... Far from being a translation or paraphrase, the Old English *Exodus* represents the rarer achievement by which a foreign story is absorbed into the native imagination and idiom" (Howe 1989: 72–3).

17   Howe (1989: 72).

18   Five major poems, or sequences of poems, comprise the corpus of Old English Old Testament poetry. These include metrical translations of the Psalms, *Genesis A, Exodus, Daniel*, and *Judith*. The standard editions of these poems are as follows: the *Metrical*

Psalms are edited in ASPR V; *Genesis A*, *Exodus*, and *Daniel* in ASPR I; and *Judith* in ASPR IV. The final poem is included in this group because even though the book of Judith was not included in the Hebrew canon, it was regarded as canonical or at least deuterocanonical in the Anglo-Saxon period, following Jerome's Vulgate. I use the term "deuterocanonical" to refer to Jewish writings that were not included in the Hebrew biblical canon, but were treated as canonical (or semicanonical) in the Catholic bible from Jerome forward. The Protestant church declared the book of Judith apocryphal after the Council of Trent. See Chapter 3.

19 Wright (2012: 121–7) provides an excellent overview of recent and past scholarship on Old English Old Testament poetry.

20 Bloom (2011:13). For a more detailed explication of "strong translation" as it might be applied to Anglo-Saxon poetry, see Chapter 2.

21 Morey (2000) offers an in-depth analysis of Middle English biblical literature and of the different methods of versification and adaptation of scripture in this later era.

Acknowledgments

I began to work on this book shortly after my father became seriously ill with pancreatic cancer. The project came as a welcome distraction during a very trying period. I now see the book in a very different light—as a celebration and commemoration of the intellectual and spiritual legacy that my father left behind. My father was a passionate teacher of Jewish religion and philosophy, Torah and Talmud. As a child and young adult, I shared this intellectual and spiritual life with him: I attended Jewish day school for the first eighteen years of my life and studied Jewish and Hebrew subjects as part of my everyday curriculum. My graduate and professional career led me on a somewhat different path in medieval studies, where I focused on early English Catholic sermons. Only recently have I come to realize that these ventures were not so very different—the methodologies I used to analyse medieval texts were never far from the techniques I learned in Talmudic study. This book is a self-conscious attempt to bring together the two worlds of Jewish learning and Anglo-Saxon studies. I only wish my father could have lived long enough to wrangle with me over my interpretations, and to see in parts of this work the indelible imprint of his teaching and *ahavah*.

I want to thank the series editors, Emma Mason and Mark Knight, for believing in this project and for giving Anglo-Saxon studies a place and voice in their cutting-edge series on *Religion and Literature*. I am also grateful to Nicholas Watson and Daniel Donahue for inviting me to present a preliminary version of my chapter on *Daniel* at the Harvard Medieval Colloquium, where I received enormously helpful suggestions from the esteemed faculty and vibrant students who attended my lecture. Selected portions of the same chapter were published separately, in a slightly different form, as "The Chosen Peoples: Spiritual Identities," in the *Oxford Handbook of Medieval English Literature*, eds. Elaine Treharne and Greg Walker (Oxford University Press, 2010), 457–77. I thank the publishers for permission to reprint these passages. I also want to thank the congregation at synagogue Beth-Hillel Beth-El in Philadelphia for inviting me to give a lecture on the *Exodus* chapter as a scholar-in-residence this past year. The questions asked of me in that forum forced me to think about my project in exciting and different ways, and to communicate my thoughts to a wider audience. I also owe a special thanks to Rabbi Neil Cooper and to David Weinstein, my father's best friend and intellectual sparring partner, for their helpful discussions. I am also beholden to my colleague Eric Cheyfitz for his willingness to discuss this topic with me in the hallways of Goldwin Smith and over lunch. I am grateful to Andy Orchard, Mark Amodio, Roberta Frank, Toni Healey, Fred Biggs, Tom Hall, Bob DeMaria, Elaine Treharne, Steve Harris, and Charlie Wright, and all my medievalist colleagues at Cornell for their long-term support. I also thank my beloved mother, Linda Zacher, and my dear friends Elizabeth Anker, Lyrae Van Clief-Stefanon, and Jacob and Lissette Schoenly, who supported me personally throughout this whole venture. Mark Amodio, Tom Hill, and Andy Galloway deserve my special gratitude for reading portions of the manuscript; they are not to blame for whatever mistakes may remain. I am also deeply appreciative of the hard work put into this book by the production team at Bloomsbury Press, and I owe a special thanks to Avinash Singh, for being both patient and encouraging at every step. My greatest debt is to my amazing husband, Peter Gilgen, who read several versions of the manuscript and offered his sharp and always brilliant comments and suggestions. I couldn't have written this book without his criticisms, and indeed without his love, patience, and support.

Introduction

Encountering the Old Testament in Anglo-Saxon England

The mechanics of reading, learning, and even hearing about the bible were very different in the Early Middle Ages than they are today. Complete copies of the Latin bible were difficult to come by and hard to use because of their size and weight.[1] When they circulated in monastic and clerical libraries, or among privileged lay individuals and intellectuals, it was most often as partial collections that each contained only a few biblical texts.[2] These partial copies were less expensive to produce and infinitely more portable than full bibles.[3] The few grand pandects containing the full sequence of texts of the Old and New Testament—such as the Codex Amiatinus (produced at the end of the seventh century at Bede's monastery of Wearmouth–Jarrow) and the late tenth-century codex now in the British Library (where its shelf mark is Royal 1. E. VII+VIII)—were housed at great monasteries.[4]

Latin texts of the bible were, of course, not understood by everyone. Thus, by the end of the eleventh century, large portions of the bible had been translated into English. Vernacular translations of the four Gospels had been produced by the second half of the tenth century, and by the beginning of the eleventh, key portions of the Old Testament had been translated, including parts of Genesis, most of Exodus, and much of Leviticus, Numbers, Deuteronomy, and Joshua.[5] These manuscript collections of Old Testament texts, known respectively as the Hexateuch (from Genesis to Joshua) and the Heptateuch (adding portions of Judges), were lavishly illustrated and beautifully appointed, presumably indicating that they served as show copies.[6] The image of the "horned Moses" on the cover of this book (reprinted from MS Cotton Claudius B.IV, fol. 136v) is one example of the rich and provocative program of biblical illumination in this tradition.[7] Moses—gigantic, beatified, and, of course, "horned"—emerges like a colossus, blessed and guided by the hand of God. The image is a fitting avatar for the present project. On the one hand, it exemplifies the originality of Anglo-Saxon exegetical and artistic minds: the sequence of images of the "horned Moses" in this relatively humble insular manuscript (MS Cotton Claudius B.IV) represents the first attested appearance of this figure in art history, preceding Michelangelo's sculpture of the "horned Moses" (housed in San Pietro in Vincoli, Rome; 1513–15) by over 500 years.[8] On the other hand, it embodies a prevailing attitude toward Old Testament Hebrews in Anglo-Saxon England. While the image of the "horned Moses" is ostensibly the ancestor of the damaging anti-Judaic stereotype of the "horned Jew," which comes to represent carnal difference and willful otherness, in Anglo-Saxon England and indeed throughout much of the Middle Ages, the "horned Moses" represents victory, power, and divine election.[9] Although later artists (such as Michelangelo) would depict Moses, still reverently, with horns emerging directly from his head, the Cotton Claudius Moses wears his as a removable headdress, indicating his spiritual, but not permanent physical, otherness.

For most people in the Early Middle Ages, the book—and perhaps especially the bible—was an "extraordinary and revered medieval icon."[10] The individual's limited access to the bible in the Early Middle Ages, however, required alternative and creative means of disseminating, reinforcing, and commenting on biblical narratives and traditions in the vernacular. Monks and clergy learned, studied, and contemplated Old Testament narratives and traditions through a variety of activities and sources.[11] Latin lections were recited regularly as part of the liturgy (in both the monastic and secular offices), read aloud in the monastic refectory, expounded upon in sermons and biblical commentaries, and contemplated privately through *lectio divina* (the meditative reading of scripture).[12] It is difficult to gauge what proportion of monks and clergy required instruction and translation in the vernacular, especially since the situation could vary dramatically according to location and time period. Alfred the Great famously complained about the fallen and wretched state of Latin learning in England in the ninth century (in his Preface to the *Pastoral Care*), as did homilists in the tenth and eleventh centuries.[13] Though the situation likely improved in the larger monasteries both during and after the tenth-century Benedictine reform, it is doubtful whether competency in Latin changed significantly in the smaller, parochial houses.

The channels for biblical learning were considerably more limited for the majority of laypeople. Except for the privileged and the wealthy, lay audiences received teaching about the Old Testament principally through sermons delivered in English, and perhaps (though this is more speculative) through parts of the liturgy recited in the vernacular.[14] There were also the visual arts available to both audiences in the form of frescoes, paintings, and sculpture in churches and on sacred objects. These artifacts not only depicted biblical scenes, but also frequently employed typology, constructed through the juxtaposition of conventionally paired Old and New Testament scenes.[15] One example of such an elaborate visual program is the impressive collection of panel-paintings alleged to have been brought back from Rome and displayed by Benedict Biscop at his joint monastery at Monkwearmouth–Jarrow between 675 and 686. Bede describes its details in his *Lives of Abbots* (*Historia Abbatum*) in sumptuous ekphrasis and asserts that the images at Jarrow were intended "not to delight the eye but to enlighten the soul," and to "benefit the unlettered by reminding them, on the one hand, of the grace of God and, on the other, of the perils of the last Judgment." [16]

From a certain perspective, these pictorial representations offer a visual analogy for Old English Old Testament poetry. The poems do not straightforwardly transmit biblical narratives and scenes: rather they encompass larger metonymic fields of scriptural tradition. In the case of the most allusive, typologically sophisticated, and obscure poetry, it seems likely that the poetry functioned as an *aide-mémoire*, designed to refresh the reader's or listener's memory of the corresponding biblical narratives. Montages of carefully chosen images and episodes were used to elicit the audience's active participation and to enable them to supply additional context drawn from their own mental store of biblical texts, liturgy, and patristic commentary.[17]

Biblical Poetry in Context: Getting Beyond the Apophatic Approach

Given the central importance conferred in present-day scholarship, companions, and primers upon heroic poems such as *Beowulf* and *The Battle of Maldon*, or elegiac and religious verse such as *The Wanderer* and *The Dream of the Rood*, it may be surprising to learn that Old Testament poetry comprises roughly a third of the extant corpus of Old English poetry. This finding is consistent with Malcolm Godden's well-documented assertion that the Old Testament was *the* chief resource and source of inspiration for Anglo-Saxon literary, visual, and theological productions. According to Godden, "poets, preachers, historians, even kings and generals found it an ever-useful storehouse of information and inspiration; its great collections of stories, poems, proverbs and prophecies provided a rich literary tradition for the Anglo-Saxons which both complemented and challenged the literary tradition of the Germanic inheritance." [18] Godden's assessment is brought into further relief by Barbara Raw's observation that few Old English poems are actually based on the New Testament: in treating subjects like Nativity, Passion, and Resurrection, Anglo-Saxon writers "did not draw primarily upon the Gospel texts: their main sources were the liturgy, apocryphal writings such as the Gospel of Nicodemus, Latin homilies and the traditions of the Church." [19]

What could explain this pronounced Anglo-Saxon preference for Old Testament sources? One answer is that Old Testament narratives were infinitely more compatible with the traditional Germanic heroic ethos than were their New Testament counterparts.[20] Their emphasis upon glory in war, fealty to one's lord, and the importance of a unified and strong nation was easily converted and translated into compelling heroic poetry.[21] Moreover, it is important to remember that early medieval cultures did not regard the Old Testament as a separate history of the Jews; rather, it was considered a vital part of their own historical past. As Godden put it succinctly, "for the Anglo-Saxons the Old Testament was in the first place a history book, a record of events in antiquity" that served as part of the larger history of Christian salvation.[22]

Yet, this is not the whole story. The argument that the Old Testament presented an apt paradigm for a past heroic ethos privileges a nostalgic reading of these poems; the implication is that the conditions of the heroic and Old Testament past are *both* superseded by a new ethos that is represented by Christianity. As we shall see, however, Anglo-Saxon poets, artists, and lawmakers continued to view the Old Testament as a source for present and future revelation, and as an influential basis for literary expressions of nation building and self-identification. The Old Testament could be read as a diagnostic of contemporary events and a means of future prognostication. The invocation of the scriptural past served as an important tool for religious, cultural, and political self-fashioning in the present.

The most serious problem for scholars studying the Anglo-Saxon biblical poetic corpus has been the difficulty of identifying specific target audiences for individual poems. Early twentieth-century scholars simply assumed that the poems—because they were written in the vernacular—were intended for the entertainment or edification of laymen. R.H. Hodgkin (1935) thus confidently asserted that such poetry was contrived in order to emphasize biblical battle scenes as a means of "stimulating the interest" of their Anglo-Saxon audiences. He argued that in early English biblical verse we can see "the form in which popular Christianity was conveyed to the ordinary Englishman,"[23] an assessment that does not engage at any level with the intellectual merits of the poems. In more recent scholarship, the pendulum has swung in the opposite direction. It has been suggested that the poems were primarily intended to edify clergy and monks who did not adequately know Latin and required biblical instruction in the vernacular. It is the contention of the present book, however, that the styles of Old English Old Testament poems range from faithful and even slavish translations (as in many of the metrical psalms and in *Genesis A*) to heavily reworked adaptations that demand advanced exegetical or catechetical interpretation (as in *Exodus*, *Daniel*, and *Judith*). It therefore stands to reason that a whole range of didactic and spiritual purposes were being served by Anglo-Saxon biblical poetry.

To date, scholars have mainly pursued one relatively safe form of analysis—namely, the study of the poems in their individual manuscript contexts. This venture has greatly illuminated the material circumstances in which certain interpretive communities would have encountered these poems. The problem with this approach is that a manuscript witness often marks but one stage in the dissemination of a poem. Moreover, the exclusive focus on manuscript studies tends to obscure such important issues as ideological or institutional pressures and motivations. To use an analogy, this manuscript-based approach could be compared to observing and studying an artwork within the context of a single exhibition, and deriving all critical insight from this artistic and institutional constellation. As an alternative, I would like to offer a reassessment of this manuscript-based approach and then consider what might be gained from an examination of the available paratextual evidence surrounding the production and dissemination of biblical poetry. To this end, I also offer a brief comparative analysis of Anglo-Saxon Old Testament poetry and Latin biblical poetry that were produced in Late Antiquity and read in Anglo-Saxon England.

Manuscript Context

The poems *Exodus* and *Daniel* are preserved in a single tenth-century manuscript, in Oxford, Bodleian Library, Junius 11 (hereafter, Junius 11), which constitutes an anthology of biblical verse.[24] The collection also contains three additional poems: *Genesis A* comes closest to the tradition of the metrical paraphrase, drawing on verses contained in Genesis 1–20. The remaining two poems are based loosely upon Apocryphal and New Testament materials. *Genesis B* is a translation of an Old Saxon poem composed on the subject of the fall of angels and of men. The poem has been embedded (with some awkwardness and repetition) within the text of *Genesis A* (at lines 235–851), either by the scribe of Junius 11 or by a previous author or redactor.[25] The second poem, *Christ and Satan*, provides a thumbnail sketch of the entire history of Christ's triumph over Satan, including brief accounts of the fall of angels, the Crucifixion, the Resurrection, Christ's appearance to his disciples, and the Harrowing of Hell. This poem is generally thought to be a late addition to the manuscript because it is demarcated by the heading *Liber II* and is paginated and laid out differently. In contrast to *Liber II*, the first part of the manuscript has been beautifully illuminated by two different artists (covering much of *Genesis A* and *B*) and spaces are left for the remaining pages of

Liber I. The visual program in this section clearly indicates that its poems were meant to be a unit.[26]

The survival of this extraordinary and unique biblical poetic anthology has prompted a great deal of speculation about its purpose and audience.[27] In 1978, Barbara C. Raw put forward the thesis—later refined by Paul G. Remley (1996)—that the five poems contained in Junius 11 were assembled in this collection because their subject matter corresponds to a series of Old Testament lections recited during the liturgy for Lent and the Easter Vigil.[28] Although the forms of the liturgy were by no means constant or uniform throughout the Anglo-Saxon period, Remley's meticulous study of developments in the liturgical service claims that such correspondence obtains, provided that the poems were written before the Gregorian reform (ca. 950).[29] The lections for the Easter Vigil include readings from Genesis 1:1–2:2, Exodus 14:24–15.1, and Daniel 3:1–24, and cover portions of text that are adapted in these Old Testament poems.[30] And in some instances, Remley demonstrates the direct influence of the liturgical lections on the poetry.

To be sure, Raw and Remley provide invaluable accounts of at least one method by which Old Testament narratives may have been popularized and disseminated in Anglo-Saxon communities—namely, through the liturgy. However, the liturgical correspondences cited by Remley are neither strong nor pervasive enough to demonstrate that the selection and arrangement of the poems in Junius 11 were intended to match this liturgical program explicitly. As my analyses of the poems *Exodus* and *Daniel* show, the texts in Junius 11 draw upon a far greater store of biblical materials and traditions than those included in any single liturgical lection or program.

A more inclusive analysis is presented by J.R. Hall, who takes into account the content of both *Liber I* and *II*.[31] He reads Junius 11 as an "epic of redemption" that narrates the course of scriptural events from Creation to the Last Judgment. Hall sees the poems as collectively following a model of salvation history, attested in Augustine's *De catechizandis rudibus* ("The First Catechetical Instruction"), which was written as a guide for catechumens preparing for baptism.[32] The manifest aim of these scriptural lections was to expose the catechumens to the entire "salvation history" from the Old to the New Testament.[33] Participative reading of the manuscript thus affords the individual the opportunity to experience subjectively all of salvation history. In this process, the active reader is invited to insert himself or herself imaginatively into the scheme of biblical history.

Hall's theory is appealing because it anchors the theme of salvation both within individual poems and across items in the manuscript. Thus, Hall argues persuasively that the poems highlight Old Testament events relating especially to the divine covenant and redemption. "The principal theme of the Abraham story in *Genesis A*," Hall argues, "is that a faithful patriarch is to be the father of a chosen people who are to inhabit Canaan." In *Exodus* this promise is realized. The poet makes it apparent that the Israelites under Moses are the offspring of Abraham and, as such, are delivered to the promised Land." [34] The saga-like dynamic of rise and fall of the Israelites continues in the poem *Daniel*, where its emplotment takes a negative turn. According to Hall's analysis, the poem begins by celebrating the success of Israel as God's chosen people, and concludes by marking the Israelites' fall into sin. The Babylonian captivity is explained as a direct consequence of Israel's failure: "Israel abandoned God and so God abandoned Israel." [35] According to Hall, *Christ and Satan* constitutes a fitting and necessary close to this Salvation epic. The poem introduces Christ's redemption, and the possibility of deliverance for all believers. Hall reconstructs a narrative trajectory for the whole of the manuscript that is deliberately supersessionist: the Old Law is fulfilled and replaced by the New. [36]

Hall's reading provides a plausible explanation for the aesthetic and spiritual vision that is developed by the manuscript's principal redactor. However, it does not offer an analysis of the poems on their own terms as individual compositions. Hall pays little attention to individual styles, modes of adaptation, or the poetic choices made by the Anglo-Saxon authors, whose work quite likely figured in other written and oral contexts before being gathered in Junius 11.

For this reason, it is of some importance to consider the status of biblical poetry that has been preserved in other contexts. The poem *Judith* is anthologized in the tenth-century MS Cotton Vitellius A. xiv, which also contains the sole extant copy of *Beowulf*. The manuscript in question comprises two separate codices, the Southwick codex and the Nowell codex, which were bound together, perhaps arbitrarily, in the late sixteenth or early seventeenth centuries. The Nowell codex contains five texts: three prose works, known as *The Life of Saint Christopher*, *The Wonders of the East*, and *Alexander's Letter to Aristotle*, followed by two poems, *Beowulf* and *Judith* (it is possible that at some point *Judith* was moved to the end of the manuscript).[37] The anthology thus combines a miscellany of genres: a hagiographic text, two travel narratives, a poem about a monster-slayer, and a biblical poem. One theory (originally proposed by J.R.R. Tolkien) is that the collection was compiled to reflect an interest in monsters and the marvelous.[38] There is much to recommend this interpretation: the *Beowulf* manuscript is richly illuminated with depictions of exotic creatures, animals, and races, of the variety usually found in the remote margins of medieval *mappae mundi* ("maps of the world").[39] These marvelous bodies appear front and center on the page, in some cases even bursting out of their frames.[40] On the basis of Tolkien's reading, it has been supposed that the two "religious" texts in this sequence are also broadly expressive of the marvelous. *The Life of Saint Christopher* presents the biography of the dog-headed giant, who converted to Christianity and became a saint, and Judith is depicted as a monster-slayer of sorts who kills her devilish adversary, Holofernes. When Judith decapitates him, she brings back his head for display (echoing the display of Grendel's arm and head in *Beowulf*).

Intriguing as this focus on the monstrous and marvelous may be, it obviates the fact that *Judith* also has a great deal in common with other Old Testament poetry from the period.[41] The poem's combination of heroic and biblical themes is consonant with the Junius 11 texts. Holofernes and his men may be monsters, but they are above all historical others who persecuted the Jews. *Judith*, like *Exodus* and *Daniel*, offers an idiosyncratic politico-theological interpretation of the biblical text from which it is derived.

Mythological and Institutional Origins

The only substantive Anglo-Saxon account of the composition, performance, and dissemination of Old English Old Testament poetry appears in Bede's legendary account of the poet Cædmon, in book IV.24 of his *Historia Ecclesiastica* (ca. 731).[42] Bede's tale narrates a well-known miracle: it explains how Cædmon, an illiterate *rusticus* (or tender of animals) living and working in the monastery Streanaeshalch (later Whitby Abbey) during the abbacy of St. Hilda (614–80), was miraculously endowed, by the grace of God, with the ability to compose religious poetry in English. The story goes as follows: Cædmon attended a feast where banqueters were taking turns singing poems. Unable to follow suit, Cædmon was ashamed and retreated to the cattle shed where he fell asleep; he was visited during the night by a "divine guest," who asked him to sing. When Cædmon replied that he had no such ability, the visitor instructed him to sing "about the beginning of created things" (*principium creaturarum*), whereupon he miraculously began to produce verses "which he had never heard before in praise of God the creator." [43] The next morning Cædmon remembered the verses and added to them "in the same manner, praising God in fitting style." [44]

Despite its status as legend, Bede's account of the poet Cædmon stands to teach us about the institutional contexts in which certain biblical poems may have been composed and transmitted in Anglo-Saxon England. The details Bede chooses to record and withhold about Cædmon's craft are significant. It seems important, for example, that Bede never relays the precise text of Cædmon's poem; instead he paraphrases it in Latin poetry. Bede explains that he is able to transmit the "sense [*sensus*] but not the order of the words [*non autem ordo ipse uerborum*] of the song," claiming that it is "not possible to translate [*transferre*] verse however well composed, literally from one language to another without some loss of beauty and dignity [*sine detrimento sui decoris ac dignitatis*]." [45] Thus, Bede provides an essentially "new" text, a paraphrase that might be called more appropriately "Bede's Latin Version of *Cædmon's Hymn*." Bede's notion of the impossibility of translation across different languages and genres reinforces the notion that vernacular biblical poetry ought to be read as *works* in their own right.

Cædmon's original English poem, whether it ever existed or not, is a phantasm, forever lost in translation. Nevertheless, the poem we refer to as "Cæmon's hymn" represents an important myth of origin for both Anglo-Saxon audiences *and* scholars, who would see this composition as the beginning of biblical verse in English, and Cædmon as the "father of English history." [46] Bede himself perpetuates this fantasy of interpretation. Although none of Cædmon's poems survive (if they were ever actually composed), Bede relates that Cædmon produced a massive corpus of scriptural poetry in the vernacular, including, as we gather from his description, verses on Genesis, Exodus, the Gospels, and Revelations.[47] As Bruce Holsinger has demonstrated, the setting of Cædmon's angelic annunciation is also fantastic: the locus of the dream in the stable and the visitation by the divine figure created a veritable "nativity scene that births both poetry and Cædmon's own future life within the institution."[48] There are also similarities between Bede's depiction of Cædmon and the legend of the seventy Jewish translators, who, in the tradition of inspired prophets, allegedly produced the Septuagint in seclusion on the Isle of Pharos.[49] In fact, Bede encourages this connection between prophecy and poetic creation when he writes that Cædmon "did not learn the art of poetry from men nor through a man [*non ab hominibus neque per hominem*] but he received the gift of song freely by the grace of God." The passage deliberately echoes Paul's self-description in his letter to the Galatians 1:1, in which he refers to himself as "an apostle, not of men, neither by man, but by Jesus Christ and God the Father, who raised him from the dead."[50] Like Paul, Cædmon is depicted as a prophet-evangelist, who is capable of inspiring rapture and reform in his audience. Bede tells us that "by his songs the minds of many were often kindled to despise the world and to long for the heavenly life" (*cuius accensi carminibus multorum saepe animi ad contemtum saeculi et appetitum sunt vitae caelestis accensi*), and that by means of these songs Cædmon "sought to turn his hearers away from delight in sin [*ab amore sclerum abstrahere*] and arouse in them the love and practice of good works [*ad dilectionem uero et sollertiam bonae actionis excitare curabat*]."[51] In Bede's view, the performative force of Cædmon's poetry has an undeniable perlocutionary effect. It carries forward "the good word" of both Testaments.

In fact, there are grounds for arguing that the whole legend of Cædmon may be regarded as a piece of institutional propaganda. Holsinger observes that it is noteworthy that Bede places Cædmon at Streanaeshalch, the same monastery where the important Synod of Whitby was held, situating it at "the centre of monastic world one of the central monastic foundations in Anglo-Saxon Northumbria."[52] The Cædmon story "explains something that needed to be explained":

it attempts to justify the "presence of vernacular poetry in active daily use within the walls of their monastery."[53] Bede for this reason emphasizes the rousing and salvational facility of Cædmon's poetry— not in the secular world, but specifically in the cloister.[54] Bede's tale of Cædmon is "the work of liturgical culture seeking to explain its unique character to a chronicler who promised to perpetuate its institutional memory."[55] Holsinger is surely right to detect a note of apology. But whether the tale of Cædmon ultimately represents a justification for the use of vernacular poetry within monastic walls, or as an explanation for the use of poetry as a tool for reform, education, and entertainment beyond them, remains unclear (thus Bede's "minds of many" [*multorum... animi*] may be intended more broadly).

On the basis of Holsinger's etiological argument, it seems prudent to ask similar questions about the production and circulation of anonymous biblical verse in later Anglo-Saxon England. One may, for instance, interrogate some of the institutional and cultural pressures and impulses that contributed to the proliferation and transmission of biblical verse. By the tenth century, large portions of the bible had already been translated into English. Why, then, were vernacular biblical poems produced alongside these texts? What educational or devotional gaps did they fill in religious or lay life? And perhaps most perplexingly, why did these biblical poems escape the customary suspicion that surrounded and regulated the production of biblical translation? From the first rendering of the Hebrew bible into Greek (in the third century BCE), biblical translations triggered anxieties about the transmission and conservation of God's sacred authority. The translator's task was to preserve the holy mystery of the word of God, without introducing dangerous changes through language variation. And yet, despite the commonality of this aim, there was no consensus as to whether the authority of the bible was best preserved by translating "word-for-word" (*verbum pro verbo*) or "sense-for-sense" (*sensum ad sensu*). Jerome gave special status to biblical translation when he advocated the strictest literalism with the aim of preserving the textual authority of God. This was Jerome's way of conserving textual meaning and saving the "essential text" from the vicissitudes of language.[56] His practice in this instance differed from his translations of secular texts, which adhered to the notion of "sense for sense." Against this deeper history of biblical translation, it stands to reason that biblical verse—composed with obvious poetic license—was treated as an altogether different genre.

Moreover, if we accept Bede's account as a diagnosis of the growing importance and ubiquity of early vernacular religious poetry, we might surmise that (like Cædmon's hymn and all of his supposed productions) the aim of biblical poetry was similarly to inspire personal devotion and reform. This was clearly the aim of the *Exodus*-poet, who announced at the beginning of his poem, in an almost prophetic or evangelical tone, that his mission was to tell of the laws of Moses, that "wondrous code," which "proclaim[s] to men reward of heavenly life for all the blessed after death, and lasting gain for every living soul. Let him hear who will." The process of reading or hearing about exemplary lives in scriptural poetry could be used to spark a spiritual process of interiorization, which might be described as a "movement from a real life represented by the text to an inner text that is intended to be lived." [57] In the case of the bible, the construction of living, inner scripture was paramount for all Christians.

Inherited Traditions: Latin Biblical Poetry

If Bede's account of Cædmon represents the only Anglo-Saxon literary account of its kind, it is not the only source from which we may draw contextualizing information. The impact of an earlier Latin corpus of biblical epic poetry in Anglo-Saxon England has been the subject of a handful of important studies by Michael Lapidge, Andy Orchard, and Roger Green.[58] Among the most influential and widely disseminated were "epic" poems by Vettius Aquilinus Juvencus (*Libri Evangeliorum*, fourth century), Caelius Sedulius (*Carmen paschale*, fifth century), Arator (*Historia Apostolica*, sixth century), and Alcimus Ecdicius Avitus (*Poematum de spiritalis historiae gestis*, sixth century).[59] These poems were composed in hexameter verse and drew heavily from classical epic poets such as Vergil, Lucan, and Statius. According to Lapidge, the study of Latin biblical poetry represented the pinnacle of advanced study in the early English educational programs:

Children were taught to read by memorizing Psalms and Wisdom books, and the mark of perfection in an oblate was that he could regurgitate the entire psalter, as is clear from numerous lives of saints. At a later stage of life the monk's occupation consisted in meditation on the bible through the agency of scriptural commentaries. It is therefore surprising, perhaps, to learn that the curriculum of medieval schools consisted not in the study of the bible *per se*, nor in meditation on patristic commentary, but in meticulous word-by-word parsing and interpretation of various poetic versions of the bible (paraphrases, as they are often called).[60]

Lapidge reconstructs the details of this school program from a variety of sources. The most important is the material evidence of dozens of surviving Anglo-Saxon manuscripts (containing copies of poems by Juvencus, Sedulius, and Arator), many of which are heavily glossed and annotated, suggesting their frequent use and study.[61] Booklists from Anglo-Saxon libraries also provide a further index of the dissemination and ownership of manuscripts that are now lost or destroyed.[62] Finally, there is the matter of textual citation—Anglo-Latin authors, such as Aldhelm, Bede, and Alcuin, quoted extensively from these poems, and sought to imitate features of meter, style, and diction in their poetry.[63]

Given this intense program of reading and studying the Latin biblical poems of this era, one might expect to find clear verbal parallels in vernacular English poetry. Yet, this task has been surprisingly difficult. Lapidge's study comparing the style of *Exodus* to the works of (especially) Avitus, Juvencus, Sedulius, and Arator remains the fullest and most persuasive, though his comparison reveals mainly similarities in style and mood rather than direct verbal parallelism.[64] Others have suggested broad generic correspondences, highlighting the fact that Latin "epic" poetry—like Old English biblical poetry—ranges from "literal" paraphrase to looser, allegorical adaptations.[65]

Even without obvious or clear verbal borrowings, there is much to be gained from a comparative study of the respective biblical poetic traditions and the intellectual and religious cultures that fostered them. It is surely important that influential patristic authors, such as Jerome, Augustine, and Isidore, candidly registered their thoughts, praise, and even occasional stylistic evaluations of these Latin biblical poems.[66] Thus, Jerome in the fourth century included Juvencus in book 84 of his work *On Famous Men*, and Isidore followed suit by including Sedulius in his own book of illustrious people in the seventh century.[67] While Jerome and Augustine openly expressed concern about the place of pagan poetry in Christian life, they (evidently) did not consider biblical verse to present a similar threat.[68] Later Christian poets likewise lauded early Latin biblical epic poetry. Venantius Fortunatus (late sixth and early seventh centuries) regarded Sedulius as both a gifted poet (calling him "Sweet Sedulius") and a religious and intellectual luminary, placing him in a list of venerated church fathers that included Ambrose, Jerome, and Augustine.[69] The almost total absence of corresponding praise and evaluation, critique and censure in Anglo-Saxon England is noteworthy.

It is also instructive to consider what is known about the conditions of performance and reader-reception of Latin biblical poetry in Late Antiquity. It is now accepted that Latin biblical poetry was intended primarily for an elite group of well-educated *literati*. The frequent and heavy-handed use of quotations from classical verse served not only to elevate biblical poetry to epic heights, but also to provide complex metrical and linguistic word-games and dense networks of literary allusions for intellectuals who were in a position to recognize and appreciate such borrowings and echoes. However, there is anecdotal evidence that suggests that biblical poetry was heard and appreciated by audiences with rather less training as well. Arator is said to have presented his *Historia Apostolica* (on Wednesday April 6, 544, just after Easter) to Pope Vigilius in the presence of bishops, priests, and deacons, and to have read parts of it aloud. The poem was so admired that the pope placed a copy in the church archives, and commissioned a public reading by the author, which took place one week later, "on the steps of St Peter [in Vincoli] in Rome, before a large company of clerics and laity, the latter including both nobility and much of the populace."[70] Although one cannot simply assume that the conditions and circumstances of performance in Late Antiquity were equivalent to those in Anglo-Saxon England, it might be fair to speculate that different early English audiences might have also appreciated the poems in different ways, according to individual training and mastery.[71]

To be sure, the comparison between Latin and English biblical verse brings to light significant ideological differences between these two traditions. In Latin poetry, the use of classical epic phrases and formulae established a definitive cultural ethos that validated and valorized the principle of *translatio studii* extending from Greece to Rome, thereby claiming an unbroken chain of poetic tradition and inspiration. In turn, Latin biblical poets saw themselves as following in the footsteps of epic writers like Vergil, Lucan, and Statius and, at times, improving upon their works by offering an authentic message of divine Truth. This is not to say that the project of Latin biblical versification was merely imitative. Christian poets were eager to establish a secure hierarchy, in which the divine plan transcended Fate, and Christ transcended Aeneas.[72]

The predominant culture that Old English Old Testament poets sought to imitate was neither that of classical Rome nor Late Antiquity, but rather the Israel of the Old Testament as transmitted through the bible, sermons, and commentary. To some extent, this can be explained by the relative linguistic difference between Latin and Old English. Latin Christian poetry could comfortably accommodate classical meter, tropes, and figures, in a way that Old English could not. However, to an equal degree, the Israelites were deliberately *chosen* as imaginary ancestors—they represented an idealized past of which the Anglo-Saxons were meant to be the new actualization. Old English Old Testament poets styled themselves first and foremost as prophets or evangelists who deliberately sought to extend and transmit the tradition of biblical encomia, complaints, and jeremiads.

These divergent textual ancestries, in turn, conditioned and shaped attitudes toward Old Testament Hebrews and Jewish practice. Latin biblical poets had peppered their poems with derogatory statements about Jews and Jewish practice.[73] The extent to which such comments ought to be read as participating in an active or deliberate tradition of anti-Judaic rhetoric has been much debated, and many scholars prefer to explain vituperative statements about Jews as merely the result of poetic convention.[74] While the brunt of these statements appears in New Testament poetry (which, arguably, employs a quasi-organic supercessionist agenda), there is also ample evidence of similar attitudes in adaptations of Old Testament materials.[75] Consider, for example, Avitus's account of Noah and the flood, at the moment when Noah releases the raven to find dry land. The poet compares the recalcitrant raven, who preferred to snack on the floating corpses rather than report back to his "patient master," to the wayward Jews. Avitus exclaims, "Jew, this is like your ignorance of how to keep faith with your Lord. Although freed by Him, you too love the flesh in this way and render no thanks to the Protector and Lord of your life. In the same way, weak and distracted, you wander off; in the same way you have broken the covenant of the law and violated perfidiously its agreement" (Avitus, *Poematum de spiritalis historiae gestis*).[76] No exposition or contextual reading can deny the palpable disgust and recrimination contained in such passages.[77]

Old English Old Testament poets, by contrast, showcased an overwhelmingly positive treatment of Jewish history, practice, and ethnicity. The Hebrews in *Exodus*, *Daniel*, and *Judith* are "a glorious race" and "God's chosen people." Only in *Daniel* do we also find reproach when the poet attributes the Babylonian captivity to the collective sins of the Jews. However, as we shall see in Chapter 2, even this disparaging view is mitigated by the poet's constant reminders that Jews remain part of the chosen people, and that they serve as important examples for righteous living. Given the quantity and intensity of anti-Judaic literature produced in both early and late medieval English texts, such views are not only surprising, but also genuinely revolutionary.[78]

Political Theology: Translating the Concept of Divine Election

A central premise of *Rewriting the Old Testament* is that translation and adaptation are fundamentally, albeit not always fully conscious, political activities.[79] Like any rewriting, Old English Old Testament poetry had its own interventionist agendas, including the transmission, mediation, and creative alteration of its biblically derived materials for religious, cultural, and political reasons. I use the concept of "political theology" to refer to an overarching hermeneutic scheme that brings to light interpretive and creative misreadings in Anglo-Saxon biblical poetry. Following the definition formulated by William T. Cavanaugh and Peter Scott, I take the term "political theology" (hereafter without quotation marks) broadly to signify "the analysis and criticism of political arrangements (including cultural-psychological, social, and economic aspects) from the perspective of differing interpretations of God's ways with the world."[80] As Cavanaugh and Scott explain, "what distinguishes political theology from other types of theology or political discourse is the explicit attempt to relate discourse about God to the organization of bodies in space and time."[81]

In fact, political theology proves to be an important and enormously helpful concept for the analysis of Anglo-Saxon vernacular biblical poetry. The central concern in all of these poems is the contractual relationship between God and his people, which is articulated by means of covenant and law that bind the individual and community to God's ordinances. God is here imagined as the absolute sovereign who establishes both the law and its limits or exceptions. Since political theology has had a recent resurgence in contemporary cultural theory, I want to briefly explain my own use of this term. It has become closely associated with the writings of Carl Schmitt (d. 1888–1985), who was a leading legal scholar during the Weimar Republic and the Nazi period. To be sure, Schmitt's support of National Socialism is rooted in his views on sovereignty and his theory of total governance.[82] His most comprehensive treatment of the subject appears in *Political Theology: Four Chapters on the Concept of Sovereignty*, in which Schmitt articulates sovereignty as a secularized theological concept, developed in association with a decisionist theory of law.[83] According to Schmitt, the "sovereign" is properly understood as "he who decides on the exception" (*wer über den Ausnahmezustand entscheidet*).[84] The elusive "state of exception" (presumably incurred by extreme emergency in war, or economic crisis, but without finite or set limitations) refers to a "response that falls outside of positive legal and constitutional order." In declaring the exception, the sovereign has the power "to set aside the positive legal and constitutional order in its entirety and to create a novel positive legal and constitutional order, together with a situation of social normality that fits it."[85] Sovereignty therefore emerges as a *Grenzbegriff* (a "limiting" or "border concept"), which "looks in two directions, marking the line between that which is subject to law—where sovereignty reigns—and that which is not—

potentially the space of the exception."[86] Although Schmitt's political theory originated with his analysis of liberal constitutionalism during the Weimar period, he imagined a much broader application. In fact, he insisted on the inevitability, and necessity, of the "exception" within all democratic systems. Although modern liberal constitutions generally do not recognize an absolute sovereign authority, Schmitt nevertheless argued that efforts to purge the exception from modern legal and constitutional theory are not only futile, but also impossible: "there can be no functioning legal order without a sovereign authority" who might suspend or overturn the material legal norms.[87]

Since a more detailed account of Schmitt's political philosophy is beyond the scope of this book, I would at least call attention to a point that is deeply relevant for it. What characterizes Schmitt's theory as *political theology*—and not merely *political theory*—is that his primary analogy and model for the sovereign is God himself.[88] Schmitt writes:

> All significant concepts of the modern theory of the state are secularized theological concepts not only because of their historical development—in which they were transferred from theology to the theory of the state, whereby, for example, the omnipotent God became the omnipotent lawgiver—but also because of their systematic structure, the recognition of which is necessary for a sociological consideration of these subjects. The exception in jurisprudence is analogous to the miracle in theology. Only by being aware of this analogy can we appreciate the manner in which philosophical ideas of the state developed in the last centuries.[89]

Schmitt's comparison between the omnipotent God and the omnipotent sovereign is rooted in both ancient Roman law and medieval theology.[90] His articulation of absolute sovereignty, in fact, comes close to the classic expression of Christian Roman emperorship enshrined in Justinian's *Corpus iuris civilis* (begun in 527 and finished in 534). That code described the role of the sovereign as *absolute*, and his will as that which alone "constitutes law." The *Corpus* takes the position that

The sovereign is "no less than the 'living law'" (*lex animata*), an application of the Hellenistic concept of the ruler as *nomos empsychos*: "let the imperial rank be exempted from all our provisions [in this constitution], because God has subjected the laws themselves to the emperor, by sending him as a living law to men." He is in short, not bound by the law, but "freed from the laws" (*legibus solutus*). This famous phrase indicates that the emperor is above human law: he is not subjected to the laws which derive from his own universal authority.[91]

Schmitt's transplantation of this classical conception of sovereignty to secular contexts (especially in the framework of twentieth-century Nazi Germany) has produced its share of skeptics and critics.[92] In the current context, my reason for adducing Schmitt's conception of political theology has less to do with the historical application of his theory (problematic as I find its connections to National Socialism), and more to do with the biblical, classical, and medieval genealogies he claims for his philosophy. It should, however, not go unmentioned that Schmitt's fetishization, and thus oversimplification, of the concept of sovereignty in premodern cultures is highly tendentious and problematic. As Claire Monagle has argued, "Carl Schmitt's model of political theology is premised upon an idealized Roman Catholic Middle Ages in which there is no separation between the political and the sacred."[93] She goes on to counter this reductive view by pointing to a multiplicity of medieval expressions of sovereignty, emerging especially after the Lateran Council of 1215. An equally powerful argument could presumably be constructed for the period before 1215, beginning with the "investiture controversies" of the eleventh and twelfth centuries, which challenged the authority of European monarchs over appointments or investitures of church officials, such as bishops and abbots.[94]

Beyond this historical criticism, Hans Ulrich Gumbrecht highlights a more general methodological problem with the use of the term "political theology" in the analysis of medieval texts and culture:

Strictly speaking, the phrase "political theology in the Middle Ages" is anachronistic.... Above all, the phrase "political theology" would have looked tautological in medieval eyes because politics without divine orientation, as an independent public use of power, was not supposed to be a practical or cosmological possibility. Likewise, the concept of theology stood in a certain tension with the pre-modern understanding that any kind of knowledge that humans could dispose of was disclosed whether by divine revelation, or by an interpretation of the world as God's creation.[95]

In addition to anachronism and tautology, the fundamental problem is surely the impossibility of identifying a uniform "political theology in the Middle Ages." Views and conceptions of sovereignty in Anglo-Saxon England looked quite different from those expressed in either Roman or Carolingian contexts, no matter how profoundly derivative Anglo-Saxon cultural and political structures are from these continental models.[96]

In the following, I make a case for recuperating the concept of political theology as a viable tool for the analysis of Anglo-Saxon biblical poetry. In the process, I invoke a different genealogy of this concept from the one proposed by Schmitt and his followers. I look back to politico-religious expressions generated in the Old Testament itself, using contemporary biblical scholarship as a guide. Several studies have been especially instrumental in shaping my methodology. Oliver O'Donovan's *The Desire of the Nations: Rediscovering the Roots of Political Theology* examines the intersections between the "political" and "theological" in the Old Testament in connection with the foundation of its nationalizing myth. I have also benefited from work on the subject of liberation theology in Puritan America; on this topic, Conrad Cherry's *God's New Israel: Religious Interpretations of American Destiny* and Michael Walzer's *Exodus and Revolution* have been especially important. The conception of America as the "New Israel" in Puritan sermons, jeremiads, and constitutional writings can be productively compared to, and contrasted with, similar Anglo-Saxon declarations (as we shall see in Chapter 1).[97] Though the political and religious pressures motivating such analogies are patently different in each case, the claim for special election in both instances marks an emergent nationalism that is constitutive of new religious and political identities.[98] Such comparisons allow provocative structural comparisons between expressions in different time periods.

The Old Testament Roots of Political Theology

Oliver O'Donovan argued that political theology is essentially a biblical invention and a key element in its story of God's relationship with his chosen people. For him, political theology "postulates an analogy—not a rhetorical metaphor only, or poetic image, but an analogy grounded in reality—between the acts of God and human acts, both of them taking place within the one public history which is the theater of God's saving purposes and mankind's social undertakings."[99] Reading the bible through the lens of political theology is *not* equivalent to reading the bible through the prism of contemporary cultural theory (such as post-colonialism or feminism), however productively we may use such paradigms to illuminate aspects of the bible.[100] On the contrary, political theology is endemic to the epic machinery and mythology that is enshrined in the Old Testament. It is engrained in the very narrative of redemption that governs God's relationship with his chosen people.[101] To be sure, when I use the term "political theology," I do not attempt to read the bible as a direct reflection of *actual* political structures. Political theology, in all its forms, belongs to the realm of ideology, not history.[102] As practitioners of the Documentary Hypothesis (JEDP) have emphasized, the Old Testament is a retrospective document, written, compiled, and redacted at several removes from the events themselves, and reimagined through a range of often competing political, theological, and religious attitudes and perspectives.[103] The proper object of study in political theology is the "theological imagination" of Israel, that is, Israel's various self-representations that are in evidence in Old Testament narratives and liturgy.[104]

At the center of the bible's politico-theological vision are God's covenants (Hebrew *britim*) with the leaders, elders, people, and kings of Israel. These include the covenants God made with Noah (Gen. 9:9–17), Abraham (Gen 17; 12:1–3), Moses together with the people of Israel (Ex. 24:4), and David (2 Sam. 7:12–13). Each covenant, in turn, has a different political profile: the covenant with Noah emphasizes God's absolutism (he may create and destroy at his will), while the promises and covenants given to Abraham (sealed by circumcision) and Moses (requiring the consent of each individual) are radically contingent upon active and willing participation.[105] The covenant with David introduces a new tension between absolute divine sovereignty and the new monarchy. The common denominator binding these covenants, however, is their strong emphasis on exclusivity and exceptionalism. The covenants uniformly distinguish between "us" and "them" (between the covenanted and the un-covenanted). From this perspective, it may be said that *all* political theology is ultimately based on this unique self-conception:

> The unique covenant of YHWH and Israel can be seen as a point of disclosure from which the nature of all political authority comes into view. Out of the self-possession of this people in their relation to God springs the possibility of other peoples' possessing themselves in God. In this hermeneutic assumption lay the actual continuity between Israel's experience and the Western tradition.[106]

O'Donovan's analysis pertains to hermeneutics (and not simply exegesis) because the concept of sovereign rule is treated as a transhistorical idea. From the Roman period forward, this unique and totalizing relationship with God as sovereign catalyzed the transmission and reconception of its core covenantal theology.

In the chapters to come, I explore how political theology as the basis of a political community is both applied and interpreted differently in each of the poems under examination. In *Exodus*, the radical dependence that marks the Sinai treaty becomes a centerpiece of the Anglo-Saxon text, and a model for communal and personal fulfillment of the covenant. In *Daniel*—as a result of a massive revision by the Anglo-Saxon poet—the terms of Israelite election are forfeited through their sins against God. Forced into Babylonian captivity, the Israelites, with the important exception of Daniel and the children in the fire, come to represent the *formerly chosen people*, much like the British before the Anglo-Saxons. For the poet, these Hebraic exceptions and exemplars (Daniel and all the faithful Jews) embody the paradigmatic template for election, which may be extended to all believers in Christ, particularly those living in Anglo-Saxon England. Finally in *Judith*, the terms of nationhood and unity are again redefined under the conditions of captivity and exile. Shifting from an emphasis on covenant to the biblical model of Holy War, the poet pronounces the Israelites God's special people and a divinely protected exceptional nation. The need for self-definition as a chosen people would continue, and even grow stronger, as the Viking attacks became more frequent and prevalent.

Constructing the Chosen Nation: Anglo-Saxon Israel

In developing a politico-theological approach to reading Old Testament poetry, I am indebted to previous scholarship on the historical perception of Jews and Jewish practice in Anglo-Saxon sermons, law, and literature. Scholars, such as Patrick Wormald, Nicholas Howe, Stephen Harris, and Andrew P. Scheil, have identified a dominant discourse in early English texts that compares Anglo-Saxon England to Old Testament Israel, and establishes the "English" as the New Israel.[107] Scheil characterizes and explains this *populus Israhel* tradition as follows:

> The *Populus Israhel*, a complex metaphor and political ideology, embraces both a figural understanding of past and present and a traditional metaphor for the vagaries of history. The Jews were once the chosen people, but now the Anglo-Saxons represent a new covenant with God, to be rewarded or punished as the occasion demanded. Jews provide a sense of history for Anglo-Saxon culture, an understanding of the relationship between past and present.[108]

The *populus Israhel* tradition may be deployed affirmatively or critically, depending on context. Moreover, this tradition coexists with a number of more sinister, anti-Judaic tropes that identify the Jews variously as the murderers of Christ, as willful infidels, or, more generally, simply as dangerous others.[109] These unsettling attitudes collectively highlight the religious, cultural, and even somatic otherness of Jews.[110] In marked contrast to these problematic cultural stereotypes, however, the overwhelming dynamic cultivated in Old Testament poetry is in fact one of identification with, and acclaim of, the Jews rather than dissociation from, or defamation of, them.

Scheil traces the origins of the *populus Israhel* tradition in Anglo-Saxon England to the writings of the Venerable Bede, particularly to his homilies and his *Ecclesiastical History of the English People*. Bede, in turn, inherited many of these conceptions about Jews and Old Testament Hebrews from commentaries, chronicles, and histories that date back to Late Antiquity, including the historical writings of Eusebius, Orosius, Salvian, and Paulinus of Nola.[111] In fact, Bede's own treatment of the *gens Anglorum* as God's "chosen people" is closely intertwined with prior claims for imperialistic exceptionalism asserted in these precursor texts. Scheil notes quite correctly that each preceding history seeks to describe its own people as the chosen elect. Indeed, he also places Old English Old Testament poetry in this same textual lineage.[112] As Scheil points out, all basic expressions of the *populus Israhel* tradition point in the same general direction: they all compare the "English" to the Israelites and map out a teleological transference of election from the Jews or Israelites to Christian believers. They also have in common a certain "constructedness": homilies, histories, and biblical poems express an ideology of unity and special election, where no corresponding "real" political, ecclesiastical, or social unity exists, or has properly materialized. Strictly speaking, it remains a rhetorical fantasy to describe a unified "English nation" (and to some extent a "unified church") before the ninth and tenth centuries.[113]

I depart from Scheil, however, by arguing that there are important cultural, historical, and aesthetic differences that shape the trope of *populus Israhel* in disparate Anglo-Saxon genres and contexts. In the following sections, I identify three important stages in the development of this theme: I label these, respectively, (1) the "ecclesiastical model" (generated by Bede, Alcuin, and Wulfstan); (2) the "sovereignty model" (developed in the age of Alfred, and continued in subsequent expressions of West-Saxon and "English" sacral kingship); and (3) the "interpretive model" (utilized by biblical translators, commentators, and poets).

Bede's Ecclesiastical Model: The Church as a New Israel

The Venerable Bede had a great deal to say—both positive and negative—about Jews and biblical Hebrews. One pervasive trope in his writings was the conception of the Anglo-Saxon people as the New Israel and God's chosen nation. In his *Historia Ecclesiastica* (ca. 731), Bede cast the migration-age Germanic invaders in the role of the conquering Israelites who overcame the sinful and unruly Britons—a view he claims to have inherited from the sixth-century British writer Gildas.[114] In his *De Excidio et Conquestu Britanniae*, Gildas explained that the British, the once-chosen people of God, forfeited their special status through sin; their punishment was the Germanic conquest of their territory. Patrick Wormald, in summarizing Bede's strategy, demonstrates that Old Testament depictions of Jews as God's chosen people provided a template and intertext for Bede's *Ecclesiastical History*:

> Once the Romans had withdrawn, the unbridled wickedness of the Britons had been faithfully chronicled by Gildas, "their own historian" (as Bede had revealingly called him). Contemptuous alike of his warnings and of a first "scourging" by Anglo-Saxon invaders, they were eventually abandoned by God, who transferred their heritage to a new favorite. Rome came again to Kent, in the person of Augustine, not Julius Caesar. The English fell heirs to what the Britons had lacked the grace to deserve.[115]

Embedded in this dense summary of Bede's project are several important assertions. In the first place, Bede viewed the experience of the post-exile Israelites who established a homeland for themselves as presenting a type for the experience of the earliest Germanic peoples who migrated to England. Moreover, Bede interpreted the Germanic invasion as following the scheme of *translatio imperii*: he saw the divine right to rule as being passed from the sinful Britons to the worthier virtuous invaders.[116]

Bede's use of this trope accommodates his presentist and futurist view of Anglo-Saxon England. The analogy matches tribal England with tribal Israel and anticipates a conception of unified nationhood in eighth-century "England," at a time when it was not yet apparent. Bede's analogy did not, therefore, pertain solely to the migration-age invaders. Rather, he extended it to include his contemporary *gens Anglorum*. The Old Testament paradigm of Israel as a nation operating under a single divinely inspired covenant provided a model for Anglo-Saxon claims to a unified cultural and religious identity that was still very much in the process of emergence.[117] Thus, in a memorable passage at the beginning of his *Ecclesiastical History* (book I.1), Bede identified the eighth-century inhabitants of Britain and compared their various languages to the five books of the bible:

> At the present time there are five languages in Britain, just as the divine law is written in five books all devoted to seeking out and setting forth one and the same kind of wisdom, namely the knowledge of sublime truth and of true sublimity. These are the English, British, Irish, Pictish, as well as the Latin languages; through the study of the scriptures, Latin is in general use among them all.[118]

Bede's account at first would appear to champion a certain cosmopolitanism: his idealized vision of a harmoniously polyglot Britain provides an obvious antitype for the catastrophe of the Tower of Babel, which had associated multilingualism with faction and discord.[119] Yet, at the same time, this seemingly evenhanded multilingualism is undermined by a hegemonic claim fusing Britain's inhabitants into a single political and cultural body. The linguistic diversity of Britain is subsumed by a powerful ecclesiastical vision of cultural and religious unity, which can claim access to the "sublime truth" and knowledge of "true sublimity." As the five books of the Old Testament are bound by one common law, so the inhabitants of Britain are united by one ecclesiastical faith and rule. The scheme is repeated in the structure of Bede's own book, for the *Ecclesiastical History* consists of five books, and thus mirrors the structure of the Pentateuch.

The entire, rather complex, analogy points to a tension that lies at the heart of Bede's *Ecclesiastical History*: at times, the Israelites are associated positively with the Germanic invaders; but at other times, they serve as mere precursors to a more comprehensive Christian nation.[120] Unfolding this apparent paradox, one may reason that if the Germanic conquerors are likened to the Jews, then their later, converted selves must represent the perfected Christian elect who have no equivalent in the original figural paradigm. For Bede, then, the idea of Jewish election simultaneously presents a model to be *imitated* and *transcended*.[121] To be sure, Bede is not primarily interested in the fall and rise of empire, but rather in the unity and triumph of the church itself.[122] Because here, and in fact throughout Bede's commentaries and homilies, Jewish chosenness is presented as a status already in transition and in question, it provides an apt vehicle for his discussion of emergent English nationhood, however mythical and imaginary its status may be in eighth-century England.

Bede's comparison provided a productive paradigm for a range of subsequent Anglo-Saxon authors. As Wormald, Howe, Harris, and Scheil have all demonstrated, Alcuin and Wulfstan adopted the same scheme of Israelite election to chastise present and future calamity resulting from sin. In his sermons, Wulfstan channels the view that just as the Israelites were handed over to their enemies on account of their sins, the Viking attacks upon the English in the late tenth century could be interpreted as a scourge sent by God to punish the English for their sins.[123] A similar trope of divine retribution presumably lurks behind the poet's cleverly ambiguous description of Grendel in *Beowulf* as both a scourge set by God and a blight acting against God. The poet's statement that Grendel "bore the wrath of God" (*godes yrre bær*, 711) surely carries both meanings.

The Political Realm: Old Testament Models and Divine Sovereignty

Bede's ecclesiastical model intersects with, but develops separately from, the ideal of divine sovereignty, which used Old Testament models of kingship in order to confer divine election upon English kings. Such claims were hardly original to the Anglo-Saxon elite[124]: similar assertions had been made by virtually every conquering people that followed in the footsteps of Rome, and also in the Holy Roman Empire. The closest cultural and textual analogues for Anglo-Saxon England were Frankish, and these can be traced at least as far back as the reign of Pippin,[125] whose anointing in 751 asserted his status as a divinely sanctioned ruler, and of the Frankish people, collectively, as the new Israel.[126] The association of Carolingian monarchs with Old Testament kings in fact initiated a whole program of legitimization. Frankish laws were brought in line with Old Testament paradigms: the *lex salica* (the Frankish law code originally written during the reign of Clovis in 507–11) was revised in 763/4 during the reign of Pippin with a new prologue containing extensive biblical quotation and allusion derived from Deuteronomy 4:6–8.[127] The prologue is read as a direct assertion about the divinely chosen status of the Franks.[128] In addition, Charles the Bald (869) reinstated the practice of anointing by bishops, a practice that symbolically forged a direct link between the Carolingian dynasty and the centralized Episcopal power.[129] What began as a trope that legitimized Frankish rule had become, by the 780s and 790s, a stable ideology that identified the empire and its people as the *populus dei*.[130]

Anglo-Saxon authors developed a similar vocabulary for asserting divine rule and imagining the people as the new *populus dei*. However, there were also important institutional differences. To begin with, Frankish anointing stressed a "gentile unity" that applied to the entire Frankish realm.[131] Anglo-Saxon England before the tenth century could claim no such unity as a single "nation"—rather the term *populus* could practically only apply to the West-Saxons (and perhaps also the Mercians) as the main centralizing powers.[132] Anglo-Saxon expressions of divine sovereignty and election were not merely imitative of Frankish examples. Although it was once supposed that Anglo-Saxon rulers, chroniclers, and historians simply absorbed their theologico-political rhetoric wholesale from earlier Frankish models, recent scholarship has, in fact, emphasized the reverse current of influence in the late eighth century—from Anglo-Saxon England to the Carolingian court. As Mary Garrison has shown, Anglo-Saxon missionaries and scholars—especially Boniface and Alcuin,[133] who taught at the Carolingian court—had a strong role in shaping the conceit of divine sovereignty as a dominant Carolingian ideology.[134] As we shall see in the analysis of *Daniel* in Chapter 2, this revised understanding of English influence correlates with the modified scheme of *translatio studii* that situated Anglo-Saxons as important innovators and transmitters of culture, literature, and theology on the continent.

From at least the ninth century onward, Anglo-Saxon kings consciously styled themselves as rulers in the form of Old Testament monarchs, thus claiming for themselves divine and elect status. The earliest recorded English coronation ceremonies for kings, the so-called *ordines*, employed a dense web of scriptural allusion to liken the newly anointed English king to Old Testament patriarchs and monarchs, and to turn the king's people into the New Israel and chosen nation of God. The blessing for the new king, drawn from the second *ordo*, testifies to this legacy:

> Multiply thy blessings upon thy servant N., whom in lowly devotion we do elect to the Kingdom of the Angles or of the Saxons, and ever cover him with thy powerful hand, that he, being strengthened with the faith of Abraham, endued with the mildness of Moses, armed with the fortitude of Joshua, exalted with the humility of David, beautified with the wisdom of Solomon... may nourish and teach, defend and instruct the church of the whole realm....[135]

The mechanics of the ceremony itself were likewise modeled on the anointing ritual of Old Testament kings. The chief paradigm used was Solomon's anointing by the priest Zadock at Gibeon; following this scriptural model, anointing bishops poured oil from a horn over the king's head.[136] Naturally, Solomon, the founder of the First Temple, provided an especially fitting figure for the unification of church and nation.[137]

Though it is difficult to assign precise dates to the composition of the earliest English *ordines*, the first *ordo* was almost certainly codified sometime in the mid-ninth century and was probably used by Alfred (reigned 871–99),[138] while the second *ordo* can be dated approximately to 880–925. The fossilization of these *ordines* during or just after the reign of Alfred is significant, since it was in this period that rule in Britain transitioned from governance by multiple kingdoms to a more centralized West-Saxon power. It is no coincidence that Alfred was the first king to use the term "English" to refer to "the English nation."[139]

The Old Testament as a paradigm for kingship was therefore not used simply for the sake of pomp and circumstance in royal coronations. Rather, the Old Testament model pervaded the iconography, literature, and law of the West-Saxon kings from the mid-ninth century onward. In the surviving regal genealogies, the kings of Wessex laid claim to rightful and divinely sanctioned rule by tracing their ancestry back not just to Woden, but also to Noah and Adam.[140] No king exploited this mythological genealogy more vigorously than did Alfred the Great, with the help of his court biographers and *literati.* In fact, Alfred's identification with King Solomon became a veritable cult of personality,[141] and thoroughly conditioned his self-presentation as a leader of religious and literary reform and as a lover of wisdom and literacy.[142] It also shaped his persona as a lawgiver. Alfred's *Lawbook* (*Domboc*), issued in the 880s or early 890s, was prefaced by a lengthy translation of most of the regulatory portions of Exodus 20–3, including the Ten Commandments. The preface, which occupied a fifth of the entire code, occasionally updated specific details for an English audience.[143] It was followed by an abstract from Acts 15:23–9, which retold Mosaic Law through an apostolic lens in order to demonstrate consonance between the old and the new dispensations. Furthermore, the division of the *Domboc* into 120 sections was symbolic: the number 120 represented the age at which Moses the lawgiver died, as well as the number of those who received the Holy Spirit after Christ's ascension in Acts I:15.[144] Although previous lawcodes (such as the revised Frankish *lex salica* and the eighth-century Irish *Liber ex lege Moysi*) had utilized the Decalogue and Mosaic Law as a model for governance, none had devoted such a lengthy or prominent position to it.[145] According to Wormald, Alfred's lawbook provided, above all, an ideological proclamation which demonstrated that "West Saxon Law—and implicitly Mercian and Kentish Law too—belonged from the outset to the history of divine legislation for humanity. The emergent kingdom of the English was thus invited, even obliged, to live as a new Chosen People."[146] Marsden, echoing Wormald, added that the prologue placed "English history in the universal scheme of Christian history, avowing continuity between Mosaic and English law, and implying a sharing of aspirations between the Israelites and the English people."[147]

In the centuries following Alfred's dynamic reign, this Old Testament analogy became deeply engrained as part of the regular iconography of Anglo-Saxon kings, as witnessed in the production of manuscript portraits, carvings, and coins that incorporated

Mosaic, Davidic, and Solomonic features.[148] This understanding of sacral kingship and sovereignty also left its mark on Old English Old Testament poetry, and in particular its conception of God as an all-wielder who takes an active role in the provenance of his chosen people. As we shall see, the *Exodus*-poet reshapes aspects of the biblical narrative to highlight God's role as a king-warrior, just as the *Judith*-poet does so to demonstrate God's intimate hand in the salvation of the Jews in exile.

Poetic Representations: The Interpretive Model of Election

Old English Old Testament poetry marks an important third stage in the development of this trope, which I label the "interpretive" model of election. The central difference in these texts is that this mode of interpretation is not bound to the revelation of a specific historical event (or range of events) in Anglo-Saxon history, but rather refers to a current and pervasive political theology expressed in these texts. Bede had been the first "English" author to describe his *gens Anglorum* as the New Israel with the express aim of establishing an idealized ecclesiastical unity in the eighth century.[149] Likewise, Anglo-Saxon monarchs and their biographers and court officials had used the trope of sacral kingship to establish and promote their rightful rule. In Old English Old Testament poetry, by contrast, this elect status was cited in order to transfer it to its own English audiences through the process of reading and hearing biblical poetry. This original point about transference is the central tenet of this book.

Each of the remaining chapters treats an example of Old Testament poetry through the lens of political theology. Chapter 1 reads the Old English poem *Exodus* as a highly sophisticated attestation of political theology. The book of Exodus has been universally regarded as the national epic of the ancient Israelites, and the *Exodus*-poet shared this view. As my analysis shows, the poem reproduces, and even expands upon, the "ethnogenetic myths" enshrined in the biblical text in order to create a firm basis for its own national identity and community. The poet focuses on the long history of the covenant (established in the Pentateuch) in order to bring to the fore the unique relationship between God and the ancient Israelites. The covenant is therefore treated as a contract to be reinstated and newly avowed by each individual. Using established mnemonic techniques associated with the medieval *ars memoriae*, the poet creates a roadmap for individual contemplation of, and participation in, the covenant.

Chapter 2 focuses on the poem *Daniel*, which freely adapts and conflates biblical narratives associated with the Old Testament and the apocryphal Daniel cycle. While the Old Testament book of Daniel emphasizes the unfaltering faith of the Israelites who adhere to their law in exile, the Anglo-Saxon poet interpolates a series of passages that emphasize the general disobedience of the Jews who violate their covenant with God and forfeit their special status of election. In emphasizing the general decline of the Israelites, the poet bypasses the text's prominent theme of *translatio imperii*, which the biblical author establishes through a series of dreams and prophecies that predict the downfall of successive nations and the eventual ascendancy of Israel over all other nations. Instead, the poet emphasizes the new theme of *translatio electionis*, that is, the transfer of chosenness away from the Jewish people who collectively have lapsed in faith to a more heterogeneous community of believers, which includes Christian converts as well as select Jews. The exemplary Jewish youths of the poem are easily readable as Christian "types." Thus, the text exposes a paradox that celebrates exemplary Jews as the former and present chosen people. In subverting the theologico-political message of the biblical account, the poet adheres to the universalist Pauline model of election. On these grounds, the status of chosenness can be plausibly transmitted and ascribed to a transhistorical Christian community that includes the Anglo-Saxons themselves.

The final chapter explores the trope of Holy War as it is revisited in the poem *Judith*. The deuterocanonical book of Judith poses complex ethical dilemmas for readers in any era: it sanctions Judith's use of sexuality as a tool for gaining military position, and it tacitly authorizes the use of guerrilla warfare as a licit military strategy. The chapter explores how the Old English poet reframes two dominant paradigms of war in the biblical text—the first is Judith's assassination of Holofernes, which she accomplishes by means of guerrilla tactics, and the second is the large-scale battle between the Israelite army and the Assyrian forces. In both cases, the poet gives new emphasis to the idea of war as divine punishment by increasing the active role of providence, and by adding an apocalyptic dimension to the eternal punishment of the heathen enemy. In doing so, the poet both acknowledges the biblical conception of "holy war" and revises aspects of it to bring it in line with patristic and medieval understandings of "just war." The poet also explores the universalizing potential of the Judith story. The book of Judith, composed during the Hasmonean period, was seen to represent a new theology and locus of Jewish self-identification: its narrative registered a new attitude toward the practice of conversion in Judaism. As we shall see, the Old English *Judith* reflects a similar understanding of *genus* and divine election: the poet systematically downplays the role of specific Jewish rituals and practices in order to place greater stress upon faith and belief—the core essentials of Pauline devotion.

Several preliminary conclusions may be drawn from the comparison of these texts. The first is that all of the poems update aspects of Old Testament narratives so that they may more effectively "speak to" Anglo-Saxon audiences. They expunge detailed descriptions about Jewish ritual and practice in order to create a more universalizing canvas for adaptation. The second, perhaps more surprising, observation is that Old English Old Testament poets were sensitive to the unique cultural, religious, and political contexts (such as exile, diaspora, and persecution) that shaped individual biblical narratives, which were composed at different times, by different authors, and with different rhetorical emphases. Such perceived differences (of time of composition, historical event, and genre) formed the basis for highly individualized modes of adaptation and translation of Old Testament narratives in Anglo-Saxon England.

Notes

1 For a recent overview of Anglo-Saxon adaptations of the Old Testament and their attitudes toward it, see the volume of collected essays, eds., Fox and Sharma (2012).

2 Marsden (1995: 1–3).

3 Marsden (1995: 1–3). Seventeen Anglo-Saxon manuscripts (compiled between the sixth and eleventh centuries) contain portions of Old Testament texts. In addition to pandects, this number includes one part-format bible, and a series of manuscripts containing isolated leaves or fragments of Old Testament texts. Marsden speculates, on the basis of the textual *stemma* he constructs, that "at least eight small Old Testament volumes and six complete Bibles" are certain to have existed in Anglo-Saxon England (Marsden 1995: 3).

4 Marsden (1995).

5 Crawford (Heptatuech 1922) has edited these prose translations.

6 For a facsimile of the manuscript, see Dodwell and Clemoes (1974); for a study of this manuscript, see Withers (2007).

7 The image is from MS British Library, Cotton Claudius B.IV, fol. 136v. It depicts Moses encouraging Joshua to assume leadership of the Israelites and to guide them through the desert to the promised land (Deuteronomy 31:7). For a study of the figure of the "horned Moses" in this manuscript and throughout the ages, see Mellinkoff (1970).

8 The iconography of the "horned Moses" famously arose from a "misreading" of the Hebrew *queren*, which may mean "horn" or "ray of light," in Exodus 34:29, a detail that describes Moses's radiance as he descends from Sinai the second time with the Ten Commandments. Jerome translates the Hebrew word as *cornuta* in his Latin Vulgate. Both the Anglo-Saxon translator and illuminator interpret this description literally. The Old English translator describes Moses as *gehyrned* ("horned"), while the illuminator depicts him as wearing a headdress with horns. Mellinkoff takes the horned headdress as a sign of virility and leadership and compares it with ancient and Germanic pagan iconography (Mellinkoff 1970: 1–2). Though in the Cotton Claudius manuscript the "horned Moses" technically should not appear until fol. 136v (where Moses descends from Sinai; cf. Exodus 34:29), Mellinkoff points out that depictions appear as early as folios 78v, 79r, and 79v. Mellinkoff also detects signs of a subsequent illuminator's correction (Mellinkoff 1970).

9 For the negative stereotype of the "horned Jew," see Mellinkoff (1970: 121–37). Mittman (forthcoming), however, highlights the gigantic size of Moses as a sign of reverence and otherness.

10 Morey (2000: 9).

11 It has been suggested that the mode of instruction, even for monks, was "almost exclusively oral." See Riché (1976: 391–2; 458–77).

12   For a discussion of monastic reading practices (including *lectio divina* and *ruminatio*), see Leclercq (2007: 71–88) and Parkes (1999: 90–102). Also see Foot's study of meditative reading in Anglo-Saxon England (2006: chapters 4 and 5).

13   For an edition and translation of Alfred's *Preface*, see Sweet, ed. 1871. There has been much discussion and debate about the actual state of learning and literacy in Alfred's day and age. Morrish (1986: 87–107) argued that Alfred exaggerated the problem for rhetorical effect. Gneuss (1986: 29–49) and Lapidge (1996: 409–39) contextualize Alfred's claim by examining waves of book production in this period. For an overview of learning and literacy during the period of the tenth-century Benedictine reform, see Foot (2006: 343–8), Lapidge (1993: 1–48), and Bullough (1972: 453–94).

14   For the various services of the liturgy in Anglo-Saxon England, see Pfaff (2009).

15   Karkov has argued that the manuscript illuminations in Junius 11 have a typological and interpretive function of their own, separate from the text. She writes that the images "both illustrate[] the poetic text and translate[]it into a new pictorial language. Like the poems they accompany, the drawings require an audience capable of reading and interpreting correctly; indeed, the need to read and interpret properly is one of the central themes of the manuscript. At every level the manuscript itself demands the active participation of each reader/viewer at each new reading" (2001: 8–9).

16   Bede, book 6, 369–70. Bede mentions the panels twice more in his homily on Benedict Biscop and in his commentary on the Temple of Solomon. See also Dodwell (1982: 85–92) and Meyvaert (1979). The tradition of study and meditation through biblical images would continue in the "picture-book bibles" (also called *Biblia pauperum*, "bibles for paupers")—which became popular in the thirteenth century (Henry 1987).

17   See, especially, my analysis of Exodus in Chapter 1.

18   Godden (1991: 206).

19   Raw (1991: 227). See, especially, the poems *The Dream of the Rood* (Vercelli Book), which is based on the Passion narrative, and *Christ I–III* (Exeter Book), which, respectively, describe scenes of the Nativity, Ascension, and Judgment. Anglo-Saxon poets recast these scenes to reflect the active and heroic agency of Christ. On the originality of these Anglo-Saxon depictions in literature and iconography, see, for example, Meyer Schapiro's (1943: 135–52) study of the Ascension motif, and Goldschmidt (1939: 709–28).

20 Godden (1991: 206–26).

21 Godden (1991: 206–7).

22 Godden (1991: 207).

23 Hodgkin (1935: 159). Hodgkin writes that an Anglo-Saxon reader's "attention was turned to the Old Testament rather than the New. He was fed on the spirit of the Old Testament as well as its stories. The new religion was coloured as a new form of warfare, to attract a pugnacious people."

24 ASPR I.

25 Doane 1991.

26 Karkov (2001: 1–44). Comparison with other illuminated biblical texts has given rise to some speculation about the content of the missing images (see her table of reconstructed images, pp. 203–6).

27 The poems survive in this unique manuscript. However, it is clear that they were copied from at least one previous textual witness (see Lucas, ed. 1994: 15).

28 Raw (1978: 1; 1984: 187–207) and Remley (1996: 78–87).

29 Hall (2002a: 22).

30 Remley (1996: 78–87).

31 Hall (2002a: 20–52).

32 Hall (2002a: 25–41).

33 Although no texts of Augustine's *De catechizandis rudibus* survive from Anglo-Saxon England, it was cited by Ælfric in his *Catholic Homilies* ii.4, 239–46 (Lapidge 2006b: 252). As Hall demonstrates, portions of Augustine's regimen were also adapted in Wulfstan's *sermo 6* (Hall 2002a: 25–41).

34 Hall (2002a: 30).

35 Hall (2002a: 33).

36 This interpretation of *Daniel* is echoed by Scheil (2004: 169–77). Scheil highlights the fall of the Israelites from favor, citing the poet's negative employment of the *populus Israhel* trope.

37 On the order and arrangement of texts in this manuscript, see Orchard (1995).

38 Tolkien (1984). See Orchard (1995, 2003).

39 See, for example, the elaborate depiction of monsters and other marvels in the so-called "Hereford map" (ca. 1285); Westrem (2001).

40 The illuminations in the *Beowulf*-manuscript have been reproduced in a searchable digital facsimile (Kiernan, *Beowulf*, digital facsimile,1991); A digital facsimile is also available online at http://www.bl.uk/manuscripts/FullDisplay.aspx?ref=Cotton_MS_vitellius_a_xv

41   Griffith, ed. (1997: 63, n. 210).

42   Colgrave and Mynors, eds. and trans. (1969: 414–27). The poem and the surrounding account were later translated into English sometime during the reign of Alfred the Great in the ninth century. Latin and Old English versions survive in multiple copies with variant readings (see O'Donnell, ed. 2005).

43   Colgrave and Mynors, eds. and trans. (1969: 416–17).

44   Colgrave and Mynors, eds. and trans. (1969: 416–17).

45   Colgrave and Mynors, eds. and trans. (1969: 416–17).

46   The growing corpus of eighth-century memorial verse and inscriptional poetry pushes the date of the Oldest English poetry back further than Cædmon's hymn (see Okasha 1971 and recently Bredehoft 2009). In any case, Cædmon's hymn deserves to share the limelight with the proverb from Winfrid's time (ca. 757–86) and recorded in the Bonifatian correspondence, written in Continental orthography, but in eighth-century West-Saxon dialect: *Oft daedlata domæ forældit,/ sigisitha gahuem, suuyltit thi ana* ("often the sluggard delays in regard to glory, to every successful venture, and thus dies alone").

47   Colgrave and Mynors, eds. and trans. (1969: 419).

48   Holsinger (2007: 149).

49   See Stanton (2002: 116–17).

50   See Stanton (2002: 116–17).

51   Colgrave and Mynors, eds. and trans. (1969: 418–19).

52   Holsinger (2007: 153).

53   Holsinger (2007: 153).

54   Holsinger (2007: 156). There is one point about which I disagree with Holsinger. He interprets the extensive corpus attributed to Cædmon as clear evidence that vernacular poetry was used in the liturgy, and cites Cædmon's instruction in "the whole series of sacred history" as representative of the daily cycle of devotion. It may be that Holsinger is right; in pre-Viking England, the forms of the liturgy were still malleable, and it may be that parts of it were performed in the vernacular. However, they also may have been recited, performed, or read in other venues outside of church, as the two reports of Arator and Aldhelm performing their biblical poetry suggest. See my discussion below, 15, and 40 n. 70 and 71.

55 Holsinger (2007: 156).

56 For a detailed account of Jerome's project of translation, see Copeland (1991: 44–9).

57 These are Augustine's words from his *Epistle* 140.6.15 (CSEL 44.166.18–23). Cf. Stock (1996: 70).

58 Lapidge (2006), Orchard (1994), and Green (2006: 351–72).

59 For "epic" poems written specifically on Old Testament subjects, see Proba's *Cento Uirgilianus* (ca. 360 AD); Pseudo-Cyprianus's *Heptateuchos* (fifth century); and Marius Claudius Victor's *Alethia* (fifth century). Of these, only the *Heptateuchos* has survived in a full Anglo-Saxon copy (Gneuss 2001: no. 159). There were also scores of Latin biblical *carmina* (by such important poets as Prudentius and Paulinus of Nola), from both Late Antiquity and the Carolingian periods, written in different metrical styles. For overviews, see Dinkova-Bruun (2007) and Orchard (1994: 161–218).

60 Lapidge (2006: 11).

61 For detailed information about these manuscripts, see Gneuss's entries (2001) for Juvencus's *Libri Evangeliorum* (7, 12, 87, 489, 540, 903); Sedulius's *Carmen Paschale* (nos. 12, 53, 253, 491, 652, 824.5, 890, 903); and Arator's *Historia Apostolica* (12, 175, 280, 488, 523.5, 620.6, 660, 890).

62 Lapidge cites further information about the dissemination and readership of these poems on the basis of booklists, inventories, and textual citations (Lapidge 2006).

63 Orchard (1994: 161–218).

64 Lapidge (1993) compares the richly descriptive style of *Exodus* lines 447–515 with a series of passages depicting the Crossing of the Red Sea in the poetic works of Avitus, Sedulius, and Arator. For Lapidge, Avitus's poem employs "violent and martial language," and attributes the bloodiness of the Red Sea to the outpouring of Egyptian blood. However, Sedulius's *Carmen Paschale* and Arator's *Historia Apostolica* represent even closer analogues, because they interpret the Crossing of the Red Sea through the distinctive typological lens of Christian baptism. According to Lapidge, "Sedulius made explicit Christ's presence at the Red Sea Crossing and explained the event as a primitive (*rude*) baptism" (22), while Arator saw the miracle of the sea, and the mingling of blood and water as a type for Christ's Crucifixion, and for the sacraments of the Baptism and Eucharist. The fact that *Exodus* employs no parallel allegorical program does not deter Lapidge.

65   Green (2006: 358–9). Green summarizes the current state
of affairs, remarking that the absence of such hard evidence
"should not be a deterrent to stating the real possibility, or rather,
probability, that the English tradition is in a real way inspired, or
certainly authenticated by Juvencus and his Latin followers. It is
only to be expected that their outstanding popularity in Anglo-
Saxon England would generate an enthusiasm to do likewise in
the vernacular" (358–9).

66   See Green (2006) for an excellent overview.

67   Green (2006: 1–9, 135). Sedulius is also given honorable mention
in the *Decretum Gelasianum*, where it states *insigni laude
praeferimus* ("we distinguish him with outstanding praise").

68   Green (2006: 12). Jerome did, however, criticize Proba for
"making Vergil speak of Christ" (Green 2006: 7). Jerome also
records a nightmare in which he is beaten for preferring Cicero to
Christ (Epistle 22.30; CSEL 54. 189–91; Green 2006: 12), while
Augustine famously discusses the dangerous lure of pagan poetry
in his *Confessions* (1.13–17).

69   Green (2006: 352).

70   Green (2006: 251). Because of the crowd's enthusiastic response,
three additional performances followed. Green adds that Arator's
"performance recalls the practice of public recitation in the heyday
of Roman literature, but no such performance is known in Late
Antiquity" (252).

71   In his twelfth-century *Gesta pontificum Anglorum* (Preest, trans.
2002: 227–8), William of Malmesbury tells a wistful anecdote
(which he claims to have found in King Alfred's own *Handbook*),
in which he depicts the Anglo-Saxon poet Aldhelm standing on
a bridge and singing biblical verse in English in order to edify the
churchgoers as entered or left mass. On the credibility of this
passage, see Remley (2005: 90–2).

72   Paraphrased from Green (2006: 71).

73   Scheil (2004: 195–8).

74   Green (2006: 268–92).

75   Green (2006: 316).

76   Shea, trans. *The Poems of Alcimus Ecdicius Avitus* (1997: 113).

77   Scheil (2004: 1970).

78   The representation of Jews in late medieval English literature
and art has been a topic of persistent scholarly attention. See, for
example, Bale (2006); Delany (2002); and Kruger (2006).

79   See, especially, Jameson (1981: 1–102).

80 Scott and Cavanaugh (2006: 1).

81 Scott and Cavanaugh (2006: 1).

82 Hollerich (2006: 107–22); Dyzenhaus (1997, 85–101) cites Schmitt's anti-liberal jurisprudence and his fervent anti-semitism.

83 Cf. "Foreword," Schmitt (1985: xx–xxi).

84 Schmitt (1985: 5). The precise meaning of Schmitt's term, *Ausnahmezustand*, has been much debated. As Strong notes, "what the first translation might seem to reinforce (the absolute and dictatorial and unlimited quality of the decision), this second might seem to mitigate. A dictionary will tell you that the word means 'state of emergency' " ("Foreword," Schmitt 1985: xiii).

85 Vinx (2010).

86 Vinx (2010: xxi). It has been argued that Schmitt's views on sovereignty and the powers of exception provide "the intellectual basis of contemporary calls for a strong executive power unhampered by constraints of legality" (Vinx 2010, citing Dyzenhaus 2006, 35–54; Scheuerman 2006).

87 Vinx (2010).

88 See further Meier (1998).

89 Schmitt (1985: 37).

90 Strong "Foreword," Schmitt (1985: xxvii).

91 Canning (1996: 8). Canning demonstrates that, in reality, the claim to absolutism in the *Corpus iuris civilis* was most likely exaggerated and idealized (see Canning on the *lex regia*, 1996: 9). However, its core ideology—rule by theocracy—remained remarkably resilient and provided the paradigm upon which all subsequent monarchies were based. The rediscovery of the *Corpus iuris civilis* in the eleventh century played an important role in the transmission of these ideas through the Middle Ages and early modern period.

92 The view that Schmitt's fascist ideology cannot be disentangled from his writings on law and sovereignty has been strongly asserted (see Wolin 1992; Dyzenhaus 1997; Scheuerman 1999). Schmitt's defenders, however, argue that his "analysis of liberal constitutionalism during the Weimar period is separable from his support for National Socialism and that it constitutes an insightful and important analysis of the political presuppositions of a well-functioning liberal constitutional system" (Vinx 2010; on this point Vinx cites Bendersky 1983; Schwab 1989; Gottfried 1990; Kennedy 2004). There has also been some attempt to recuperate aspects of Schmitt's work from both a leftist and liberal point of view, following the early lead of Jewish luminaries like Hannah Arendt and Walter Benjamin who knew Schmitt and engaged with his political ideas (Strong "Foreword," Schmitt 1985: xiv).

93   Monagle (2010: 115).

94   In England, several such critical moments called into question the proper offices of "church" and "state." The most important was the struggle over investiture between Pope Gregory VII and Henry IV in 1075. However, an earlier incident occurred between Henry I of England and Pope Paschal II in the years 1103–7. See Cantor (1993: 286).

95   Gumbrecht (2011: 84).

96   At the most basic level, there is the acknowledged difference between rule by multiple kings (and later Wessex dynasty) in Anglo-Saxon England and the concept of Empire transmitted from Rome to Frankish rule.

97   Howe (1989: 1–7) compares the Anglo-Saxon migration myth to Puritan ideologies concerning colonization. See Chapter 1 of this book.

98   Cheyfitz 1991 offers an account of the imperialistic trope of election as it developed in connection with European-American expansion. He investigates the "language of empire" that translates native inhabitants into "savages," "cannibals," and "Indians."

99   O'Donovan (1996: 2).

100   Although proponents of Marxism tend to argue that its "political perspective" represents "the absolute horizon of all reading and interpretation" (Jameson 1981: 17), their approach still hinges on the modern conceptions of commodity and economy, both of which cannot be applied willy-nilly to ancient societies.

101   O'Donovan (1996: 3).

102   Brueggemann (2006).

103   The "Documentary Hypothesis" (sometimes called JEDP) articulates the view that "the Pentateuch and book immediately following were artfully created by combining a number of older documents into a single, sustained account" (Gabel et al. 1986: 346). These documents refer to the four main sources that were edited or redacted together. The acronym JEDP stands for the Yahwistic, Elohistic, Deuteronomic, and Priestly traditions. See Coogan et al., ed. (2001: 3–7) for an overview.

104   Brueggemann (2006: 9).

105   Walzer (1985: 90–93, 107) develops the notion of a "radically contingent" Covenant of Sinai, based upon faith and observance.

106 O'Donovan (1996: 45–46). While nations both before and after ancient Israel viewed themselves as "chosen peoples," what made Israel's covenant with God unique was that "there [was] no precedent for a treaty between God and an entire people or for a treaty whose conditions are literally the laws of morality" (Walzer 1985: 74).

107 As Harris (2003: 131–56) argues, the self-fashioning of the English as a chosen people cast in the footsteps of Israel was a theme that continued well into the post-Conquest era, at which point it competed with other Norman ethnogenetic myths that claimed special descent from the Trojans.

108 Scheil (2004: 19).

109 For a more in-depth analysis of these tropes, see Scheil (2004: 1–20).

110 Scheil's investigation of the somatic difference of the Jews in Anglo-Saxon contexts remains the most comprehensive to date (2004: 195–330).

111 Important precursor texts include Rufinus's Latin translation of Eusebius of Caesarea's *Ecclesiastical History* (Greek 263–340 AD; trans. 345–410/11 AD), Paulus Orosius's *Historiarum adversum paganos libri VII* (ca. 417 AD), Salvian of Marseille's *De gubernatione Dei* (ca. 439–51 AD), and poems by Paulinus of Nola (early fifth century). See further Hanning (1996), supplemented by Scheil (2004).

112 Scheil (2004: 152).

113 See Wormald (1983, 1994). One could, of course, take this claim much further to debate the applicability in the first place of the concept "nation" in this period by invoking the work of Benedict Anderson (*Imagined Communities: Reflections on the Origin and Spread of Nationalism*). For engagement with Anderson's ideas in relation to Anglo-Saxon England, see Harris (2003: 38–9).

114 For discussions of Bede's use of this theme of chosenness, see, especially, Wormald (1994: 1–23 at 1, 12–16; and 1983: 121–25), Scheil (2004: 111–42), Harris (2003: 45–82), and Zacher (2010).

115 Wormald (1994: 14).

116 Zacher (2010: 77–8).

117 As a matter of fact, Bede cultivated the ideal of a united "English people" far in advance of any such political reality (cf. Wormald 1983: 105; 1992).

118 *Haec in praesenti iuxta numerum librorum quibus lex diuina scripta est, quinque gentium linguis unam eandemque summae* *ueritatis et uerae sublimitatis scientiam scrutatur et confitetur, Anglorum uidelicet Brettonum Scottorum Pictorum et Latinorum, quae meditatione scripturarum ceteris omnibus est facta communis.* Colgrave and Mynors, eds., trans. (1969: 16–17).

119   Zacher (2012a: 78).

120   Scheil (2004: 109).

121   Zacher (2012b: 463–65).

122   See Zacher (2012b: 466–74) and Chapter 3.

123   Harris (2003: 180). On the appearance of similar tropes in the writings of Ælfric, see Godden: 225.

124   For the adoption of the entwinement of the theme of Old Testament election with genealogies going back to Trojan ancestry, see Tanner (1993).

125   According to Wallace-Hadrill (1971: 48–50), the Frankish kings began to cultivate a view of themselves as inheriting the divine right to rule as early as the seventh century in the reign of Clovis. On the potential influence of the Frankish model upon English expressions of chosenness (beginning with Bede), see Wormald (1994: 11–15).

126   Pratt (2007: 73).

127   Pratt (2007: 73), Nelson (1986: 290–2), and Garrison (2000: 129–30). The original edition of the code was commissioned by the first king of all the Franks, Clovis I (ca. 466–511), sometime between 507 and 511.

128   Garrison (2000: 129).

129   Garrison (2000: 124).

130   This important observation about the influence of Anglo-Saxon scholars on Frankish conceptions of nationhood is Garrison's (2000: 150–54).

131   Nelson (1986: 283–307).

132   Pratt (2007: 73).

133   Norman F. Cantor (1993: 167–8) describes Boniface's connection to the Frankish kingdom as follows: he was "one of the truly outstanding creators of the first Europe, as the apostle of Germany, the reformer of the Frankish church, and the chief foment[e]r of the alliance between the papacy and the Carolingian family."

134   Garrison (2000: 158).

135   Legg (1901:24).

136   Pratt (2007: 76).

137 It is a testament to the staying power of this imagery that the essential elements of the coronation service used in modern times in England can still be traced back to these earliest Anglo-Saxon services. The anointing ceremony in particular is still based upon the Solomonic ideal. The following description is given of the coronation ceremony of Queen Elizabeth II in 1953: "Four Knights of the Garter hold a canopy over the Chair and, concealed from view, the Archbishop anoints the Sovereign with holy oil on the hands, the breast and the head. This is the most solemn part of the coronation service, for by anointing the monarch is set apart or consecrated for the duties of a Sovereign. Meanwhile the choir sings the anthem [used by] Zadok the Priest, the words of which (from the first book of Kings) have been sung at every coronation since King Edgar's in 973. Since the coronation of George II in 1727 the setting by Handel has always been used" ("Guide to the Coronation Service at Westminster Abbey," http://www.westminster-abbey.org/our-history/royals/coronations/guide-to-the-coronation-service, last accessed December 16, 2012; missing text supplied in square brackets).

138 There are records of earlier anointings in Mercia and Northumbria, but there is no evidence that the ceremony was codified by this point (Legg 1901: 24).

139 See Wormald (1994, 1995). Technically speaking, Æthelstan was the first to style himself a *rex totius Britanniae*, or the "king of all of Britain." On the significance of this regal designation, see Wormald (1983: 110–12). In the earliest charters of Æthelstan's reign, his subscription appears as *Angul Saxonum rex* or *rex Anglorum* (as in Sawyer 396, 397, 399, 400, 403, and 405), whereas by 931 he more commonly subscribes as *rex totius Brittanniae* (see Sawyer 416, 421, 422, 430, 438, 446, and 448 for his subscription).

140 For an overview of these genealogies, see Anlezark (2002). The relevant genealogies are contained in the B and C versions of *Anglo-Saxon Chronicle* for the year 855; in Asser's *Life of King Alfred*, ch. 1 [d. 893]; and in the *Chronicle of Æthelweard* III.3 [d. 1000]).

141 Wormald (1999: 416–30) and Pratt (2007: 170). This use of Solomonic iconography for kings was largely the invention of Anglo-Saxon England. According to Nelson, "although Solomon was cited in the Carolingian *ordine*, under Hincmar Old Testament symbolism was diluted by parallels with baptism and Episcopal consecration. This was an identifiably West Saxon form of Solomonic posturing, of significance specific to West Saxon rule" (Pratt 2007: 76; see also Nelson 1986: 355 ff.).

142 In an oft-cited passage from his *Life of Alfred*, Asser compares Alfred's wisdom and learning to that of King Solomon: "In this respect he resembled the holy, highly esteemed and exceedingly wealthy Solomon, King of the Hebrews, who, once upon a time, having come to despise all renown and wealth of this world, sought wisdom from God, and thereby achieved both (namely, wisdom and renown in this world), as it is written 'Seek ye therefore first the Kingdom of God, and his justice, and all these things shall be given to you' [Matthew vi. 33]" (Stephenson 76–77). As Pratt has shown in a detailed reading of this passage (2007: 152–3), the incident in question is a dream attributed to Solomon in the aftermath of his accession, in which God appears to him and offers to grant him any request. When Solomon asks for an "understanding heart in order to judge his people," God grants him his wish, and also grants him riches, wealth, and glory. He also "stimulat[ed] his intelligence from within."

143 Wormald (1999: 417–29).

144 Wormald (1999: 417–18).

145 Wormald (1999: 419–20) demonstrates that a similar collection of extracts is found in the eighth-century Irish *Liber ex lege Moysi*, which circulated in manuscripts of Irish law, and was probably known in England at the time of Alfred's reign.

146 Wormald (1999: 426).

147 Marsden (1995: 401). Cf. Foot (2002: 55).

148 Chaney (1970) and Karkov (2004). In a forthcoming article, Adam S. Cohen explores the Davidic iconography associated with King Edgar and proposes a new reading of his portrait.

149 Withers (1999) makes the provocative argument that the Old English manuscripts of the Heptateuch record an obsessive interest in the Old Testament history of the covenant. In a study dedicated to the textual layout of the Old English prose *Genesis*, he shows that it includes a series of rubrics that are not witnessed in the Vulgate tradition. The rubrics, acting as chapter titles, effectively "divide the story of Genesis into a series of holy biographies of the patriarchs Noah, Abraham and Joseph" (111).

1

Exodus: Reconstructing the Ethnogenetic Myths of the Hebrews

Are these the folk whom from the brittish Iles,
Through the stern billows of the watry main,
I safely led so many thousand miles,
As if their journey had been through a plain?
Whom having from all enemies protected,
And through so many deaths and dangers well directed,
I brought and planted on the western shore,
Where nought but bruits and salvage wights did swarm
(untaught, untrain'd, untam'd by vertue's lore
That sought their blood, yet could not do them harm?

— II.149–581, MICHAEL WIGGLESWORTH, 1662

In his poem "God's Controversy With New England," Michael Wigglesworth describes the journey of the pilgrims to the New World as a second Exodus and the people of New England as a "New Israel." The colonists who settled in America are depicted as God's transplanted people, liberated from "deaths and danger" in the British Isles and protected from the wild inhabitants of New England. Implicated in this teleological trope is a narrative of progress: the chosen sojourners bring the hope of Truth and light to the "untaught, untrain'd, [and the] untam'd." [1]

The story of the Israelites' sojourn in Egypt and their eventual emancipation provided an attractive and remarkably elastic template for a wide range of liberation theologies in Western history and literature.[2] The series of events included the medieval crusades, the revolutionary campaigns of the peasant's revolt in Germany, the protestant sermons of John Calvin and John Knox, and the parliamentary speeches of Oliver Cromwell.[3] Moreover, the Exodus narrative in later centuries lived on as a secular tale of "moral progress" and "transformation." Thus, it was productively adopted in the context of communist politics in defense of Leninist politics in the writings of Ernst Bloch.[4] In later periods of American history, the story of the Exodus was revisited and reused in the counterideologies of the abolitionist movement in the South, and in subsequent equal rights movements.

What provided the foundation for this comparison was the common understanding of the book of Exodus as the paradigm *par excellence* of political theology. Exodus was the national epic of the Israelites. It codified the special relationship between God and his chosen people by means of a mutual compact. As Michael Walzer has argued, Moses's primary role in the flight from Egypt was not religious, but rather political.[5] God had commissioned him not only to liberate the Israelites from slavery, but also to transform this chosen nation (physically and psychologically) into a free people. Moses "didn't do this merely by breaking their chains, but also by organizing them into a 'political society' and giving them laws."[6] Thus, in Walzer's formulation, it was Moses who brought the Israelites "positive freedom," that is, "not so much ... a way of life free from regulation, but rather a way of life to whose regulation they could, and did agree."[7] The transition from Egypt to the wilderness and eventually to the promised land offered a teleological progression from *problem* to *struggle* to *resolution.* The bible's mythologized travel across space was readily reconstructed "as a movement from one political regime to another."[8]

These interpretations and adaptations of the Exodus story from the late medieval period through the modern era may well provide a clue as to how and why Anglo-Saxon writers and preachers adapted this narrative to their own ideological purposes. In this chapter, I explore the ways in which the biblical narrative is rewritten and recast in the

Anglo-Saxon poem *Exodus*. A frequent claim in *Exodus* scholarship is that the poem focuses exclusively on a single scene—the crossing of the Red Sea, as narrated in Exodus 12–15:1—to which is added a brief digression, narrating parts of Genesis (lines 362–446). Against this view, I would like to argue that the poet's sweeping politico-theological vision extends well beyond this episode, and in fact, beyond the nationally circumscribed narrative contained in the biblical book.[9] The poet traces and draws upon the whole history of the "authentic Israel"—which is to say, the Israel of the covenant, from Abraham to Jacob to Judah and to David, in all of its different political and cultural manifestations—from the first covenant forged during the nomadic period, to the conquest of Canaan, to the tribal period, and finally to the monarchy. The promise of the covenant is not something applied through mere analogy in the poem. As we shall see, the poet employs a range of mnemotechnical devices that encourage personal reflection and meditation upon the covenant as personal contract. The aim is to create a meditative template that allows each of its readers to experience the terms of the covenant individually. A montage of images drawn from the biblical Exodus acts as a rhetorical *ductus* designed to lead the mind through its network of images. Though the poet initiates the process of meditation, it is completed by the "inner teacher" of the rational soul, described in detail at the end of the poem.

Importing Exodus

Exodus has been celebrated as one of the most lively, erudite, and innovative poems in Old English. Lucas claims that "*Exodus* stands out by virtue of the sheer brilliance of its writing," and Greenfield comments that *Exodus* is "one of the most stirring and exciting of Old English poems" written in epic tone and style.[10] The poem has been praised for its variety of styles and rhythms, ranging from animated description to vivid narration and lively speech.

The poet's technique of adaptation, expansion, and intertextual combination is epitomized in the energetic passages describing the Parting of the Red Sea (447–515). These sixty-eight lines expand upon two brief verses in Exodus 14:27–8[11]:

27) And when Moses had stretched forth his hand towards the sea, it returned at the first break of day to the former place: and as the Egyptians were fleeing away, the waters came upon them, and the Lord shut them up in the middle of the waves. 28) And the waters returned, and covered the chariots and the horsemen of all the army of Pharao, who had come into the sea after them, neither did there so much as one of them remain (trans. here and throughout from the Douay-Rheims bible).

Due to the length of the Old English passage, I excerpt two representative portions from the beginning (458–75) and end of the sequence (494b–506):

	Þær ær wegas lagon	
mere modgode	(mægen wæs adrenced),	
streamas stodon.	Storm up gewat	460
heah to heofonum,	herewopa mæst;	
laðe cyrmdon	(lyft up geswearc)	
fægum stæfnum.	Flod blod gewod:	
randbyrig wæron rofene,	rodor swipode	
meredeaða mæst.	Modige swulton,	465
cyningas on corðre.	Cyrm swiðrode	
wæges æt ende;	wigbord scinon.	
Heah ofer hæleðum	holmweall astah,	
merestream modig.	Mægen wæs on cwealme	
fæste gefeterod,	forðganges nep	470
searwum æsæled,	sand basnodon,	
witodre wyrde,	hwonne waðema stream,	
sincalda sæ,	sealtum yðum,	
æflastum gewuna,	ece staðulas,	
nacud nydboda,	neosan come,	475
fah feðegast,	se ðe feondum gehneop.	
....		
	Flodweard gesloh	
unhleowan wæg,	alde mece,	495
þæt ðy deaðdrepe	drihte swæfon,	
synfullra sweot.	Sawlum lunnon	
fæste befarene,	flodblac here,	

siððan hie onbugon   brimyppinge,
modwæga mæst.   Mægen eall gedreas,   500
ða þe gedrecte,   dugoð Egypta,
Faraon mid his folcum.   He onfond hraðe,
siððan grund gestah,   Godes andsaca,
þæt wæs mihtigra   mereflodes Weard--
wolde heorufæðmum   hilde gesceadan,   505
yrre and egesfull.

Where the paths previously lay, the sea now raged (the troop was drowned), streams stood still. The storm flew up high to the heavens, as did the greatest of battle cries. The loathly Egyptians cried out with doomed voices (the skies grew dark). Blood permeated the flood: the shield-ramparts were broken, and the greatest of sea-deaths lashed against the heavens. Brave kings perished amid their troops. Their cry subsided at the sea's edge; battle shields gleamed. The wall of the sea, a valiant sea-stream, climbed high above the warriors. The troop was fettered fast in death, bound by their armor without the power of advance. The sands awaited their appointed fate, as to when the streams of the waves—that perpetually cold sea accustomed to its own natural course, a naked messenger of distress, a hostile warlike spirit that crushed enemies—should return to seek its eternal foundations with its salty waves.

    ...

    The Guardian of the Flood struck the unprotected wave with an ancient sword, so that the troops and the hosts of sinners perished by its death-swing. Surrounded, the flood-pale army of Egyptians lost their souls after they were subdued by the sea's rising and by the greatest of raging waves. The whole troop fell, the host of the Egyptians, all of those who were afflicted, Pharaoh together with his people. The adversary of God understood quickly after he sank to the ground, that the Guardian of the Sea-flood was the mightier. Angry and terrible, [Pharaoh] had wished with the sword's embrace to decide that battle.[12]

The passage pulses with epic energy and excitement. As Lucas notes, the poet fills the verses with extra "alliterative pyrotechnics" and produces "a breathless staccato-like effect" that dramatically conveys the crashing of the waves.[13] There is also occasional rhyme: the self-rhyming phrase *Flod blod gewod* ("blood saturated the flood"; 463b) marks the mixture of blood and water, providing a common etiology for the Red Sea. The poet also packs the sequence with nonce words and poetic compounds that give precise shape and meaning to his vision of the sea wall. It is called *se holmweall* ("sea-wall"; 468); *se blodegesa* ("blood-terror"; 478); *se famigbosma* ("the foamy-bosomed [sea]"; 494); *nacud nydboda* ("naked messenger of distress"; 475); and *se meretorr* ("sea-tower"; 485).

However, the most striking change is the poet's addition of martial imagery that pervades the entire poem. God is depicted as a warrior, and the sea and wind as his willing soldiers. The poet's militaristic vocabulary and tone have been attributed to various sources and influences: Lucas identifies Germanic-heroic diction and phrasing, while Lapidge suggests broad parallels with the biblical poetic traditions of Late Antiquity.[14] Although these influences may well be heard in the poem, the most compelling source for these lines is the "Song of the Sea" in Exodus 15.1–18, which offers a poetic, and, by most accounts, older variation of the events narrated in Exodus 14. Surprisingly, Moses's "Song" has never been proposed as the main source for the episode of the crossing of the Red Sea in *Exodus*.[15] This "Song of Moses" celebrates God as a "warrior-King," whose demeanor is more reminiscent of Poseidon than the veiled and distant Lord of Exodus 14. He is described as a man of war (*Dominus quasi vir pugnator*) who crushes the Egyptians with the strength of his right arm and drowns them with a single blast of air from his nostrils. Several of these details are reduplicated in the passage from *Exodus* quoted earlier: in it God is described as a "guardian of the flood" (*Flodweard*; 494) and the "Guardian of the sea-flood" (*mereflodes Weard*; 504), who punishes with a "slaughterous grasp" (*wælfæðm*; 486, cf. Exodus 15:6, 12, 16) and a "holy hand" (*halige hand*; 485–7). As in the biblical Exodus 15:14 and 16, terror itself is animated and represented as an unremitting weapon: in the Old English, the Egyptians experience "flood-terror" (*flodegesa*; 447), while the ocean is described as being furious in mind or intention (480). The biblical example in Exodus 15:9 likewise anticipates the poet's sudden shift in perspective to the Egyptian victims in the midst of the crashing flood. In line 503 we are told that Pharaoh, the "adversary of God" (*godes andsaca*), had attempted to win the day by the sword ("angry and terrible [Pharaoh] had wished with the sword's embrace to decide that battle"). This line corresponds roughly to Exodus 15:9, which states, "The enemy said: I will pursue and overtake, I will divide the spoils, my soul shall have its fill: I will draw my sword, my hand shall slay them" (*dixit inimicus persequar et conprehendam dividam spolia implebitur anima mea evaginabo gladium meum interficiet eos manus mea*).

It has often been noted that the Old English poet omits Moses's "Song of the Sea" at the end of the Red Sea crossing and substitutes instead a far more pedestrian and brief homiletic injunction to keep the covenant (in lines 554–64). Another way to read this substitution is to treat Moses's biblical "song" as a substantive model for the entire Old English poem. The prosimetric composition witnessed in Exodus 14 and 15 provides a direct stylistic paradigm for the versification and variation of *Exodus*.[16] It also presents a powerful model for the poem's political vision. Walter Brueggemann has called the biblical "Song of Moses" the paradigmatic event in the Old Testament, in which "YHWH is rendered as the great force and agent who confronts the absolute political power of Pharaoh, and through a series of contests delegitimates and finally overthrows the imperial power of Egypt."[17] The God of Exodus offers an attractive contrast to Pharaoh's regime— he offers abundance instead of scarcity, freedom instead of slavery, and a covenant instead of a monopoly of power. This same contrast between God and Pharaoh resonates through the *Exodus*.

The "Tribal Digression": The Chosen Line

The *Exodus*-poet's theologico-political vision comes into full focus in a passage that I would like to call the "tribal digression." It is here that the poet brings to the fore his understanding of the Israelites as the chosen people of God. In the biblical Exodus, a mere two verses are devoted to Israel's crossing of the Red Sea:

21) And when Moses had stretched forth his hand over the sea, the Lord took it away by a strong and burning wind blowing all the night, and turned it into dry ground: and the water was divided. 22) And the children of Israel went in through the midst of the sea dried up: for the water was as a wall on their right hand and on their left.

Once Moses parts the waters, the children of Israel—*filii Israhel* in the Vulgate—cross the dry path to safety as a single unit. In the Anglo-Saxon *Exodus*, by contrast, the description runs to some 62 lines and contains an elaborate account of how the first three tribes of Israel entered and crossed the Red Sea. The entire passage is quoted next in order to highlight a number of interpretive cruces. It will be noted that many of the pronouns in the passage are ambiguous. My translation preserves these ambiguities and provides suggested solutions in brackets:

Æfter þam wordum	werod eall aras,	
modigra mægen;	mere stille bad.	300
Hofon herecyste	hwite linde,	
segnas on sande.	Sæweall astah,	
uplang gestod	wið Israhelum	
andægne fyrst,	yðholmes hleo.	
Wæs seo eorla gedriht	anes modes,	305
fæstum fæðmum	freoðowære heold.	
nalles hige gehyrdon	haliges lare	
siððan leofes leoþ	læste near	
sweg swiðrode	ond sances bland.	
Þa þæt feorðe cyn	fyrmest eode,	310
wod on wægstream,	wigan on heape,	
ofer grenne grund,	Iudisc feða,	
on onette	uncuð gelad	
for his mægwinum.	Swa him mihtig God	
þæs dægweorces	deop lean forgeald,	315
siððan him gesælde	sigorworca hreð,	
þæt he ealdordom	agan sceolde	
ofer cynericu,	cneowmaga blæd.	
Hæfdon him to segne,	þa hie on sund stigon,	

ofer bordhreoðan   beacen aræred   320
in þam garheape   gyldenne leon,
drihtfolca mæst,   deora cenost.
Be þam herewisan   hynðo ne woldon
be him lifigendum   lange þolian,
þonne hie to guðe   garwudu rærdon,   325
ðeoda ænigre.   Þraca wæs on ore,
heard handplega,   hægsteald modige
wæpna wælslihtes,   wigend unforhte,
bilswaðu blodige,   beadumægnes ræs,
grimhelma gegrind,   þær ludas for.   330
Æfter þære fyrde   flota modgade,
Rubenes sunu;   randas bæron
sæwicingas   ofer sealtne mersc,
manna menio,   micel angetrum
eode unforht.   He his ealdordom   335
synnum aswefede,   þæt he siðor for
on leofes last   (him on leodsceare
frumbearnes riht   freobroðor oðþah,
ead and æðelo);   næs he earg swa þeah.
Þær æfter him foron   folca þryðum   340
sunu Simeones   sweotum common,
þridde þeodmægen   (þufas wundon
ofer garfare)   guðcyste onþrang
deawig sceaftum.   Dægwoma becwom
ofer garsecge,   Godes beacna sum,   345
morgen meretorht.   Mægen forð gewat.
Þa þær folcmægen   for æfter oðrum
isernhergum   (an wisode
mægenþrymmum mæst,   þy he mære wearð)
on forðwegas,   folc æfter wolcne,   350
cynn æfter cynne.   Cuðe æghwilc
mægburga riht,   swa him Moises bead
eorla æðelo.   Him wæs an fæder,
leof leodfruma,   landriht geþah,
frod on ferhðe,   freomagum leof.   355
Cende cneowsibbe   cenra manna
heahfædera sum,   halige þeode,

Israela cyn,   onriht godes,
swa þæt orþancum   ealde reccað,
þa þe mægburge   mæst gefrunon,   360
frumcyn feora,   fæderæðelo gehwæs.

After these words, the multitude arose, a mass of brave Israelites. The sea remained tranquil. The chosen troops raised their shining linden shields and standards as they reached the sand. That sea-wall of water stood upright for the duration of one day for the Israelites. The company of nobles was of a single mind—they held the covenant fast in their breast. Not at all did they scorn the instruction of the Holy One. Following the song of dear [Moses], and close upon his footsteps, the harmony and the combination of their psalmody grew stronger. Then, the fourth tribe went first, the infantry of Judah, warriors in a single troop, they journeyed out in haste into the water-stream, over the green ground on an unknown path before their kinsmen. Thus, mighty God had offered [Judah] a profound reward for that day's work, after he had given him the victory of triumphant works, in order that [Judah] should have chief authority over the kingdom, the glory of generations of kinsmen. When [the soldiers of Judah], the greatest of noblemen, marched into the sea, they bore a sign as a beacon upon their shields within that spear-troop, a golden lion, the bravest of beasts. Because of that battle leader [Judah] they would not endure humiliation for long—not as long as their leader was still alive, and they reared spears in battle against any nation. The battalion was at the vanguard, fighting with ferocious hand-play. Where Judah went there were brave young warriors, soldiers unafraid of slaughter by weapons, or bloody sword-wounds, or the rush of the army, or the grinding of boar helmets. After that first battalion went forth, the sea-troop—the sons of Reuben—raged; those sea-vikings bore shields over the salty marsh. The troop of men, a powerful host, went unafraid. [Reuben] had destroyed his chief authority with sins, so that he went later in the track of dear [Judah]. His own brother [Judah] had taken away from him the right of the first-born to the nation, his blessedness and his right lineage; nevertheless he was not cowardly. After them went the sons of Simeon, among the throng of people, advancing in a troop, the third tribal power. Standards waved above the martial company. They pressed ahead among the chosen troop with dewy spears. The portent of day appeared over the ocean, one of God's beacons, the sea-bright morning. The troop went forth. The tribal powers went one after another as iron-clad troops. Because he was famous, [Judah] alone guided the most powerful group of combatants onto the paths forward, the people after the cloud, tribe after tribe. Each one knew the rightful order of his tribe, as Moses commanded them concerning the lineage of nobles. There was one father for them all. [Jacob], the dear founder of the people, old and wise in spirit and beloved by his noble kinsmen, had seized his land-right. [Jacob], one of the patriarchs, thus engendered generations of brave men, a holy people, the tribes of Israel, who were entirely deserving of God, just as ancients tell skillfully, those who inquired most about the lineage and the origin of this people, and about each person's paternal ancestry.

Few scholars have paid attention to this original and puzzling expansion. Lucas correctly identifies the inspiration for these lines as Genesis 49:8–12, which relays Jacob's address to his twelve sons before his death and identifies the following details as the most salient: Reuben is ejected from favor as firstborn because he slept with his father's concubine, while Simeon and Levi are disqualified because of their slaughter of the men of Sichem.[18] Lucas assumes that the order of the tribes (Judah, Reuben, Simeon) simply reflects "the order of seniority except for the presence of Judah."[19] Like most critics, he treats these lines as colorful background that serves to intensify the poem's martial imagery. He concludes that the fighting is described in relation to the tribe of Judah—and not the other tribes—"simply because it goes first," and subsumes this sequence within what he perceives to be the poem's larger typological framework.[20] Furthermore, Lucas detects in this passage a series of baptismal images. He explains that "this mode of representation is to be explained only by reference to the exegetical tradition of interpreting the Crossing of the Red Sea as an allegory for Baptism. The Christian Catechumen approaches Baptism as a soldier fighting off assailants (sins)."[21]

This interpretation, however, misses the key point of the digression, namely, that Judah has been granted sovereignty over his brothers. The poem's perspective can better be discovered if we understand how the poet read and reframed Genesis 49: 1–10. In this biblical episode, Jacob's death speech is called a "benediction" to his sons, but what Jacob actually delivers is a *prophecy*: Jacob foretells the good and bad fortune that will befall his sons, and ultimately, the twelve tribes of Israel. In verses 8–10, he predicts that Judah's brothers will bow to him and pay him tribute and homage, and that Judah will retain the scepter "till he come that is to be sent" (*donec veniat qui mittendus est*)—a detail usually taken to refer prophetically to the reign of David, the Lord's anointed. Biblical scholars have traditionally explained this anachronistic reference to David by treating it as a late interpolation, supplied by a Deuteronomic redactor.[22] Central to this interpretation is the presence of the anachronistic Hebrew phrase *shivtei yisrael* (the "tribes of Israel"), which represents a political division that has not yet come to pass at this point in the Genesis narrative. Jacob's speech thus effectively lays out the future history of Israel in order to legitimize Judah as the forbear of the Davidic line.[23]

The Old English poet faithfully retains this political message in full. In lines 314–18, we are told that "mighty God had offered [Judah] a profound reward [*lean*] for that day's work after the triumph of victorious works, in order that he should possess noble status [*ealdordom*] over the kingdom, the glory of generations of kinsmen [*blæd cneowmaga*]." Here, the *lean* is extended to all subsequent generations of Judah. The identification of Reuben's sons as *flotan* and *sæwicingas* ("sailors" and "sea-vikings"; 331, 333) furthermore echoes Genesis 49:4 where it is stated that Reuben's offspring will be *effuses... sicut aqua* ("poured out like water"), thereby losing their inheritance in the process. Simeon's aforementioned revenge on Sichem, moreover, accounts for the detail of the already bloodied spears (344). In contrast with his brothers, Judah emerges as both righteous and valiant. The imperial representation of Judah as a lion's whelp in Genesis 49: 9—a detail that prophesizes his rise to power— is incorporated into the poet's description of the lion standard that Judah takes into battle.[24]

The Old English poet also revises certain details of the Vulgate passage. In the process of recalling Genesis 49, he imposes his own unique political vision. Lines 335–9 state that Reuben lost his *ealdordom* ("chief authority") through sin, and that Judah usurped

Reuben's birthright and the associated benefits of sovereignty. As a matter of fact, from a strict scriptural perspective, the poet's account is inaccurate. Genesis 49 makes it clear that Joseph (not Judah) inherits the birthright; Judah, however, is distinguished as the *expectatio gentium* ("the hope of nations")—the source from which all subsequent kings of Israel will descend (see further 1 Chronicles 5). By contrast, the Old English poet conflates the issues of birthright and sovereignty in order to emphasize the supreme status of Judah as the New Israel, and thereby also foreshadows the rift between the kingdoms of the North and the South, narrated in 2 Kings 17.

But why, one may ask, does the poet depict Judah as a usurper? The answer is that the poet intends to link Judah's fate directly with that of his father, Jacob, who notoriously usurped his birthright from his older brother, Esau. Subsequently, God changes Jacob's name to Israel to commemorate his status as the progenitor of God's chosen nation. This story is briefly rehashed in lines 356–61 of *Exodus*. Most scholars have identified the subject of 356–8 as the first patriarch, Abraham, whose Hebrew name means "father of the nation." It is better, however, to read the subject as Jacob because he (unlike Abraham) commandeered his birthright from his brother. The key phrase "seized his land-right" (*landriht geþah*; 354) echoes the action of Judah, who is said to "have taken away the birthright" (*frumbearnes riht ... oðþah*; 338). Jacob is not just "one of the patriarchs"; rather, he is the "single father" (*an fæder*) and the "progenitor" (*leodfruma*) of these twelve sons, and subsequently of all the "generations" (*cneowsibbum*) of the tribes of Israel. The poet directs us to this interpretation by encoding the popular patristic Hebrew etymology for the name "Israel"—*yesher el*, or "rectitude of God"—in the phrase *onriht godes* ("what is proper to God" or "right of God"; 358). The final lines of "the tribal digression" contain the poet's political vision: like the esteemed *ealde* ("ancients," or possibly "prophets") who proclaim Israel's lineage and paternal ancestry, the poet remembers the Exodus story as a political theology that identifies Judah as the future of Israel.

This politico-theological interpretation sheds new light on the opening lines of this sequence. Like the *Beowulf*-poet who periodically joins the vision of present harmony with future discord, the *Exodus*-poet looks ahead to later events, which will involve political conflict

(305–9).[25] At present, the company of nobles is still of one mind and the troops hold dear the covenant as one *herecyst* ("chosen army"). However, in the future there will be division, and Judah will emerge as the inheritor of the special status as God's chosen people. Yet, unlike *Beowulf*, the political vision constructed in *Exodus* is not one of destruction or downfall. On the contrary, it is a prediction of faith and renewal. In fact, for biblical exegetes quite generally the renewal of the covenant served as the preeminent paradigm for the organization of political and ecclesiastical bodies in a lasting contract with God. As Oliver O'Donovan has explained, the "hope of a new national life for Israel was the hope of a restored world order," and the "future of [this] one nation was a prism through which the faithful looked to see the future of all nations."[26]

A closer look at the opening of *Exodus* (1–7) shows us that the poet's politico-theological vision includes his present and future Anglo-Saxon audiences, for they are part of the "generations of men" (*wera cneorissum*) who hear the divine law through this poem:

Hwæt, we feor and neah	gefrigen habað	1
ofer middangeard	Moyses domas,	
wræclico wordriht,	wera cneorissum,—	
in uprodor	eadigra gehwam	
æfter bealusiðe	bote lifes,	5
lifigendra gehwam	langsumne ræd,—	
hæleðum secgan.	Gehyre se ðe wille!	

Listen! Far and near throughout the world we have heard men proclaim the ordinances of Moses, those wonderful laws, to the generations of men, of the reward of life in heaven for each of the blessed after the baleful journey, and of everlasting counsel for each living soul. Let him hear, who will!

Usually, this passage is read through the lens of Christian typology, treating the "baleful journey" (*bealusið*) as both the Exodus proper and the turbulent journey of life, and the *bot* as the "reward" that has been granted through Christ's sacrifice (5).[27] Yet this reading obviates the central message of redemption that is at the heart of the political theology of the Old Testament Exodus: God protects and redeems his special people provided that they keep and honor his covenant. One meaning of the Hebrew *yishua* ("redemption") is "payment in a contract," a meaning also encapsulated by the term *bot* in Old English. In the context of *Exodus*, this redemption is not associated strictly with Christian soteriology, but rather with the observance and constant renewal of the social and political covenant that binds every individual to God. In hearing the poem and heeding its message, Anglo-Saxon audiences become the community bound by God's covenant.

The God of Presence: Mediation and Meditation

As discussed earlier, the God of *Exodus* is recast in highly personal terms: he is depicted first and foremost as a king, a warrior, a judge, and a giver of laws. These relationships are reflected in symbols used to represent his presence among the Israelites. In Exodus 13:21-2, God appears at the Red Sea in the form of a pillar of cloud by day and fire by night. Moreover, these indicators of divine presence are mirrored elsewhere in Exodus in the miracle of the burning bush (3:2), in the cloud that appears at Sinai (19:9), and in the cloud of presence at the Tabernacle (33:9 and 40: 34-8). Exodus also contains a series of theophanies in which God appears privately to Moses, to the people, and to the chosen elders. When God is not present, his authority is conveyed through the power of his word: in the very laws given at Sinai and in the covenant itself.

The poet of the Old English *Exodus* faithfully reproduces several of these symbolic and physical manifestations of the divinity. In fact, in a highly original and complex passage, the poet layers these depictions in an artful montage that rewrites two lines of verse in the bible as twenty-six lines of Old English verse. Exodus 13: 21-2 is as follows:

21) And the Lord went before them to show the way, by day in a pillar of a cloud, and by night in a pillar of fire; that he might be the guide of their journey at both times. 22) There never failed the pillar of the cloud by day, nor the pillar of fire by night, before the people.

The corresponding Old English passage in *Exodus* (71–97) is as follows:

	Þær halig God	
wið færbryne	folc gescylde,	
bælce oferbrædde	byrnendne heofon,	
halgan nette,	hatwendne lyft.	
Hæfde wederwolcen	widum fæðmum	75
eorðan and uprodor	efne gedæled,	
lædde leodwerod,	ligfyr adranc	
hate heofontorht.	Hæleð wafedon,	
drihta gedrymost.	Dægsceldes hleo	
wand ofer wolcnum;	hæfde witig God	80
sunnan siðfæt	segle ofertolden,	
swa þa mæstrapas	men ne cuðon,	
ne ða seglrode	geseon meahton	
eorðbuende	ealle cræfte,	
hu afæstnod wæs	feldhusa mæst,	85
siððan he mid wuldre	geweorðode	
þeodenholde.	Þa wæs þridda wic	
folce to frofre.	Fyrd eall geseah	
hu þær hlifedon	halige seglas,	
lyftwundor leoht;	leode ongeton,	90
dugoð Israhela,	þæt þær Drihten cwom,	
weroda Drihten,	wicsteal metan.	
Him beforan foran	fyr ond wolcen	
in beorhtrodor,	beamas twegen,	
þara æghwæðer	efngedælde	95
heahþegnunga	Haliges Gastes	
deormodra sið	dagum ond nihtum.	

There, Holy God shielded the people against the terrible heat, he spread out a covering over the burning heavens, and a holy veil over the sweltering loft. A cloud, with its wide embrace, had evenly divided the earth and heavens and led the host [of Israelites]; it quenched the fiery flame, searing and heavenly bright. The warriors marveled, the most joyous of troops. The shelter of the day-shield moved across the heavens; the wise Lord had covered over the path of the sun with a sail in such a way that men dwelling on earth could not detect the mast-ropes, nor could they see by any means the sailyard, or how the greatest of tents was fastened, after He honored those loyal subjects with glory. Then the third encampment came as a comfort to that people. The army saw how the holy sails, the bright marvel of the sky, towered above them. That people, the troop of Israel, perceived that the Ruler, the Lord of hosts, had come there to determine a camping place. Before them went the fire and cloud, as two pillars in the bright heavens, each of which shared in equal parts the high service of the Holy Spirit and the journey of the brave-minded men both day and night.

Parts of this passage read almost like an imagist poem. Its vivid stockpiling of images is linked by only the barest narrative structure.[28] The cloud of presence is superimposed upon an image of the Tabernacle itself, that "greatest of tents" (*feldhusa mæst*; 85). The basis for this convergence is likely biblical: like the cloud-pillar itself (in Exodus 13), the mist of Divine Presence (the *shekinah*) surmounts the Tabernacle (described in Exodus 25–6, 35–6, 38–40) in order to lead the Israelites through the desert.

These two images of the cloud-pillar and the Tabernacle combine with a third representation of a ship. In lines 81–2, we are told that the sun was covered with a wondrous *segl* ("sail"), whose *mæstrapas* ("mast-ropes") and *seglrode* ("sailyard") are made invisible to the eyes of men. In this context, the *nett* ("net"; 74) and *segl* (81) may refer to both the rigging of a ship and "the velum that divided the holy place before the altar from the holy of holies behind it" (Exodus 26: 33).[29] James Earl explains the image of the ship as a reference to the common patristic trope that compares life to a sea journey,[30] while Lucas interprets it as a reference to the "Ship of the Church."[31] For Lucas, the interpretation "Ship of the Church" is supported by a range of symbolism derived from the Mass. For example, he detects in the compound *seglrode*, the simplex *rod*, meaning "rood, or cross."[32] He likewise reads the *beam* as a reference to both the "pillar" and "the Cross" (even though the plural *beamas* appears in 94, 121, 249, suggesting multiple fixtures).[33] Lucas, moreover, interprets the kennings *heofonbeacen* ("heavenly beacon"; 107b) and *heofoncandel* ("heavenly candle"; 115) as veiled references to the Paschal candle.[34] These details are, however, more obviously supported by the solutions "pillar" and "sun," derived from the Exodus narrative itself.

While many of the individual details and complexities of this passage have been decoded, it remains a challenge to identify a governing formal principle by which these images are arranged. Lucas reads the passage as an extended instance of *ambiguum* (the rhetorical use of words in more than one sense), since *segl* may refer simultaneously to "sail," "curtain," and "veil," and *beamas* to "pillar" and "cross."[35] For him, this device serves to generate an "allusive condensation of meaning" that was intended to "form a tapestry of ideas embroidered as on a back-cloth in a coherently unified pattern."[36] He does not, however, indicate what this elaborate tapestry might have been meant to depict.

Placing these poetic images in a new cultural and aesthetic context allows us to see that these superimposed images are linked by means of highly sophisticated biblical allusion and wordplay. These images conjoin to form what we might call a "picture of puns" (a term I borrow from Mary Carruthers) that is generated by multiple expressions of the word-concept *arca* ("ark").[37] The standard patristic interpretations include the Ark of the Covenant (in the Tabernacle), the Ark of Noah (the archetype for the Ship of the Church), and the Jerusalem Ark (the Temple). Such collages were frequently used as mnemonic and meditative devices in ancient and medieval *ars memoriae*.[38] The most elaborate examples involving meditations on the biblical *arcae* can be found in twelfth-century writings. Of these, the most famous is Hugh of St. Victor's *De arca Noe mystica* (or *De pictura Arche*).[39] In her study of this treatise, Carruthers describes the concatenation of all three *arcae* (the Ark of Noah, the Ark of the Covenant, and the Ark of Jerusalem) in the single image of a triple-tiered ark:

> The basic structure of Hugh's Ark *pictura* is a three-tiered set of rectangular boxes: the *arca* as a "chest," a pun which associates the Genesis Ark with the Ark of the Covenant, described in Exodus, for which God also gave measurements and in which were stored the texts of the Law (on which the righteous man meditates day and night, according to Psalm 1). The mental painting is driven by sound-associations, homophones and polysemous words as

much as it is by coloring and shape. Puns transform the treasure chest of memory into the salvational ark of Noah, into a treasure chest (the ark of Moses) that contains the matter of salvation (God's law) which, stored in the chest of memory and thus available for meditation, will redeem and save, as the citadel (arc-) of "Jerusalem" will save God's people—provided they remember to "measure the pattern." And the triple-tiering of the Ark, as Hugh paints its mental image, fashions—literally—this triple pun on *arca* (Noah's ark, Moses's ark, Jerusalem ark) from the material in the "ark" of his memory. Hugh's *pictura Archae* is a picture constructed by puns.[40]

Hugh's verbal picture is intended as a *ductus*, that is, a device that is used to lead the mind through this cluster of intertwined images; a "*ductus* insists upon movement, the con*duct* of a thinking mind on its *way* through a composition."[41] The stated aim of this kind of meditative work was to implement chains of stories to facilitate a habit of mind. Carruthers offers an elegant simile to describe the workings of such a *ductus*:

> Like a tuning-fork, the textual trope reverberates in the cultural-made-personal memories of those who read it. So a reader's memory, not confined by worries about "the author's intended meaning," is freed to roam its memorial symphony, "gathering up" harmonies and antitheses in the compositional activity which Hugh St. Victor described as "meditation," the highest kind of study, that "takes the soul away from the noise of earthly business" (such as grammatical commentary) and "renders his life pleasant indeed" who makes a practice of it. Interpretation can then become a form of prayer, a journey through memory.[42]

The practical goal of this kind of meditation was to generate in the heart and mind "a treasure-chamber" of biblical images and associations that can be retrieved by recollection. In the work of memory, this "treasure-chest of memory" could be symbolized by the *arc* ("ark"), or an *armarium* (a "book cupboard"), or both.[43]

We might think of the concatenation of images in Hugh's *De pictura Arche* as a linguistic equivalent to at least one Anglo-Saxon

artistic work—namely, the famous *pictura* of the Tabernacle in the early
eighth-century Amiatinus Codex, one of the rare surviving examples
of an Anglo-Saxon *pandect* (i.e. a complete bible) produced at Bede's
monastery of Jarrow. The Tabernacle picture appears at the beginning
of the codex, spread across two folio leaves, where it occupies the
conventional *locus* of the meditational *pictura* (Figure 1).[44] What
makes this a meditative image (rather than a mere illustration) is
that the structure is altered to incorporate conventional mnemonic
devices, drawn from a variety of biblical and Greek influences.[45]
The incorporation of a cross into the picture of the Tabernacle
brings to mind the verse from Paul's Epistle to the Hebrews 8:3,
which establishes Christ as the "true" Tabernacle.[46] The Tabernacle
illustration also incorporates a cosmic pattern and mnemonic
scheme: the artist includes the Greek anagram ADAM (with a letter
placed at each of the four sides of the rectangle), which stands for
the Greek names for the four compass points of the world (*Arctos*,
Dysis, *Anatol*, and *Mesembria*), thus orienting the reader within

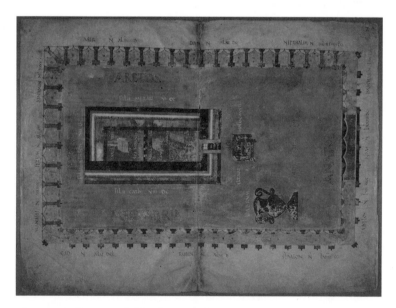

Figure 1 *Florence, Bibliotheca Medicea Laurenziana, Amiatino 1, fols
2v–3r. The Codex Amiatinus. Diagram of the Tabernacle.*

these cosmic coordinates. The *pictura* represents an experiment in perspective. As Carruthers has explained, the Tabernacle is pictured at once from three different perspectives: it is "seen both from the interior (where the columns are in front of the curtain) and the exterior (where the curtain covers the columns). The artist provides yet a third dimension by means of a 'bird's eye' view of the sacred vessels and the *sancta sanctorum.* " [47] These colliding perspectives force the mind to wander through and around the Tabernacle complex, providing a *ductus* for contemplation. This mnemotechnical picture visualizes the potent injunction in the Benedictine Rule to "build a temple within the self," and is later echoed by John Cassian's counsel to "build in your heart the sacred tabernacle of spiritual knowledge." [48]

When compared to such meditative and aesthetic *picturae*, the literary image of the pillar/Tabernacle/ship in *Exodus* may be seen to provide a comparable *ductus*, which leads the mind through image-based associations that have their basis in conventional exegesis.[49] This association is facilitated by the conventional translation of all three aforementioned Latin *arcae* as Old English *earce (f)* in biblical commentaries and glosses. Returning to the passage in *Exodus* 71–97, we may see that the Tabernacle and ship in fact represent two *arcae*—namely, the Ark of the Covenant (contained in the Tabernacle) and the Ark of Noah, which is, as already mentioned, the standard patristic type for the "Ship of the Church." The Ark of Noah is the more prominent image in this context because it is described elsewhere in the poem as the vessel that bears the *maðmhorda mæst* ("greatest of treasure hoards"), carrying within its *bearm* ("bosom") the precious exemplars for all living creatures and plants. It makes little difference that the vessel in lines 71–97 is described as a ship with sails, rather than an ark. The images of the tent and the ship are sketches intended to inspire further mental *catena* that draw on a combination of biblical reference and memory.

The "image-pun" in *Exodus* also bears comparison with two illuminations of Noah's Ark in Junius 11, in the portion of the manuscript that contains the poem *Genesis A*. On p. 66 of the manuscript, Noah's Ark is depicted as a cross between a Viking ship and a church-like structure, which contains a "tower capped with a weathercock to either side of the central structure, enhancing its ecclesiastical appearance" (see Figure 2).[50] This triple-tiered

Figure 2 *Oxford, Bodleian Library, Junius 11, p. 66. Noah's Ark.*

structure realizes the typological connections between Noah's Ark and the Ship of the Church. Five pages later, a second artist depicts the disembarkation of Noah and his family (on p. 73; Figure 3), this time depicting the Ark as a "tub" or "sarcophagus."[51] This image could be taken as a mnemonic picture for the "treasure-chamber of memory," for it overlays two perspectives that lead us inside and out of the Ark, as well as rows of equally sized cubicles that look like

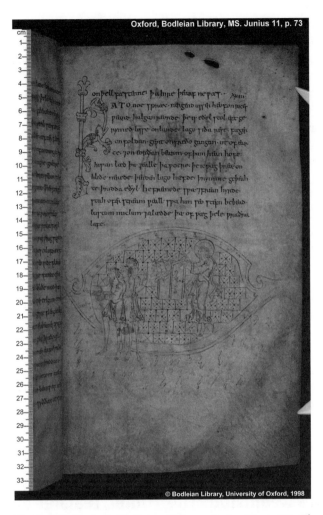

Figure 3 *Oxford, Bodleian Library, Junius 11, p. 73. The Disembarkation of Noah and His Family.*

shelves or containers. When placed together these two images map a process of interiorization.

In the case of *Exodus*, the verbal image of the sailing ship allows the poet to connect his "picture of puns" to all subsequent images of the Israelites as "seafarers" crossing the Red Sea.[52] It also unites the verbal *pictura* as a whole to the subsequent description of the

Temple, portrayed as "a holy temple ... the holiest and highest and most famous among men, the greatest and most splendid of all temples the sons of men have built upon the earth" (alh haligne,/.../ heahst and haligost, hæleðum gefrægost,/mæst and mærost, þara þe manna bearn,/fira æfter foldan, folmum geworhte; 392–6). This image of the Temple, the permanent home of the shekinah, completes the meditative arc that links the Ark of Noah, the Ark of the Covenant, and the Ark of Jerusalem in the poem.[53]

Furthermore, we can place the Exodus-poet's verbal picture of puns firmly within the tradition of medieval memory work. The poet himself connects all three biblical arcae (Latin)/earce (Old English) to the concept of "the ark of memory." The poet refers to the patriarchs and the faithful Israelites as arcae or "treasure chambers" in their own right. Noah is said to "bear the Covenant in his breast" (hæfde him on hreðre halige treowa; 366), and the Israelites are permitted to pass safely through the walls of the Red Sea because they "held the Covenant fast in their embrace" (fæstum fæðmum freoðowære heold).[54] Finally, in one dazzling development at the end of the poem, which I will discuss shortly, the poet asserts that it is the spiritual imperative for every mind to hold the precepts of God "bright within the breast" (beorht in breostum), and to interpret them with the "key of the spirit." All these images complete the poet's assertion that the pillar/Tabernacle/ship guided the Israelites not just through the journey (and the text) of the Exodus, but also to and through the "via recta," the "path of life" itself (riht stræte and lifweg; 126).

lifes wealhstod: The "Inner Teacher and Translator"

Michael Walzer has provocatively claimed that the covenant is the particular "political invention of the Book of Exodus."[55] Although the first covenant was forged with Abraham (and an earlier promise given to Noah), Walzer demonstrates that the Exodus covenant enacted at Sinai is distinctive. The main difference is that "the earlier covenants have the form of absolute and unconditional promises delivered by God," whereas the covenant at Sinai is radically dependent on contingencies. In Exodus 19:5, God states, "If ye will obey my voice indeed, and keep my covenant, then ye shall be a peculiar treasure unto me."[56] This idea of personal responsibility and accountability is anticipated in Exodus 13:3–16, where it becomes the responsibility of each and every individual "to remember this day on which you came out of Egypt" and to pass this remembrance on to subsequent generations. As this verse exhorts, it was with "a strong hand that the Lord brought *us* forth out of the land of Egypt, out of the house of bondage" (my emphasis).[57]

This idea of the personal covenant helps to illuminate a passage in *Exodus* that has been especially resilient to decipherment because of its many textual cruces. After the drowning of the Egyptians, and after the Israelites have crossed the shore safely, Moses pauses to make a speech (anticipated in 516–22), which is delayed by a lengthy interruption or meditation (523–42):

Þanon Israhelum	ece rædas	
on merehwearfe	Moyses sægde,	
heahþungen wer,	halige spræce,	
deop ærende.	Dægworc ne mað,	
swa gyt werðeode	on gewritum findað	520
doma gehwilcne,	þara ðe him drihten bebead	
on þam siðfate	soðum wordum.	
Gif onlucan wile	lifes wealhstod,	
beorht in breostum,	banhuses weard,	
ginfæsten god	Gastes cægon,	525
run bið gerecenod,	ræd forð gæð;	
hafað wislicu	word on fæðme,	
wile meagollice	modum tæcan,	
þæt we gesne ne syn	godes þeodscipes,	
Metodes miltsa.	He us ma onlyhð,	530
nu us boceras	beteran secgað,	
lengran lyftwynna.	Þis is læne dream	
wommum awyrged,	wreccum alyfed,	
earmra anbid.	Eðellease	
þysne gystsele	gihðum healdeð,	535
murnað on mode,	manhus witon	
fæst under foldan,	þær bið fyr and wyrm,	

open ece scræf   yfela gehwylces,
swa nu regnþeofas   rice dælað,
yldo oððe ærdeað.   Eftwyrd cymeð,   540
mægenþrymma mæst   ofer middangeard,
dæg dædum fah.

Then on the shore of the sea, Moses, the illustrious man,
delivered to the Israelites, in holy language, a profound message
and eternal counsel. He did not conceal that day's work, each
decree, which men still find in scripture—namely, those which
the Lord commanded to them on that journey, with true words.
If the "interpreter of life," radiant within the breast, the guardian
of the body, wishes to unlock those ample benefits with the key
of the spirit, the mystery will be explained, and that counsel will
go forth; it holds wise words in its embrace, and wishes earnestly
to teach minds, so that we will not be devoid of God's fellowship
or the mercy of the Creator. It illuminates more for us now that
learned book scholars tell us of better and more lasting heavenly
joys. This delight is transitory, cursed with sins, granted to exiles, it
is the anticipation of all who are wretched. Homeless, we occupy
this guest hall with sorrows, we mourn in mind, we are aware
of the house of sin fast beneath the earth, where there is fire
and worms, the open and eternal pit of all evil, where those arch-
thieves—old age and sudden death—share dominion. The Day of
Judgment comes, the greatest of powerful glories in the world, a
day hostile to evil deeds.

The passage beginning at line 523 is enigmatic: who or what is the
lifes wealhstod? Most editors and translators treat this "interpreter
of life" and "keeper of the body" as the Christian mind, intellect,
or soul.[58] The *ginfæste god* ("ample benefits") are taken to refer
to Old Testament teachings, which can be unlocked by means of a
spiritual key, that represents Christian exegesis. The implication is
that without Christian hermeneutics the divine "counsel" (*ræd*; 526)
and "mystery" (*run*; 526) contained in the Old Testament text would
remain sealed, veiled, and incomplete. The act of "interpretation"
performed by the *wealhstod* is therefore the analysis of the
biblical Exodus through the lens of typology and allegory. As Lucas

explains, "the word [*wealhstod*] clearly implies elucidation of the correspondence between two sets of information, in this context the correspondence between literal and allegorical and the typological connection between historically separate events or personages."[59] For him, the passage exemplifies "the Pauline distinction between the Letter and the Spirit (2 Cor. 3:6)."[60] Lucas, thus, would situate this entire passage within a recognizable Christian hermeneutic paradigm: the Old Testament represents the letter of the law that is superseded and fulfilled by the spiritual meaning contained in the New Testament.

Dorothy Haines offers an interesting, but ultimately limiting, variation, suggesting that the *lifes wealhstod* is Christ himself.[61] She cites examples from patristic literature in which Christ is said to possess the *clavis David* ("key of David"), which unlocks the spiritual meaning of scripture. This reading aptly supports the didactic function of the *wealhstod* who teaches minds, and also the New Testament idea that Christ dwells within his believers (see, e.g. Romans 8:10, Galatians 4:19, Colossians 1:27, and Ephesians 3:16–17). However, Haines's interpretation does not explain why Christ is figured as the guardian of the *banhus* ("body") rather than the soul or the heart. It also does not take into consideration the passage that immediately follows this one (531–42), which elaborates upon the imprisoned condition of the soul in this earthly and transitory life. The *gystsele* ("guest hall") of line 535 must represent the temporary body on loan to us in this life, a condition that renders the soul temporarily deprived of its rightful or native homeland in heaven.

The two solutions proposed by Lucas and Haines do not explain all the facets of the *wealhstod*. There is another, which does not necessitate a radical departure from the literal interpretation of Exodus. The *wealhstod* can be understood as a figure for intellection that is based closely upon Augustine's conception of the "inner man." In his *De civitate Dei*, 13.24.2, Augustine asserts that every man is the sum of two parts: "a man is not just a body or a soul, but a being made up of both body and soul ... the soul is not the whole man, but the better part of man; the body is not the whole, but the inferior part of a man." Every rational being contains both an "inner man" (*homo interior*) and an "outer man" (*homo exterior*). By "inner man," Augustine refers principally to "the rational soul and its relation to and experience of God." It is in this "secret place of the rational soul" in which God is to be sought and worshipped, as in a temple (*De Magistro* 1.2). The "outer man," by contrast, refers "not to the body alone, but also its own peculiar kind of life, from which the structure of the body and all the senses derive their vigor and by which they are equipped to perceive external things" (*De Trinitate* 12.1). If "the inner man is endowed with understanding, the 'outer man' is endowed with sense perception" (*De Trinitate* 11.1). Augustine draws inspiration for this conception from several Pauline epistles, including 2 Corinthians 4:16, which states that "even though our *outer man* is decaying, yet our *inner man* is being renewed day by day" (*De Trinitate* 11.1).

As the better part of every rational soul, the "inner man" plays a vital role in cognition. In his tract *De Genesi ad litteram,* Augustine identifies three types of vision engaged in this process—corporeal, spiritual, and intellectual. These have been summarized as follows:

> The first, corporeal vision (*visio corporalis*) is concerned with the bodily eyes and sense perception...; the second, spiritual vision (*visio spiritualis*), with the inward perception, in terms of images stored in the mind or memory, of what has been sensed externally; the third, intellectual vision (*visio intellectualis*), is concerned purely with what the mind knows and sees interiorly, unmediated by external sense perception and without corporeal images... since God is invisible in nature, he will be seen not by any of our senses, but by the heart.[62]

Using this threefold, hierarchical division, Augustine devises a model of communication that enables the "outer man" to correspond with the "inner man." The soul, according to Augustine, operates by means of a kind of courier service that relays stimuli from the outside world within.[63] It is importantly "not the *body* that perceives, but the *soul* by means of the body; and the soul uses the body as a sort of messenger [*nuntio*] in order to form within itself the object that is called to its attention from outside world" (*De Genesi* 12.24.51; italics mine).[64] The "inner man" interprets these sense perceptions in the following manner: "after the eyes have taken their object in and announced it to the spirit, in order that an image of it may be produced there, then, if it is symbolic of something, its meaning is either immediately understood by the intellect, or sought out; for there can be neither understanding nor searching except by the functioning of the mind" (*De Genesi* 12.11.22).[65] This operation of the "inner man" is in many ways analogous to the function of memory, which Augustine so memorably described in the *Confessiones* (10.14.21) as the "stomach of the mind"—that is, the internal processing plant that stores sense memories and allows them to be brought up again for rumination.[66]

It is, however, also a vital concept for Augustine that genuine contemplation is impossible without divine illumination. In Augustine's major writings on the soul, he states that Christ is the "the inner teacher who illuminates the inner man."[67] Augustine develops this idea from Ephesians 3:16–17, which asserts that God grants understanding of his "manifold wisdoms" in order that the "inner man" might be strengthened by his Spirit and that "Christ may dwell by faith" in the hearts of men.[68] These biblical verses find a close parallel in Augustine's *De magistro,* where he asserts that "God is not just what we long to see, but what powers the eye which sees. So the light of God is not just 'out there,' illuminating the order of being, as it is for Plato; it is also an 'inner light.' God cannot be understood by teaching alone, but rather, he "is to be found in the intimacy of self presence."[69]

Could not, then, the *lifes wealhstod* in *Exodus* be read as the equivalent to the rational soul working in accordance with the divine? Like Augustine's "inner man," the function of the *wealhstod* is to "translate" or "interpret" precepts imported from external sources, such as books, teachers, and experiential sense perceptions. This process enables spiritual mysteries and divine counsel to be "unlocked" so that they may "go forth" to the soul for true intellection. The soul, in turn, uses what it has understood and comprehended to reform the behavior of the lower cognitive strata—represented in our poem by the *mod* ("mind"; 528)—in accordance with God's precepts.

It is important for our discussion that Augustine develops the core elements of this model of communicability between outside and inside in his tract on the literal interpretation of Genesis (*De Genesi ad litteram*). For Augustine, spiritual understanding of the bible is impossible without the literal level of interpretation, which (according to his own definition) includes "the eternal truths that are taught, the facts that are narrated, the future events that are predicted, and the precepts or counsel that are given" (*De Genesi ad litteram*, I.1).[70] In *Exodus*, these precepts and counsels are elegantly represented by the *ræd* ("counsel" or "teaching") that "goes forth" in 526. We can be sure that *ræd* is grounded in Mosaic law rather than allegorical Christian hermeneutics, since the word appears three more times in this precise context in the poem. Thus, in the opening lines of the poem we are told that "the laws of Moses" (*Moyses domas; 2*) provide "lasting counsel" (*langsumne ræd*; 6) for every living person. The word *ræd* appears again in lines 269–72, as Moses offers those who have forgotten God's precepts "a better counsel" (*beteran ræd*), which refers to the proper service of God through prayer. Finally, the word appears at the end of the passage about the *wealhstod*, where it states, "so spoke the mildest of men, in a loud voice, mindful of counsel, made great in strength" (*swa reordode ræda gemyndig/ manna mildost, mihtum swiðed,/hludan stefne*; 549–51). This *ræd* would seem to refer to Moses's entire speech, which, we are told, provides a *muðhæl* (553), literally a "mouth healing," or perhaps "a spiritual salve" for those who listen. In each of these instances, *ræd* refers to precepts delivered within a Mosaic framework.

It is worth contemplating this passage in detail, because it offers a paradigm for reading and interpreting *Exodus* as a whole. In its brief and enigmatic complexity, the passage on the *wealhstod* provides a manual for autodidacticism and offers a paradigm by which the "inward eye/I" might interpret and understand scripture and contemplate the divine. Similar models of private erudition and contemplation are readily found in the works of Augustine. In his *De magistro*, the doctor of the church ponders the strengths and limitations of earthly teachers (*magistri*), eventually concluding that the individual can only attain true contemplation and understanding when the "inner man" is engaged in intellection.[71] Augustine's model of communication between the "inner man" and the "outer man" likewise found an important echo in his conception of the "inner dialogue" and "the soliloquy," which was to become his preferred mode of contemplation, philosophical engagement, and spiritual askesis in such texts as the *Confessions* and the *Soliloquies*.[72]

It seems entirely fitting that *Exodus* brings to a close the physical journey of the Israelites, which transports them from slavery to freedom, by contemplating a complementary spiritual journey inward—an *ingressus* (as opposed to *exodus*)—toward the divine. Perhaps the poet was aware of a longstanding analytical tradition, initiated by the Jewish philosopher Philo (20 BC–50 AD) and reiterated often by subsequent patristic authors,[73] in which Philo first represented Moses as a figure for the *vita contemplativa* itself, "represent[ing] the man who has been initiated into the life of the spirit, and for whom the immaterial world alone has meaning."[74] According to Philo, Moses began his life as a homeless castaway on the Nile "shut up ... in a casket, coated with pitch, which is a figure of the body," who, nevertheless, was "seized with a desire for immaterial reality," and thus freed himself from earthly bonds and "transformed the world into his city and fatherland."[75] Philo's Moses acts much like the poem's soul, which seeks permanent housing in heaven and rejects the temporary guesthouse of the body. According to Philo, this movement from the earthly to the heavenly and the physical to the spiritual was reduplicated by the Israelite nation collectively as they freed themselves from slavery. Philo thus established Israel as a figure for the soul, which liberated itself from enslavement to the pleasure of the senses—that is represented by Egypt.[76] Using the analogy of the "eye of the mind" turned inward to the soul and toward God, Philo explains the movement from sensuous perception to true contemplation in terms that are strikingly reminiscent of Augustine's description of cognition, and also the poet's account of the *wealhstod*[77]:

> when the mind is open to divine things, it needs nothing else for its contemplation, for in spiritual matters the most penetrating eye is the mind in solitude; but when matters of the senses, the passions or the body concern it—and of all of these the land of Egypt is the symbol—then there is every necessity for all the powers and resources of speech." (Philo, *De Migratione Abrahami* 76–7)[78]

In these examples, the Old Testament provides the necessary grounds for pure contemplation. Self-contemplation is, for Augustine and for our Anglo-Saxon poet, a primary vehicle for self-governance, knowledge, and perfection. It is with this context in mind that Moses's final speech on the shore of the Red Sea makes sense. In place of the biblical "Song of the Sea" we find the following injunction to the Israelites, and to his listening and reading audience:

Wile nu gelæstan   þæt he lange gehet
mid aðsware,   engla Drihten,
in fyrndagum   fæderyncynne,   560
gif ge gehealdað   halige lare,
þæt ge feonda gehwone   forð ofergangað,
gesittað sigerice   be sæm tweonum,
beorselas beorna.   Bið eower blæd micel!

The Lord of Angels wishes to fulfill now what He had promised long ago in days of old to our forefathers with a covenant; if you will hold his holy teachings, you may hereafter overcome every enemy, and conquer every powerful court and every beer-hall of warriors between the two seas. May your glory be great!

The passage reiterates the terms of the Sinai Covenant (updated specifically for a English audience, as indicated by the reference to beer-halls) suggesting that if we keep the covenant, we may overcome all enemies and achieve lasting blæd. The "glory" or "fame" (blæd) promised here has special resonance: it describes the glory in heaven that is promised to each of the righteous souls in 542–6, where "there is light and life and the glory of bliss" (þær is leoht and lif, eac þon lissa blæd). It is also echoed in the political blæd promised to Judah in 314–18: "thus, God Almighty gave them great reward for that day's work, granting them glory of triumphant deeds, that they might have dominion over kingdoms and sway their kinsmen" (swa him mihtig god/þæs dægweorces deop lean forgeald,/siððan him gesælde sigorworca hreð,/þæt he ealdordom agan sceolde/ofer cynericu, cneowmaga blæd). Through this promise of blæd to all righteous believers, the poet unites his political project and quest for redemption, bringing it in line with the complex ethnogenetic myth of the Exodus itself.

Conclusion

In this chapter, we have seen that the Anglo-Saxon *Exodus* offers more than a backward-looking celebration of Israel as the once-chosen nation of God and the Germanic migration as its double. The poet adopts the political theology contained in the biblical Exodus and applies it to contemporary Anglo-Saxon ideals and realities. As such, the central biblical theme of divine election serves as a contemporary instantiation of a political theology derived from scripture itself. To accept the covenant is to follow in the footsteps of Judah through the Red Sea. In this sense, the Anglo-Saxon *Exodus* can be read as manifesto that has perlocutionary force, and thus a performative aspect to it: it functions as an invocation to join in the ranks of the chosen who keep the covenant, as well as a directive to orient oneself in body and spirit toward God, just as the Israelites of the biblical Exodus had.

Notes

1 As the poem's title suggests, the tone shifts markedly as the settlers fall into sloth and carnality: the colonists become a "Carnall Brood of the Israelites," a "fleshly generation" that turns away from God's teachings and willfully rejects the Gospels. The speaker adopts the homiletic rhetoric of the jeremiad: "This O New-England hast thou got/ by riot, & excess" (387–8).

2 On the partially indigenous tradition on liberation theology in Latin America, see Guttiérez (1974).

3 Walzer (1985).

4 Walzer (1985: 3–4); Steffens (1926) uses the figure of "Moses in Red" to stage a defense of Leninist politics.

5 Walzer (1985: 12).

6 Walzer (1985: 12).

7 Walzer (1985: 53).

8 Walzer (1985: 10–11).

9 *Exodus* is a free and highly innovative paraphrase and interpretation of Exodus 13:20–14:31 (Lucas 1994: 51), but it is also a dense network of intertexts. The so-called "patristic digression" narrates the stories from Genesis of Noah's Ark

(362–79), Abraham's near sacrifice of Isaac (380–446), and perhaps also Joseph (140–1 and possibly the lacuna at lines 142–7). The poet's description of the Jerusalem Temple (389–96) shows familiarity with parts of Kings and Chronicles (Lucas 1994: 52). Other sporadic details are incorporated from the Books of Numbers, Psalms, and Wisdom (Moore 1911; Lucas 1994: 54–5). As my analysis demonstrates, Exodus 15:1–18, "The Song of the Sea," provides a stylistic archetype for *Exodus* as a whole.

10   Greenfield (1965: 155), as cited by Lucas (1994: 44).

11   Lucas (1994: 447–515, n. 132).

12   My translations here and throughout, unless otherwise specified.

13   Lucas (1994: 45).

14   Lapidge (2006a: 25ff).

15   Echoes of the "Song of the Sea" have been noted at other moments in *Exodus*. For echoes of this *canticum Moysi* in Moses's short speech in lines 554–64, see Irving (1972: 322); Remley (1996: 177, n. 25); and Tolkien (1981: 64, 69). In the Hebrew Bible, Moses's canticle in Exodus 15 is written with a special layout and format—the lines are dispersed across the page in three interleaving columns almost like a concrete poem, so that the words of Moses are configured to form a textual image. The outer two columns are thought to represent the two walls of the sea, while the third middle column is seen to depict Israel advancing through the center of the sea-ramparts. The point is not to suggest that the Anglo-Saxon poet knew this precise tradition (I do not know of any Latin commentary that points out the canticle's unique Hebraic format), but rather to suggest that the canticle was widely recognized for its powerful imagery in both traditions, and that the Anglo-Saxon poet brought a similar attitude to his poem.

16   After all, the "Song of the Sea" was among the best-known portions of Old Testament text during the period: it was recited as part of the liturgy as a variable canticle in the Divine Office at Monastic and Secular at Lauds, and during the liturgy for the Easter Vigil. See further Harper (1991: 257) and Remley (1996: 84). According to Remley, the canticle was so well known in Anglo-Saxon England that it was memorized and recited by heart. His evidence is a series of manuscripts from Anglo-Saxon England in which the incipit of the *canticum Moysi* is provided, but not the rest of the text (see Remley 1996: 199–211). Remley makes this keen assertion in support of his larger argument that the poems in the Junius manuscript were adapted from the liturgy for the Easter Vigil.

17 Brueggemann (2006: 10).

18 Lucas (1994: 310–46, n. 117).

19 Lucas (1994: 310–46, n. 117).

20 Holthausen (1905) finds only late parallels for the order in which the Israelites enter the sea, in Peter Comestor's twelfth-century *Historia Scholastica* (Exodus, cap. 31; PL 198: 1158) and in the fifteenth-century *Le mystère du Viel Testament*, neither of which appears to borrow directly from the Anglo-Saxon *Exodus*. On this tradition, also see Moore (1911: 144).

21 Lucas (1994: 46).

22 See, for example, Coogan *et al.* (2001: 78–9).

23 See, for example, Coogan *et al.* (2001: 78–9).

24 Wright (2002: 319–22).

25 One such famous passage in *Beowulf* (67–85) is the description of the creation of Heorot, which is immediately followed by a reference to its destruction by fire.

26 O'Donovan (1996: 23–4).

27 Earl (2002: 142).

28 See Lucas's edition (1994) for extensive notes.

29 Lucas (1994: n. 76).

30 Earl (2002); also see Moore (1911: 107).

31 Lucas (1994: 89, n. 80b–84) demonstrates that both conceptions are patristic commonplaces, though they do not derive from exegesis associated with Exodus.

32 Bosworth and Toller (1882) define the word *segl-ród* (f.) as "a sail-yard" and link it to Old High German *segal-ruota*, "antenna." They compare this compound with *segel-gird*, which may refer to a "sail-yard, yard of a ship" or "the cross rod from which a banner hangs."

33 Lucas (1994: 91) points out that the formula *wuldres beam* ("beam of glory") used of the cloud pillar in 568 likewise recurs in the poems *The Dream of the Rood*, line 97, and *Elene*, line 217, to refer to the Cross.

34 Lucas (1994: 94).

35 Lucas (1994: 47).

36 Lucas (1994: 48, 51). Roberta Frank suggestively compares the style of this passage to Norse skaldic poetry (Frank 1987, 1988: 191–205).

37 Carruthers (1998: 271). As we shall see, this specific wordplay works beautifully in Latin (*arca*) and in Old English (*earc*), but not in the original Hebrew (where Noah's Ark is described as a *teivah*; the Ark of the Covenant as an *aron*; and the Ark of Jerusalem as the *beit hamikdash*).

38   Carruthers (1998: 221–76).

39   Carruthers (1998: 245–6) describes Hugh's ark as a type of *ekphrasis*. Some scholars have supposed that Hugh's model is based upon an actual painting (like the plan of St. Gall), but Carruthers maintains that it is more likely engaged in " 'painting' rhetorical *picturae*" (1998: 245). Hugh leads us to scan the picture from different viewpoints, and thereby to commit it to memory by mingling it with our own previously retained images.

40   Carruthers (1998: 244–5). As she points out, there may also be an additional architectural pun that links these various imaginings: "the word for an architectural arch is *arca* or *archa*, a homophony that completes an associational chain to the word for Ark or the chest in which the precious law (on which one meditates day and night) is enclosed—that is, one's memory chest. So the *intercolumnia* in a church, formed by sets of *arche* or arches, is a perfect unit or scene for memory work" (Carruthers 1998: 270).

41   Carruthers (1998: 77–81 at 78).

42   Carruthers (1998: 147–8).

43   Caruthers (1990: 43). Also see O'Reilly (2001: 14–15).

44   Carruthers (1998: 236).

45   Carruthers (1998: 236).

46   Carruthers (1998: 236).

47   Carruthers (1998: 237).

48   Cassian *Conferences* XIV [SC 54, p. 193], quoted by Carruthers (1998: 270).

49   To my knowledge, there has not been any work on the art of memory in Anglo-Saxon texts. It seems to me, however, that there is ample material that would appear to reflect such practices. Several Anglo-Saxon manuscripts contain extensive tables representing the dimensions of Noah's Ark, alongside lists of the ages of the world, the Temple of Solomon, the Tabernacle, etc. (for individual manuscripts, see Gneuss (2001): nos. 56, 90, 363, 385, 435, 451, 882). These charts and tables collectively suggest the use of such documents for meditative purposes.

50   Karkov (2001: 90).

51   Karkov (2001: 92); Gatch (1975: 00). Also see Head (1997: 73), who discusses the use of perspective in the image. It is, of course, vital

to my argument that the Old English term *earc* may also be used
to represent a "chest" or "treasure chamber." See the Bosworth-
Toller supplementary entry for *earc*.

52 Throughout the poem, the Egyptians are described as "landmen"
(*landmenn*; 179) and "natives" (*ingefolca*; 142). The Israelites
are described as being homeless and in exile (see 137–40a). The
analogy suggests that just as the Israelites are in exile from the
holy land, so every Christian is in exile until he or she reaches
heavenly home.

53 This latter connection between the Temple/Tabernacle was
reflected in other Anglo-Saxon texts: it represented a fluid image
for Bede in his commentaries (*De Tabernaculo* and *De Templo*)
since both arks served as a template for the heavenly Jerusalem.

54 By contrast, the Egyptians are said to "eat" or "destroy" the
covenant: "then *they* [=Egyptians] slew *his* [=Moses's] kinsmen,
brought strife down on them, and destroyed/ consumed the
covenant" (*ða heo his mægwinum morðor fremedon,/wroht
berenedon, wære fræton*; 147).

55 Walzer (1985: 74).

56 Walzer (1985: 77–8).

57 This injunction to tell the story of Exodus as a personal story
of redemption is the central imperative of the Passover *seder*
as represented in the *haggadah*. The exhortation is repeated
with an even greater emphasis upon personal responsibility in
Deuteronomy 5.2–3 and 6:20–1, where the command is to "tell
what God did for *me* when *I* came out of Egypt."

58 Most editors and translators (including Krapp [1931, ASPR 1],
Lucas [1994], and Bradley [1982]) place lines 523–48 in the
mouth of the narrator, even though we are told specifically at
lines 517 and 549 (at the beginning and end of the sequence)
that Moses spoke these words. In order to make sense of these
speech markers, it has been argued that lines 523–48 represent
the narrator's own interpolation, and that Moses's actual speech
begins only in lines 554–64, which are based on the canticle
of Moses (in Exodus 15). The main reason for ascribing these
words to the narrator—and not to Moses—is that the passage
has traditionally been read as asserting the superiority of spiritual
interpretation associated with Christian hermeneutics, over the
letter of the law—a perspective that would hardly suit Moses.
In the following, I propose a different interpretation of these
lines that is more suitable to the context in which they are either
spoken by, or about, Moses as a spiritual guide and teacher.

59   Lucas (1994: 143, n. 523).

60   Lucas (1994: 143, n. 523).

61   Haines (1999: 481–98).

62   Harrison (1999: 768).

63   This idea is echoed by Alcuin in his treatise (composed ca. 801–4) *De Ratione Animae*, IV: "Now let us consider the remarkable speed of the mind in shaping material which it takes in through bodily senses, from which, as though acting through a kind of messenger-service [*nuntios*], whatever it takes in of sensible things known or unknown at once with indescribable speed it forms within itself figures of them, and hides these 'in-form-ations' in the treasury of memory" (*Nunc autem consideremus miram velocitatem animae in formandis rebus; quae percipit per carnales sensus a quibus quasi per quosdam nuntios quicquid rerum sensibilium cognitarum vel incognitarum percipit. Mox in seipsa earum ineffabili celeritate format figuras informatasque in suae thesauro memoriae recondit*; Curry, ed. and trans. 1966, 48 and 79). On the importance of Alcuin's text in Anglo-Saxon England, and especially in shaping Anglo-Saxon theories of "the mind," see Godden (2002).

64   Taylor, trans. *The Literal Meaning of Genesis* (1982: 214).

65   Taylor, trans. *The Literal Meaning of Genesis* (1982: 191–2).

66   Augustine's comparison of the process of memory to a stomach has been discussed in many places. See, for example, Mendelson (2000). For a broader discussion of the monastic practice of *ruminatio* ("spiritual rumination"), see Leclercq (2009: 71–88) and Parkes (1999: 90–102).

67   Rist (1994: 37, n. 36).

68   Ephesians 3:16–17: "That he [God] would grant you, according to the riches of his glory, to be strengthened by his Spirit with might unto the inward man: That Christ may dwell by faith in your hearts" (*Ut det vobis secundum divitias gloriae suae virtute corroborari per Spiritum eius in interiore homine habitare Christum per fidem in cordibus vestris*; Rist 1994: 37). See also *De magistro* 1.2; 11.38; 12:40 *De vera religione* 39.72; *Retractationes* 1.12, as identified by Rist. On the role of *solus magister* (in *Confessions* xi.8 and 10 and *De Magistro* 14, 45–6) in relation to the articulation of the exterior world, see Gilgen (2012: 98f).

69   Taylor (1989: 134).

70   Taylor, trans. *The Literal Meaning of Genesis* (1982: 19).

71 "When we have to do with things which we behold with the mind, that is, with the intelligence and with reason, we speak of things which we look upon directly in the inner light of truth which illumines the inner man and in inwardly enjoyed. There again if my hearer sees these things himself with his inward eye, he comes to know what I say, not as a result of my words but as a result of his own contemplation. Even when I speak what is true and he sees what is true, it is not I who teach him. He is taught not by my words but by the things themselves which inwardly God has made manifest to him" (*De Magistro*, 40; trans. Burleigh, *The Teacher*, 1953: 96).

72 On Augustine's use of the soliloquy as a contemplative strategy, see Stock (2010). On the relationship between the *Soliloquies* and the *Confessions*, also see Gilgen (2012: 82–92).

73 Daniélou (1960: 217–26) traces the evolution of this interpretation of Moses and the Israelites from Philo to Clement and Origen, and beyond.

74 Daniélou (1960: 203).

75 Daniélou (1960: 203, quoting Philo).

76 Daniélou (1960: 206).

77 I suspect the similarity is due to a common Platonic root.

78 Quoted by Daniélou (1960: 207).

2

Daniel: The Translation of Divine Election

Throughout the Middle Ages, the biblical book of Daniel was regarded as the paradigmatic expression of *translatio imperii*, a literary scheme that asserted the divinely sanctioned transfer of power and authority from one empire or regime to another.[1] In the book of Daniel, the theme of *translatio imperii* is established through a series of visions and dreams, in which the rise and fall of successive empires is foretold. The famous instance appears in book 2, when Nebuchadnezzar dreams of an enormous statue forged from a series of metals: a head of gold, a chest and arms from silver, a middle and thighs from bronze, legs of iron, and feet of mixed iron and clay. The Israelite prophet Daniel interprets this sequence of materials as representing the rise and fall of four successive kingdoms: Babylon, Media, Persia, and Greece.[2] Daniel also predicts the rise of an unnamed and indestructible fifth kingdom, which is understood in the context of the biblical book to be the eternal kingdom of Israel. The very scheme of *translatio imperii* is repeated several times in the narrative with variations. In book 5, the mysterious writing on the wall (*Mene, Mene, Tekel, Parsin*), representing different weights and currencies in descending order of value, reduplicates the same succession of kingdoms.[3] The pattern recurs in book 7, where Daniel has a surreal dream about four hybrid beasts that destroy each other in succession,[4] and another about the combat of a mystical goat and ram (book 8) whose multiplying and dividing horns symbolize the same basic political sequence.[5]

In her meticulous textual study, Ulrike Krämer demonstrates that the conception of such a translation in the book of Daniel in fact became the foundational paradigm for all history writing from the patristic period to the eighteenth century.[6] The longevity and appeal of this scheme undoubtedly have to do with its inherent flexibility and applicability to different political conditions and regimes. Authors from Late Antiquity forward utilized the translation topos in order to construct their own political community as the eternal and unconquerable fifth kingdom.[7]

This transfer of power was generally connected to the related scheme of *translatio studii* that marked the corresponding transmission of culture, knowledge, and learning. As Édouard Jeauneau explains,

> The *translatio studii* is a consequence of the *translatio imperii*.... The transmission of learning from one place to another implies the translation of texts from one language to another. In a world where books are the necessary vehicle of learning, it is obvious that learning cannot travel unless conveyed by books. And books cannot be understood, unless they speak the language of the country into which they are received.[8]

In the Middle Ages, the scheme of *translatio studii* was commonly used to plot the transmission of philosophy and learning from Greece to Rome, and then to a new center of secular or religious learning. Thus, in the thirteenth century, the University of Paris, the very center of medieval scholasticism, was proclaimed a "New Athens." Although Athens and Rome presented the most obvious models for cultural and imperial imitation, they were not the only available paradigms. Other ancient and medieval authors turned to the book of Daniel to represent Babylonia as the original wellspring of learning and philosophy.

One of the earliest attestations of the trope of *translatio studii* appears in Josephus's *Historiae antiquitatis Iudaicae* (1.167–8), in which he claimed that Abraham, born in Ur of the Chaldeans as stated in Genesis 11:31, introduced arithmetic and astronomy to Egypt, and that the Egyptians in turn passed it onto the Greeks. Josephus used this genealogy to assert that "learning was not born in Greece, but in the land of the Patriarchs and the Prophets."[9] This mythology reaching back to Abraham linked the whole of Western political intellectual history and culture to Israel of the bible. A wealth of thinkers from Augustine in the fourth century to Peter Comestor in the twelfth cited versions of this lineage.[10] In one especially complex passage, Otto von Freising (twelfth century) wound together the twin tropes of *translatio imperii et studii* in order to map out a divinely ordained and teleological passage of authority and wisdom from the East (in Babylonia) to the West (under Germanic rule), a pattern that remained influential in the philosophy of history into the early nineteenth century. In this text, the basic scheme of *translatio imperii* in the book of Daniel (which plotted the succession of Babylon, Media, Persia, and Greece) again provides the *terra prima* for this itinerary:

> The power (*principatus, imperium, regnum*) passed from the Babylonians to the Medes and the Persians, from these to the Macedonians, from the Macedonians to Rome, from Rome to Constantinople (*Ab Vrbe ad Graecos*), from Constantinople to the Franks (*a Graecis ad Francos*), from the Franks to the Lombards (*a Francis ad Lonbardos*), finally from the Lombards to the Germans (*a Lonbardis rursum ad Teutonicos Francos*). Similarly Wisdom began in the east, in Babylonia, and was hence transferred (*translatam*) to Egypt [and then advanced westward].[11]

As Otto von Freising's elaborate program suggests, the tropes of *translatio imperii et studii* could be molded and manipulated to claim a wide variety of intellectual, cultural, and political genealogies going back to classical Athens, or Christian Rome, or patriarchal Chaldea.

The twin tropes of *translatio imperii et studii* are well attested in Anglo-Saxon literature. As we have already seen in the Introduction, writers such as Bede, Alcuin, and Wulfstan employed the scheme of *translatio imperii* to explain the Germanic conquest of Britain, and later, to rationalize the Viking attacks that weakened England. Etienne Gilson locates a parallel intellectual itinerary of *translatio studii* in the works of the Anglo-Saxon writer Alcuin of York, who lived and taught at the court of Charlemagne.[12] Alcuin promoted himself as "a missionary of learning, whose duty was to transfer [an entire] cultural heritage from Northumbria to Gallia." [13] As Alcuin writes in his *Epistle 170*, it was his dream to build, with the help of Charlemagne, a new Athens in Francia: "*Forsan Athenae noua perficeretur in Francia.*" [14] Whereas the Old Athens would remain famous for the insights of its philosophers, the New Athens would "be taught by Christ himself." [15] The transfer of reading and learning—the dynamic of *translatio studii*—Gilson reminds us, was never simply metaphoric: it entailed the massive transfer of books and scholars from one place to another—in the case of Alcuin, from England to Francia. [16] Focusing on the Anglo-Saxon Alcuin as a seminal figure, Gilson establishes Anglo-Saxon texts and culture as important institutions and way stations in the dissemination of the trope of *translatio studii*.

Scholars of the tenth-century Old English poem *Daniel* have sought to identify a similar program of *translatio imperii et studii*. And indeed at first glance, *Daniel* appears to be an obvious match: the poem describes the rise and fall of three sovereign entities in succession—the nation of the Israelites, the Babylonians, and the Chaldeans. [17] Thus, Earl Anderson has argued that the "organizing theme of *Daniel* ... has to do with the medieval historiographical and political concept of *translatio imperii* and with the closely related tradition about the Hebrews as the *populus dei* who through sin lost their favored position and eventually were superseded by the *populus christianus*." [18] Anderson reads the rhetoric of supersession in the poem as absolute; there is no redemption for the fallen Israelites. [19] Against Anderson's interpretation, it has been argued that the central geographical and imperial details that comprise this political scheme in the biblical book are absent in the Old English *Daniel*. [20] The poet omits the main sources of political allegory in Daniel 1–5, which is the political allegory embedded in Nebuchadnezzar's first dream of the statue and the details of the writing on the wall, both of which provide the central foundation for the comparison to four successive empires.

However, rather than displace the theme of *translatio* altogether, the poet focuses on a different sort of transfer. At its core, *Daniel* is a loose and innovative adaptation of books 1–5 of the book of Daniel, as well as parts of the apocryphal Song of Azarias derived from the liturgical canticles (rather than directly from the bible). Although the poem stays in constant contact with its biblical source, it simultaneously rewrites and displaces the narrative's original theologico-political agenda. Whereas the Old Testament book of Daniel emphasizes the unfaltering faith of the Israelites who adhere to their law in exile, the Old English poet, by contrast, describes the general disobedience of the Jews who violate their covenant with God and forfeit their special status. By emphasizing the decline of the sinful Israelites, the poet undermines the biblical *locus classicus* of *translatio imperii*, which establishes the downfall of Babylonian rule and its three successive empires, and the eventual ascendancy of Israel over all other nations. In its place, however, we may locate the theme of *translatio electionis*—a term I have coined to mark the transmission and expansion of *the status of election* from the nation of Israel to a more heterogeneous community of believers, which includes Christian converts as well as select Jews.[21] The poem's novel focus on the transmission of *election* deliberately interferes with the exclusive nationalistic claims of the biblical text, where the status of *chosenness* is reserved uniquely for the people of Israel.

The focus on *translatio electionis* brings to the fore a further central aspect of translation put into practice in the poem. The poet's highly significant manipulations and revisions of the classical tropes of *translatio imperii et studii* indicate that *Daniel* ought to be understood as a "strong translation" in its own right. Thus, whereas in the biblical text, Daniel and Nebuchadnezzar narrate their own dreams, in the poem, by contrast, authority is invested in the narrator, who speaks frequently as a reporter of information derived from an unnamed oral source, and—more remarkably—at times also as an eyewitness to the biblical events that lead up to the sacking of Jerusalem and the Babylonian captivity. As a witness, interpreter, and transmitter of biblical history, the narrator assumes and supplements Daniel's role as prophet and thereby establishes himself as a voice of authority in the process.

Adapting Daniel

The biblical book of Daniel is a composite text in at least three respects. The oldest version of the book of Daniel is preserved in two languages: Daniel 2:4b–7:28 is written in Aramaic, and the remaining portions are written in Hebrew. The book was also almost certainly woven together from texts written at different points in time. Chapters 1–6 were likely composed during the Persian (539–333 BCE) or early Hellenistic (333–168 BCE) periods. These sections, describing the experiences of Daniel and his friends at the Chaldean court (during the Babylonian exile), reflect a period in which Jews could live at peace with their non-Jewish neighbors, and imperial rule was "ignorant and dangerous" rather than "malevolent."[22] By contrast, chapters 7–12 "depict extreme hostility to foreign governments." In fact, the use of apocalyptic imagery in this section reflects "ongoing universal tribulation," rather than specific conflicts that are limited in time and scope.[23] These portions were probably written "on the eve of the Maccabean revolt against the assimilations policies of Antiochus [IV Epiphanes] and his allies in Jerusalem's priestly circles."[24] The same division is also reflected in the changing role of the text. In the first six books, Daniel is depicted as an interpreter of dreams; these are narrated by Nebuchadnezzar himself or by an omniscient narrator. In books 7–12, however, Daniel is depicted as a prophet and a dreamer, and he narrates the majority of this portion of the narrator. Both of these changes in focalization mark and coincide with the division between the "early" and "late" books, and between an ethos of relative peace in exile and one of threat in the long term.

The Old English poem was adapted mainly from the materials in Daniel 1–5. The action begins as the three Hebrew youths—"wisest in the books of the law"—are invited to the court. Their arrival is followed by Daniel's much abbreviated interpretation of Nebuchadnezzar's first dream; Nebuchadnezzar's attempted punishment of the youths in the furnace (which contains a version of the apocryphal "Canticle of Azarias")[25]; Daniel's interpretation of Nebuchadnezzar's second dream; and an account of Nebuchadnezzar's madness and exile. The poem ends abruptly just after Daniel interprets the miraculous writing on the wall (book 5). The poem's unpolished ending has occasioned much debate about whether the poem is actually complete as it stands, or whether it is fragmentary.[26]

In addition to following the general plot of the eponymous biblical text, *Daniel* also draws extensively on other scriptural resources. As we shall see, the poet makes significant changes to the focalization of the text that bring it closer in style to the later visionary books

7–12 of Daniel. He also draws freely and widely from a range of textual sources in other parts of the Old Testament that give shape to the governing theme of *translatio electionis*. The most influential passages are from Deuteronomy 7, but the poet's politico-theological vision encompasses the wider history of "chosenness" in the Pentateuch. These additions to the biblical text also alter the ostensible doctrinal purpose of the book of Daniel. If the latter espouses a distinctively anti-assimilationist discourse that champions the retention of Jewish law and ritual in exile, the Old English poem omits these requirements. For the poet, faith and belief are the sole criteria by which election is judged and made available.

The Old Testament Model of Election

In order to understand what is at stake in the literary *translatio electionis* in *Daniel*, it is necessary to explain the terms of Israel's exclusionary status as conveyed in the Old Testament. God "chooses" (from the verb *eligere*) Israel as his special people for the first time in Deuteronomy 7:6–10:

6) Because thou art a holy people to the Lord thy God. The Lord thy God hath chosen thee, to be his peculiar people of all peoples that are upon the earth. 7) Not because you surpass all nations in number is the Lord joined unto you, and hath chosen you, for you are the fewest of any people: 8) But because the Lord hath loved you, and hath kept his oath, which he swore to your fathers: and hath brought you out with a strong hand, and redeemed you from the house of bondage, out of the hand of Pharaoh the king of Egypt. 9) And thou shalt know that the Lord thy God, he is a strong and faithful God, keeping his covenant and mercy to them that love him, and to them that keep his commandments, unto a thousand generations: 10) And repaying forthwith them that hate him, so as to destroy them, without further delay immediately rendering to them what they deserve.[27]

In addition to having been "chosen," the Latin terms designating special election are *sanctus* ("holy") and *peculiaris* ("peculiar" with the additional sense of "private" or "special"). The latter designation comes closest to the original Hebrew *segullah*, which can mean either "specific" or "treasured." In Hebrew, this term highlights the special value placed upon the people in question and participates in the pervasive rhetoric of growth, health, and abundance associated with Israel's status of election. Thus, in the remaining passages of Deuteronomy 7, God promises to increase the nation, to provide an abundant harvest, to remove sickness, and to enable Israel to "destroy and consume" all other peoples (which is to say the seven nations mentioned in 7:1). In this passage, we witness the cultivation of the Old Testament's central political theology: God is depicted as the ultimate sovereign, and his covenant as a political contract.[28] Assigning this unique status to Israel, the passages in Deuteronomy also insist on the otherness of the surrounding nations who practice idolatry and are therefore cut off from the blessings of Israel. This distinction between Israel and its others is subsequently reinforced by the emphatic injunction to refrain from intermarriage in 7:2–3.

An important correlative to this passage appears in Deuteronomy 26:16–19, which communicates the radical contingence of Israel's covenant.[29] The status of Israel's election is dependent upon the strict observance of God's command (including ceremonial laws and religious customs) and is therefore subject to annulment:

> 16) This day the Lord thy God hath commanded thee to do these commandments and judgments: and to keep and fulfill them with all thy heart, and with all thy soul. 17) Thou hast chosen the Lord this day to be thy God, and to walk in his ways and keep his ceremonies, and precepts, and judgments, and obey his command. 18) And the Lord hath chosen thee this day, to be his peculiar people, as he hath spoken to thee, and to keep all his commandments.[30]

This passage makes it clear that Israel must *choose* the Lord and his ways in order to *be, and continue to be, chosen*.

It should be said that the Deuteronomic conception of election represents only one formulation of Old Testament chosenness. As Israel's internal political and religious structures changed, the conditions of election shifted markedly over the course of the period covered by the Pentateuch and its supplementary Jewish writings. One such redefining moment cited frequently by Old Testament prophets and New Testament authors alike is the split of Israel into the northern kingdom of Israel and the southern kingdom of Judah. The "new" Israel, having fallen into the sin of idolatry (against which Deuteronomy 7 states a warning injunction), is cut off from election. Thus, 2 Kings 17:18 states, "And the Lord was very angry with Israel, and removed them from his sight, and there remained only the tribe of Judah." Although the people of Judah likewise break "the commandments of the Lord their God," they are spared because they continue to observe "the customs that Israel had introduced." [31] Eventually the tribe of Judah, joined by the tribe of Benjamin, inherits the status as the Lord's chosen people.

The New Testament quite naturally cites this fissure between the old and new Israel as sufficient grounds for further reinterpretation of the concept of chosenness. For the New Testament authors, it stood to reason that if special election could be lost through sin, it could also be transferred to new groups of true believers. For Paul, the newly chosen people included only the remnant of Jews who believed in Christ as well as the new gentile believers, whom he called "the circumcised" and "the uncircumcised," respectively. Peter, echoing this rhetoric, explains to his formerly gentile readers (in 1 Peter 2:9–10): "9) But you are a chosen generation, a kingly priesthood, a holy nation, a purchased people: that you may declare his virtues, who hath called you out of darkness into his marvelous light: 10) Who in time past were not a people: but are now the people of God. Who had not obtained mercy; but now have obtained mercy." Citing and co-opting the language of Deuteronomy 7:6–10, Peter extends the range of chosenness to universal proportions.[32]

After the emergence of a separate sect that eventually became Christianity, this rhetoric sharpened and changed considerably: the church fathers changed the trope of expansion to reflect a dynamic of replacement. Already in the second and third centuries, Marcion and Tertullian strongly emphasized the Jewish forfeiture of election through sin. Augustine, however, opposed this purely teleological conception of the Old Testament in relation to the New. As Paula Fredriksen has argued, he advocated a return to the Pauline model of universalism—the model that included a remnant of the Jews in its salvational scheme.[33] Augustine's views on the matter were tied to his conviction that The Old Testament was essential for understanding the New, with which it stood in a complex typological relationship, and that, correspondingly, the Jews represented vital witnesses to the "living letter of the Law" in Christ.[34] In this question, as the following reading of *Daniel* aims to show, the Anglo-Saxons proved to be Augustine's spiritual offspring.[35]

The Theme of *translatio electionis*

The *Daniel*-poet establishes the theme of *translatio electionis* in the first 78 lines of his poem, which constitute a free expansion of just two lines in the Old Testament text (Daniel 1:1–2)[36]:

> 1) In the third year of the reign of Joakim, king of Juda, Nebuchadnezzar, king of Babylon, came to Jerusalem, and besieged it. 2) And the Lord delivered into his hands Joakim, the king of Juda, and part of the vessels of the house of God: and he carried them away into the land of Sennaar, to the house of his god, and the vessels he brought into the treasure house of his god.

These biblical verses report in the briefest detail Nebuchadnezzar's siege of Jerusalem; his holding captive of the people of Judah; and his profane use of the holy vessels of the Temple of Solomon. By contrast, the Old English passage tells in great detail of Israel's special election[37]:

Gefrægn ic Hebreos	eadge lifgean	1
in Hierusalem,	goldhord dælan,	
cyningdom habban,	swa him gecynde wæs,	
siððan þurh metodes mægen	on Moyses hand	
wearð wig gifen,	wigena mænieo,	5
and hie of Egyptum	ut aforon,	
mægene micle.	Þæt wæs modig cyn!	
Þenden hie þy rice	rædan moston,	
burgum wealdon;	wæs him beorht wela.	

Þenden þæt folc mid him   hiera fæder wære   10
healdan woldon,   wæs him hyrde god,
heofonrices weard,   halig drihten,
wuldres waldend.   Se ðam werude geaf
mod and mihte,   metod alwihta,
þæt hie oft fela folca   feore gesceodon,   15
heriges helmum,   þara þe him hold ne wæs,...

I have heard tell of the Hebrews living blessedly in Jerusalem, controlling their gold-hoard, maintaining their kingdom, as was natural for them, since through the might of the Creator an army was delivered into Moses's hand, a company of warriors, who went out of Egypt with great strength. That was a courageous people! For a while they were allowed to govern their kingdom, to manage their strongholds; they had magnificent prosperity. For a while the people strove to keep their Father's covenant among them. God was a shepherd to them, the Guardian of the heavenly kingdom, the Holy Lord, the Wielder of Glory. He, the Creator of all things, gave courage and strength to their community, so that they were able to destroy the lives of many people, (and of) the generals of the army, who were not loyal to Him...

No direct source has been identified for these lines. However, the passage echoes the terms of divine election, as set out in Deuteronomy 7:6–10. True to this source, the *Daniel*-poet explains Israel's blessedness as being contingent upon the observance of "their father's covenant" (*hiera fæder wære*; 10).[38] As in the biblical text, the righteousness of the Israelites is rewarded with political sovereignty and economic prosperity: they are permitted to live blessedly in Jerusalem, to hold their kingdom, to wield its treasures, and to gain victory over all those who are not "loyal" (*hold*) to God. The poet depicts this state of chosenness as being "natural" or "rightful," as the phrase "as was natural for them" (*swa him gecynde wæs*) indicates.

    Whereas the opening sequence depicts the nation of Israel in the best possible light, the subsequent passages demonstrate the tenuousness of this privileged status. Beginning with line 17, Israel is shown to fall into sin (17–32)[39]:

oðþæt hie wlenco anwod   æt winþege
deofoldædum,   druncne geðohtas.
Þa hie æcræftas   ane forleton,
metodes mægenscipe;   swa no man scyle   20
his gastes lufan   wið gode dælan!
Þa geseah ic þa gedriht   in gedwolan hweorfan, [40]
Israhela cyn   unriht don,
wommas wyrcean.   Þæt wæs weorc gode!
Oft he þam leodum   lare sende,   25
heofonrices weard,   halige gastas,
þa þam werude   wisdom budon.
Hie þære snytro   soð gelyfdon
lytle hwile,   oðþæt hie langung beswac[41]
eorðan dreamas   eces rædes,   30
þæt hie æt siðestan   sylfe forleton
drihtnes domas,   curon deofles cræft.

...until pride invaded them at their banquets, in the form of drunken thoughts with devilish deeds. Then they at once abandoned their profound knowledge of the law, the might of the Creator. Thus no man shall cut off his spirit's love from God! Then I saw that company, the people of Israel, turn to error, (and) perform acts of unrighteousness and sin. That was a pain for God! Often He, the Guardian of the Heavenly Kingdom, sent His teaching to that people (and) to the holy spirits who preached wisdom to the company. They believed the truth of that wisdom for a little while, until a deeper longing for the joys of the earth seduced them away from eternal counsel, so that they abandoned the judgments of the Lord (and) chose the Devil's craft.

The sudden shift from blessedness to wretchedness is marked by *oðþæt* ("until") in line 17a. Although the Israelites used to be *gecorene* ("chosen"), they have now lost that privilege as a community, for they "chose the devil's craft" (*curon deofles cræft*).[42] As indicated in Deuteronomy 26:16–19, the status of Israel's election is contingent upon the strict observance of God's command (including all ceremonial laws and religious customs).

One might suppose from this expansive treatment of the sins of Israel that the poet has adopted comprehensively the pre-Augustinian narrative of forfeited election. However, the opening passages of the poem also set up an important contrast between the demoted Israelites, on the one hand, and Daniel and the three Hebrew youths, on the other hand. In order to stress this distinction, the poet expands and reinterprets the biblical text. In fact, the word "chosen" does not appear anywhere in Daniel 1–5.[43] Yet *gecorene* ("chosen") appears three times in the Old English *Daniel*. In all instances it refers to the Hebrew youths. In line 90, we are told that the youths were "young and good in *godsæd*... chosen by God" (*ginge and gode in godsæde... metode gecorene*). This interpretation of the youths was possibly inspired by the Hebrew etymologies embedded in their names—Hannania means "the mercy of God," Azarias, "the help of God," and Mishael (possibly) "who is like God."[44] The poet's theme of chosenness helps explains the nonce compound *godsæd* (literally "God-seed"; 90b). This term has posed problems for translators—the *Dictionary of Old English* suggests that it might mean "divine progeny," with the sense of "among God's children" though the exact meaning is uncertain. In fact, the compound may be understood as an adaptation of the phrase *de semine regio* ("from royal seed") in Daniel 1:3, which refers to human rather than divine rule. By attributing divine lineage to the youths, the poet may have associated the physical perfection of the youths with that of the priestly class, the "chosen" of God, who are described in Leviticus 21:17–23 as being *de semine Aaron sacerdotis* ("of the seed of Aaron the high priest"). The Aramaic text further supports the thesis of a double sense in the Old English, since the corresponding phrase *mizerah hamlucha* ("of royal seed or offspring") may refer either to God or to earthly kings. Patristic exegetes were apparently familiar with both options, since Jerome points out in his commentary on Daniel—a text that some have supposed the Anglo-Saxon poet knew intimately[45]—that the Septuagint translated this phrase simply as "the chosen ones."[46]

As indicated, the word "chosen" appears twice more in the Old English *Daniel*. First, in line 145, when Daniel comes to

Nebuchadnezzar's court to interpret the king's initial dream (145–57). This dream, we are told, exceeded the interpretive abilities of even the wisest men at the Babylonian court:

> Ne meahte þa seo mænigeo on þam meðelstede 145
> þurh witigdom wihte aþencean
> ne ahicgan, þa hit forhæfed gewearð
> þætte hie sædon swefn cyninge,
> wyrda gerynu, oðþæt witga cwom,
> Daniel to dome, se wæs drihtne gecoren, 150
> snotor and soðfæst, in þæt seld gangan.
> Se wæs ordfruma earmre lafe
> þære þe þam hæðenan hyran sceolde.
> Him god sealde gife of heofnum
> þurh hleoðorcwyde haliges gastes, 155
> þæt him engel godes eall asægde
> swa his mandrihten gemæted wearð.

Then the crowd in the meeting place could not process or interpret any of it through prophecy, since it was denied that they might explain the dream or the mysteries of fates to the king; that is, until the Prophet came into the hall, Daniel to judgment; he was chosen by the Lord, wise and steadfast in truth. He was the leader of that wretched remainder who had to obey the heathens. God gave him a gift from the heavens, so that an angel of God told him everything just as that earthly lord had dreamed it.

In the bible, Daniel is introduced together with the three youths, but in the Anglo-Saxon poem he makes a rather dramatic separate entrance. His arrival provides a remedy for the people. The oðþæt ("until") that first appeared in line 17 to introduce the downfall of Israel is repeated here (line 149b) to show a second reversal of fortune. In the Vulgate, Daniel, having been endowed with the gift of interpreting all visions and dreams, vision[es] et somni[a], takes it upon himself to interpret Nebuchadnezzar's dream. In the poem, by contrast, Daniel is chosen by God to become the interpreter of Nebuchadnezzar's dream. Daniel's election is choreographed to mirror that of the three youths. As their names reflect their relationship with God, so does Daniel's—his name means "judgment of God," an etymology that the Old English collocation of *Daniel* and *dom* ("judgment") repeatedly invokes.[47]

The central lines 149–51 are repeated almost verbatim at the end of the poem, when Daniel is called upon to read the writing on the wall in the hall of Balshazzar. Here we find the final occurrence of the word "chosen" in *Daniel*, when we are told that no one could interpret the characters "until Daniel came entering the hall, chosen by the Lord, wise and steadfast in truth" (*oðþæt Daniel com, drihtne gecoren,/snotor and soðfæst, in þæt seld gangan*). In the Vulgate, the Queen invites Daniel to construe the writing. In the poem, however, Daniel is described as being "chosen by God" (*drihtne gecorene*). Thus, his election and wisdom are contrasted with the limited knowledge of the "rune-savvy men" (*runcræftige men*; 733) who, ironically, cannot read these divine "runes"—if indeed *runcræftig was* the intended meaning of having such abilities.

It would seem, then, that whenever the word *gecoren* appears in *Daniel* it is always tied to the allocation of divine wisdom. By citing the Deuteronomic observance of law as the mere precondition for chosenness, to which is then added the reception of God's wisdom, the poet subscribes to a recognizable Christian hermeneutics that privileges the spirit over the letter. The overarching principle of *translatio electionis*, however, comes to completion in a rather unexpected place. In the Old English version of the Daniel story, Nebuchadnezzar becomes not just a convert, but also a spokesman for God. Though he is never described as *gecoren* (for he is not a Hebrew), he takes on the properties of the elect youths, and he too becomes endowed with divine wisdom. The emphasis on knowledge in the process of his conversion is clear: whereas the Israelites were said "to turn to error" (*in gedwolan hweorfan*; 22), we are told that Nebuchadnezzar "turned again [*eft onhwearf*; 626] from the madness of his intellect" and, finally, "his spirit turned [*ahwearf*; 629] to the memory of God." These "turning" points mark a true *conversio* for Nebuchadnezzar. As he recovers his kingdom, he reverses the pattern of the "fall" that was enacted by the sinful Hebrews, and he regains control of his "treasure" (*gestreona*) and "kingdom" (*rice*). The crowning moment of this *translatio electionis*, which shifts the status of chosenness from the sinful Israelites to God's spokesman, occurs in lines 640–61:

Þa wæs eft geseted	in aldordom	640
Babilone weard,	hæfde beteran ðeaw,	
leohtran geleafan	in liffruman,	
þætte god sealde	gumena gehwilcum	
welan swa wite,	swa he wolde sylf.	
Ne lengde þa	leoda aldor	645
witegena wordcwyde,	ac he wide bead	
metodes mihte	þær he meld ahte,	
siðfæt sægde	sinum leodum,	
wide waðe	þe he mid wilddeorum ateah,	
oðþæt him frean godes	in gast becwom	650
rædfæst sefa,	ða he to roderum beseah.	
Wyrd wæs geworden,	wundor gecyðed,	
swefn geseðed,	susl awunnen,	
dom gedemed,	swa ær Daniel cwæð,	
þæt se folctoga	findan sceolde	655
earfoðsiðas	for his ofermedlan.	
Swa he ofstlice	godspellode	
metodes mihtum	for mancynne,	
siððan in Babilone	burhsittendum	
lange hwile	lare sægde,	660
Daniel domas.		

Then the guardian of Babylon was set up again in governance. He held to a better custom, a clearer belief in the Lord of Life— namely that God gave to every man prosperity and punishment, as he himself saw fit. The prince of the people was not held back by the mutterings of his wise men, but he preached widely [with?] the might of the Creator where he had the power of proclamation among his own people. He told about his journey, his wide wanderings with wild beasts, until a sensible understanding of the Lord God came upon him, into his spirit, when he looked up to the heavens. Fate was cast, the miracle made known, the dream fulfilled, the torment overcome, the judgment judged, just as Daniel had warned before that the leader of people would experience a miserable exile on account of his pride. So he zealously brought good tidings, [with?] the powers of the Lord before mankind, after Daniel had for a long time been uttering his teachings, his judgments to the citizens of Babylon.

The subject of the passage is unclear—who is this bringer of "good tidings": Daniel or Nebuchadnezzar? It would seem that that the grammatical subject "he" refers to Nebuchadnezzar, since we are told in the Vulgate that he preached the glory of the Lord, and in the poem that "he preached widely" (he wide bead). But the poet has left the pronouns ambiguous—perhaps deliberately. Godspellian generally takes the accusative of thing and dative of person. However, line 658a seems to imply that the subject has spoken "by means of the powers of the Lord" (metodes mihtum), since the feminine noun miht appears as an instrumental plural (see further line 647a). The passage implies a transfer of status—just as Daniel interpreted through God's intercession, so now Nebuchadnezzar carries on "the judgments" (domas) of Daniel through the powers of God.[48] The choice of godspellian is striking: either the poet intended the neutral sense "bringing good tidings," or else he wanted to highlight evangelical and missionary activity. While the poet used the terms "messenger" (spelboda; 229b, 464b, 532a, 742a) and "those who bear his tidings" (þ[a] þe his spel berað; 478b) for Daniel and the youths, he chooses this more acutely Christianized term for Nebuchadnezzar. Nebuchadnezzar's conversion follows the Pauline scheme of translatio electionis, since it indicates that all true believers may be brought into God's fold. By emphasizing the service of faith as the main criterion for chosenness, the poet highlights an important facet of the Pauline ideal.

The theme of translatio electionis, as it is developed in Daniel, ultimately differs from the models of "ecclesiastical" and "sacral" election that were analysed in the Introduction. Bede had used the transfer of election to underscore the status of his gens Anglorum as a divinely and singularly chosen people, united under one ecclesiastical regime. In contrast to this closed model of chosenness, the Daniel-poet offers a paradigm that is reframed within a more comprehensive, universal Christian context. This change is reflected in the details of the poem. As we saw earlier, the first part of the book of Daniel was written in the post-exilic period, and one of its primary didactic aims was to enforce anti-assimilationist practices. The author of *Daniel*, however, obviates this message by diminishing the attention to specific Jewish ritual and practice, and by suppressing details in the biblical Daniel that earmark the Jews as "special" or "peculiar" in a restrictive and exclusive sense. Thus, the emphasis on the observance of Jewish dietary laws is dropped, and the poet alters (703–11) the description of the Jewish vessels taken by the Babylonians from the Ark of the Covenant. These artifacts are called *huslfætu*, which in most other contexts would be translated as "eucharistic vessels." Although the simplex *husl* originally meant "holy," the word is far more commonly associated specifically with the "eucharist." Bede uses the term *huslfætu* at least twice to represent the vessels of the mass in his *Historia Ecclesiastica* (book I.16 and V.18). For the *Daniel*-poet, such aspects of Jewish ritual are easily reimagined within a broader Christian framework. In keeping with this change, the poet also adjusts the language he uses to describe Israelite "nationhood." The language of the composite Hebrew and Aramaic "original" text of the book of Daniel includes references to both "Jews" (Aramaic *yihudaiye*; Latin *Iudaeos*; in Daniel 3:8 and 12) and "Israelites" (Hebrew: *b'nai yisrael*; Latin *filios Israhel*). By contrast, the *Daniel*-poet writes about "Israelites" or "Hebrews." Only in one instance is the reference to the Jews kept—when the *blæd Iudea* is mentioned—that is, either the "glory of Judah" or "the glory of the Jews" (707b–8a). By shifting the focus generally to *Hebreos*, a term that tends to emphasize tribal affiliation, the poet expands the concept of chosenness beyond the bounds of biblical history to include his own Christian audience.

Translatio Auctoritatis

In addition to the transfer of chosenness, there is a complementary aspect of textual translation that deserves comment: the "transfer of authority." To this purpose, let us return briefly to the enigmatic verses in *Daniel* 17–32. At this point in the narrative, a perplexing change of perspective takes place: the narrator inserts himself into the text as an eyewitness. Though in every other instance he gathers information simply by hearing it told (he uses the phrase "I have heard" [*gefrægn ic*] four times in the poem at lines 1a, 57a, 458a, 738a), at 22 he explains that "then I *saw* that company turn to error" (*Þa geseah ic þa gedriht in gedwolan hweorfan*). This change is of great importance. *Hearing* implies the narrator's temporal and (possible) spatial distance from events in the poem. By contrast, his status as an eyewitness would seem to close, or at least narrow, this gap. The speaker's function as a *spectator* is highlighted by other elements that have generally, and perhaps hastily, been treated as scribal errors and emended in modern translations. For example, in line 22, Farrell's edition substitutes the seemingly more logical deictic *þa* ("then") for the manuscript's second-person accusative *þe* ("you"). Moreover, Farrell goes on to substitute the first-person plural *hie* ("they") in place of the first-person singular *me* ("me") in line 29. The unemended verse in the manuscript, *oðþæt [me] langung beswac* ("until longing seduced me"), implicates the narrator himself in the sins of the Israelites, and strongly resembles that moment of pure affect in *The Dream of the Rood* in which the narrator professes to share in the pain of the Cross by saying "I was all stirred up with sorrow" (*eall ic wæs mid sorgum gedrefed*).[49] The comparison with *The Dream of the Rood* draws attention to the articulation of visionary discourse in *Daniel*. In the former text, the phrase *geseah ic* forms a signature mode of visionary experience; the phrase appears five times in close proximity to testify to the first-hand experience of divine wonders[50]:

1 *Geseah ic wuldres treow … wynnum scinan* ("I saw the tree of glory … joyfully shine"; 14–15).

2 *Geseah ic þæt fuse beacen / wendan wædum ond bleom* ("I saw that clear beacon change its coverings and colors"; 21–2).

3 *Geseah ic þa frean mancynnes / efstan elne mycle* ("I saw the lord of mankind hasten with great zeal"; 33–4).

4 *þa ic bifian geseah / eorðan sceatas* ("Then I saw the corners of the earth tremble"; 36–7).

5 *Geseah ic weruda god / þearle þenian* ("I saw the god of hosts cruelly stretched out"; lines 51b–52a).

Through these attestations, the dreamer in *The Dream of the Rood* is established as an important eyewitness to Christ's passion, and as a credible reporter who transports the details of his dream to his reading and listening audience. The speaker in *Daniel* employs *geseah ic* in a similar vein. Although there is no parallel occurrence of a first-person eyewitness in the Vulgate (books 1–5), we can find a structural echo in Nebuchadnezzar's dreams, which he introduces by saying each time "I saw" (in Latin *vidi* or *videbam*). In the Old English, by contrast, both of his dreams are conveyed through third-person narration. By removing the language of dream-visions away from the protagonists in *Daniel*, and transferring it to the narrator himself, the poet establishes the narrator as a visionary figure in his own right, and as one who is, moreover, qualified to comment on the sins of Israel.

What are the reasons for this change of focalization? The poet's intention seems to have been to endow the narrator with the gift and authority of authentic prophetic speech. In the subsequent lines 33–78, the narrator deploys the typical accusatory and chastising rhetoric of the Old Testament prophets to good effect. He describes the plundering of the holy vessels of the temple as a punishment for the sins of Israel and establishes Nebuchadnezzar's conquest as an instrument of divine wrath. At the same time, however, the narrator's "I saw" differs from the Old Testament prophets' use of the same phrase. In the books of the prophets, the claim "I saw" is always the mark of a theophany—that is, a direct and spontaneous encounter with the divine.[51] Whereas biblical authors "showed little interest in the subjective experience of the visionary," the narrator of *Daniel* uses "I saw" precisely to introduce his very own visionary experience.[52]

By transferring the prophetic perspective to the narrator, the poet establishes him as an *interpres* ("interpreter") in both senses of the word: he is "a go-between" or "intermediary" as well as an "interpreter, translator, and expounder."[53] He mediates the biblical story of Daniel for the audience outside of the poem, even as he reports the recent events surrounding the Babylonian captivity and sack of Jerusalem to the listening public in the poem. In this double role, he takes over the prophetic office of Daniel himself, who in Books 1–6 is "an interpreter of dreams and visions, symbols and *aenigmata*," but in books 7–12 acts as a prophet who receives revelation directly from God. As both an eyewitness and reporter, the narrator becomes an important link in the process of *translatio electionis*. As we have already seen, it is difficult to assess his precise temporal relation to the actions in the poem. If he is in fact speaking as a Christian looking back to the biblical past, then the extension of the pattern of "conferred election" beyond the biblical communities in Daniel has been accomplished. Through the project of transference, the poem leaves open a space for the chosenness of its English audience beyond the pale of the poem.

This novel reading of features that have been consistently emended in earlier interpretations of the Old English *Daniel* requires us to reevaluate its opening line. Many Old English poems begin with the collective "we have heard" (*we gefrugnon*), but *Daniel* begins atypically with a privileged claim to personal knowledge: "I have heard" (*Gefrægn ic*), an introduction that appears in only one other long poem, namely, *The Phoenix*.[54] While the narrator claims to have heard part of his story from an oral source, he does not name his informant. As a point of contrast, we might compare the beginning of *Daniel* with the opening lines of *Exodus*, which begin by announcing its textual origins (1–7):

Hwæt! We feor and neah gefrigen habað   1
ofer middangeard Moyses domas,
wræclico wordriht, wera cneorissum,—
in uprodor eadigra gehwam
æfter bealusiðe bote lifes,   5
lifigendra gehwam langsumne ræd,—
hæleðum secgan. Gehyre se ðe wille!

Listen! Far and near throughout the world we have heard men proclaim the ordinances of Moses, those wonderful laws, to the generations of men, of the reward of life in heaven for each of the blessed after the baleful journey, and of everlasting counsel for each living soul. Let him hear, who will!

The speaker of *Exodus* credits two sources of information: one oral and one textual. The undisputed authority in both cases is the bible, which is called "the ordinances of Moses," and described as "wonderful laws" (*wræclico wordriht*). He also includes in this textual community all "the generations of men, and every living soul." The stated purpose is to transmit the biblical ordinances forward to his contemporary audience in the capacity of an evangelist. The poet's words *Gehyre se ðe wille* eloquently ventriloquize the words of Matthew 11.5: "He that hath ears to hear, let him hear."

The comparison with *Exodus* exposes a radical revision of authority in *Daniel*, in which the poet overwrites and displaces the *locus classicus* of biblical authority. Through the narrator's intervention, we are offered a parallel version—not an exact rendering—of the biblical story, which is interpreted through the lens of a much wider history that also encompasses events beyond the historical time of the biblical Daniel. As a *strong translation*, the poem claims a novel status as an original and independent text that calls attention to its own condition as a work that stands in need of interpretation and exegesis.

Ecce Auctor: Translation, Authority, and Biblical Poetry

My reading of *Daniel* raises an important methodological question that is especially acute in this poem: How should we discuss or evaluate textual authority in Old English Old Testament poetry? On the one hand, there is the problem of sources. Although the Vulgate appears to have been the predominant source for most of the Old Testament poems, we do not know with sufficient precision which other versions and traditions were utilized. On the other hand, there is the matter of classifying textual *auctoritas*. Without specific dates and authors at our disposal, it is difficult to categorize the conditions of, and claims to, authorship. To some extent, *Daniel* shares this problem with other medieval writings. The medieval conception of *auctoritas* is treated as the extreme other of contemporary "authority." Jocelyn Wogan-Browne explains the stakes as follows:

Contemporary understandings of authorship often revolve around either the notion of individual genius (derived from the Romantic conception of the "artist") or that of property rights over a text (as expressed in laws governing copyright or plagiarism). Authorship in the Middle Ages was more likely to be understood as participation in an intellectually and morally authoritative tradition, within which … a writer might fill one of several roles, copying, modifying, or translating, as well as composing.[55]

In the past thirty years, or so, medievalists have pushed back assertively on this narrow conception linking authorship with modernity. One important milestone has been Alastair Minnis's *Medieval Theory of Authorship*, which traces the emergence of the medieval human *auctor* to the thirteenth century.[56] Minnis uses the term specifically to denote "someone who was at once a writer and an authority, someone not merely to be read but also to be respected and believed."[57] He defines a*uctoritas* as a performative condition: its very dynamism was engrained in popular etymons, which included the Latin verbs "*agere* 'to act or perform,' *augere*, 'to grow,' and *auiere* 'to tie.'"[58] Accordingly, an *auctor* thus "'performed' the act of writing, brought something into being, caused it to grow."[59] Before the thirteenth century, *auctores* were typically characterized as ancient authors, whose works had been cited, read, and believed for centuries. The status of *auctor* was therefore conferred only retrospectively. However, with the age of scholasticism (and in particular with the work of Alexander of Hales), a new model of authorship emerged. The status of *auctor* became something that could be cultivated or asserted in the process of writing a text.[60] The decisive change, according to Minnis, was the invention of the Aristotelian *accessus*, which applied Aristotle's formal causes to the process of translation and textual production itself. Of course, God remained "the ultimate *auctor* of holy writ" and the primary "efficient cause," but human authors could now be identified as "instrumental efficient causes" working with a degree of autonomy under the authoritative "unmoved mover."[61] In Minnis's words, "the result was the emergence of an inspired but fallible author who was allowed his individual authority and his limitations, his style and his sins."[62] The entire process marks a type of *translatio auctoritatis*, a term that Minnis uses to invoke the classical scheme of *translatio imperii*.[63]

Although Minnis's argument has been widely accepted,[64] it leaves us with an obvious question: How did *early* medieval writers view textual production and translation and define their relationship to established *auctores* such as Augustine or Boethius? [65] More to the point, how did writers express and grapple with their own interventions as interpreters of the language and the meaning of the bible? In her influential book, *Rhetoric, Hermeneutics, and Translation in the Middle Ages,* Rita Copeland provides a compelling account of the practices of translation from the classical to the late medieval periods. Within this larger frame, she observes gradations of *auctoritas.* Although the concept of the *auctor* is a thirteenth-century invention, it does not emerge all of a sudden. Rather, it should be seen as an incremental development that takes its departure from earlier modes of translation and biblical exegesis. It is therefore quite important that Copeland attributes to patristic commentary and early medieval literature a hermeneutic and rhetorical identity of its own. As she shows, "patristic criticism borrow[ed] the terminological apparatus of Cicero and Horace ... in order to generate a theory of translation directed almost entirely at meaning and at signification outside the claims of either source or target language."[66] In the process, patristic hermeneutics "rejected the classical motives of contestation, displacement, and appropriation"; instead it aimed at "a communality of source and target in terms of the immanence of meaning."[67] Copeland consequently distinguishes between "patristic" or "primary translations," which use exegesis to comment on and maintain a firm connection to the target text, and "secondary translations," which present themselves as independent works.[68] "Primary translation" represented the dominant form of translation in patristic and early medieval writing and continued to be employed even in nonbiblical texts up to the fifteenth century, while "secondary translation" emerged in its true form only in the thirteenth century.

Without a doubt, there are perceptible differences between late and early medieval practices and theories of translation. However, this does not mean that Copeland's characterization of early medieval translation as a transparent process of recuperation and preservation ought to be accepted without further modification. In fact, Robert Stanton challenged this account in *The Culture of Translation in Anglo-Saxon England.* He argued that written vernacular initially appeared in a service relationship to Latin, that is, as a mere tool for translation, but it eventually "acquired a hermeneutic status and authority in its own right." [69] One measure of this partial autonomy is that the very act of writing in the vernacular constituted a significant "rupture in an expected linearity of Latin literary and textual reception." [70] In so arguing, Stanton brings us back to the truism that every translation of a work must, to some extent, also be regarded as an act of transference rather than mere transmission. Stanton pushes this idea further still by suggesting that beginning with the works of Alfred, the valorization of English as a viable mode for literary production deviates from Copeland's assessment that "primary translation is concerned mainly with recuperating a truthful meaning beyond the accidents of human language and linguistic multiplicity." [71]

Minnis and Copeland provide important and useful frameworks for the study of the history of authorship and translation. But in the process they shortchange emergent, not-yet-dominant modes of textual production. *Daniel*, for example, represents a convincing precursor to Copeland's "secondary translation." In the beginning of the chapter, we noted that the poem performs a "radical misreading" of the core politico-theological scheme articulated in the biblical Book. Later, we noted that the narrator of *Daniel* also rewrites his source by co-opting the role and voice of the eponymous Old Testament prophet. By claiming to be an eyewitness to the described events, he appears as an interloper in biblical history. His claim of being able to "see" the sinful activities of Israel commandeers novel textual authority. Because of this double intervention, *Daniel* stands as one of the most important and extreme examples of "strong translation" in Anglo-Saxon England, and more generally in the early medieval period.

Conclusion

Daniel performs a radical "misreading" of its biblical source. While the Old Testament book of Daniel (chapters 1–5) emphasizes the unfaltering faith of the Israelites who adhere to their law in exile, the Old English poet interpolates a series of passages that emphasize the general disobedience of the Jews who violate their covenant with God and forfeit their special status of election. By focusing on decline, the poet obviates the prominent theme of *translatio imperii*, which is established in the bible through a series of dreams and prophecies that predict the downfall of successive nations and the eventual ascendancy of Israel over all other nations. In its place, the poet substitutes the scheme of *translatio electionis*, that is, the transfer of chosenness away from the Jewish people that collectively has lapsed in faith to a more heterogeneous community of believers that includes Christian converts as well as select Jews. On these grounds, the status of chosenness can be plausibly transmitted and ascribed to a transhistorical Christian community that includes the Anglo-Saxons themselves. Moreover, as a "strong translation," *Daniel* represents a bold experiment in narratology. The poet manipulates the conventions of time, space, and focalization in the target biblical text in order to realize a substantially different kind of revelation that is influenced by the medieval dream-vision genre.

Notes

1   Portions of this chapter appear in an earlier publication on the subject of "chosenness" as a trope in Anglo-Saxon literature (see Zacher 2010). I recast and rework my analysis of *Daniel* here to reflect the book's larger engagement with biblical poetry and the depiction of Old Testament Jews.

2   Coogan *et al.* (2001: 1268).

3   Coogan *et al.* (2001: 1265). Coogan explains the currencies as follows: "*mene* (heb. 'mina') is a large weight and is related to the word 'count'; *tekel* (heb. 'shekel'), related to the word 'weight,' is one-sixtieth of a *mene*; *parsin* are two spheres with one sphere (or *peres*) equaling a half-shekel; it is interpreted as meaning 'divide.'"

4   Coogan *et al.* (2001: 1267). The fourth beast is the most spectacular, with its growing and dividing horns, representing further political division. One of the horns has eyes and a mouth that speaks arrogantly (7: 8).

5   For the complex political allegory represented by the ram and the goat, see Coogan *et al.* (2001: 1269–70).

6   "Von herausragender Bedeutung für die Ausprägung dieses Translationsgedankens war das biblische Danielbuch, das mit seiner

Leitidee der nach einem göttlichen Plan aufeinanderfolgenden und z.T. durch translatio miteinander verbundenen vier Weltreiche mit anschließendem Weltengericht und der Errichtung eines fünften, göttlichen und ewigen Reiches ein 'unbestrittenes Gerüst für die Geschichtsschreibung' bis zum Ende des 18. Jhdts. bildet" (Krämer 1996: 7, quoting Koch 1982: 276).

7   Krämer focuses mainly on French literature from the twelfth to the sixteenth centuries; however, she cites and relies on the early medieval examples in the Carolingian era.

8   Jeauneau (1995: 8).

9   Jeauneau (1995: 18–19).

10 The genealogy was repeated by luminaries such as Isidore of Seville, Hrabanus Maurus, Freschulf of Lisieux, Remigius of Auxerre, and Otto of Freising (see Jeauneau 1995: 20–1). It gave rise to the legend that Plato himself was educated in Egypt and learned philosophy from the prophet Jeremiah. As Jeauneau (19) points out, Augustine himself espoused this view for a time. Thus, he mentions the meeting between Plato and Jeremiah in his *De doctrina Christiana* 2.28.43, though he corrects this view in *De civitate Dei* 8.11. Josephus also traced the "origin of sciences" back to the sons of Seth, before the flood (in his *Historia antiquitatis Iudaicae* 1.70–1; as cited by Jeauneau 20).

11 Otto von Freising (*Historia* I prol. and 5 prol., ed. Hofmeister: 7 and 227). Summarized here by Jeauneau (1995: 20).

12 Gilson *De translatio studii* (unpublished lecture): 3, as discussed by Jeauneau (1995: 3).

13 Gilson (1955: 171–96); see also Jeauneau (1995: 6–7).

14 Alcuin, *Epistula* 170 (PL 100:282; MGH *Epistulae* 4: 279.20–6), cited by Jeauneau 1995: 11. Gilson "Alcuin and the Flowering of Carolingian Learning" (unpublished lecture): 7.

15 Jeauneau (1995: 11) and Gilson "Alcuin and the Flowering": 7.

16 Jeauneau (1995: 11) and Gilson "Alcuin and the Flowering": 7. and Lapidge (2006b: 148–54).

17 Anderson (1987) argues that the trope of *translatio imperii* appears intact in *Daniel*.

18 This pattern of rise and fall is repeated in a variety of ways in the poem. For example, there is a demonstrable link between scenes of drunkenness at the beginning, middle, and end of the narrative, where in turn the Israelites, Nebuchadnezzar, and Belshazzar each fall prey to this same offense (Isaacs 1968: 148–51). Other critics have focused similarly on the theme of pride as a constant

impetus for moments of rise and fall in the poem, making the argument that the downfall of Nebuchadnezzar and Belshazzar at the middle and end of the poem, respectively, mirrors the pride of the Israelites at the beginning of the poem (Caie 1978).

19   For Anderson, this overarching trajectory encapsulates within it other "moral issues" noted by other critics of *Daniel*, such as the poem's prominent emphasis upon punishment for pride and drunkenness (sins that are committed first by the Jews and then by the Chaldean kings Nebuchadnezzar and Balshazzar), and also the poem's use of various thematic tensions between, for example, obedience and disobedience; good counsel and the *deofles cræft*; and finally, adherence to God's covenant instead of the practice of devil worship.

20   Remley (1996: 248–52).

21   Zacher (2010).

22   Coogan (2001: 1253).

23   Coogan (2001: 1253).

24   Coogan (2001: 1253).

25   In keeping with the Vulgate text, the poem also includes a version of the apocryphal "Canticle of Azarias," which appears in lines 279–429. A version of this "song of Azarias" appears as an independent poem in the Exeter manuscript. The texts are close enough to suggest that they are derived from a common textual tradition. See further Farrell (1974: 45) and Remley (2002).

26   Farrell (1974: 33).

27   6) quia populus sanctus es Domino Deo tuo te elegit Dominus Deus tuus ut sis ei populus peculiaris de cunctis populis qui sunt super terram 7) non quia cunctas gentes numero vincebatis vobis iunctus est Dominus et elegit vos cum omnibus sitis populis pauciores 8) sed quia dilexit vos Dominus et custodivit iuramentum quod iuravit patribus vestris eduxitque vos in manu forti et redemit de domo servitutis de manu Pharaonis regis Aegypti 9) et scies quia Dominus Deus tuus ipse est Deus fortis et fidelis custodiens pactum et misericordiam diligentibus se et his qui custodiunt praecepta eius in mille generationes 10) et reddens odientibus se statim ita ut disperdat eos et ultra non differat protinus eis restituens quod merentur.

28   Brueggemann (2066: 10–13).

29   The term "radical contingence" upon observance of the covenant is Walzer's; see the Introduction and Chapter 1.

30   16) hodie Dominus Deus tuus praecepit tibi ut facias mandata haec atque iudicia et custodias et impleas ex toto corde tuo et

ex tota anima tua 17) Dominum elegisti hodie ut sit tibi Deus et ambules in viis eius et custodias caerimonias illius et mandata atque iudicia et oboedias eius imperio 18) et Dominus elegit te hodie ut sis ei populus peculiaris sicut locutus est tibi et custodias omnia praecepta eius.

31   2 Kings 17:19–20: "19) But neither did Judah itself keep the commandments of the Lord their God: but they walked in the errors of Israel, which they had wrought. 20) And the Lord cast off all the seed of Israel, and afflicted them and delivered them into the hand of spoilers, till he cast them away from his face."

32   The subject of Paul's "universalism" has been treated in great detail. See, for example, the study by Badiou (2003).

33   Fredriksen (2008: esp. 243–5). This point is vital for understanding Augustine's doctrine on the Jews and the Old Testament. Fredriksen writes that Augustine's assertion was "revolutionary" in that it "stood centuries of traditional anti-Jewish polemic, both orthodox and heterodox, on its head." Pre-Augustinian Christianity had stressed the Jews' "literal-mindedness" in observing the Law. This perceived obstinacy "had long provided Christian critics with absolute proof of Israel's turpitude: as their own worst enemy (so went the argument), the Jews through their insistent loyalty to fleshly ancestral practices indicted themselves. Instead of understanding the Law 'spiritually,' Jews had understood 'carnally' and thus remained enmeshed in the fleshly 'works of the law,'" (244). Augustine, however, argued strenuously against this view. Fredriksen summarizes his position as follows: "The Jews had not erred in their mode of observing the Law and enacting its mandates 'in a fleshly way' *secundum carnem*, rather than *secundum spiritum*, 'according to the spirit.' On the contrary, they had done just what God had commanded them to do (*Against Faustus* 12.9)" (244).

34   On the concept of the Jew as "witness," see, especially, Cohen (1999).

35   Augustine's influence on Old English literature and poetry has been well documented. See, especially, Huppé (1959).

36   The relationship of the Old English *Daniel* to various biblical versions is still unclear. The case has been made for the poem's dependence upon several versions, including two distinct Greek versions (the Theodotian and the Septuagint versions), two distinct Old Latin versions, and the Vulgate. A still helpful study of the poem's relationship to the Old Latin texts can be found in Hofer (1889). For a comprehensive summary of all previous scholarship on the issue, and a meticulous consideration of the verbal correspondences between *Daniel* and these biblical versions, see Remley (287–333), who concludes that the *Daniel*-poet probably had direct knowledge of the Vulgate; that he directly consulted a continuous Old Latin exemplar; and that he had indirect knowledge of the Septuagint. Since the poem shows the most sustained correspondences with the Vulgate, I use this as the base text for my comparison. For a list of the poem's departures from the Vulgate text of Daniel 1–5, see Bjork (214).

37 All quotations from the Old English *Daniel* are from Farrell (1974).

38 Bjork (1980: 215) explains the importance of the theme of the covenant in *Daniel*. He argues that just as the covenant is broken by the Hebrews at the beginning of the text (an act that results in the scattering of the Jews throughout the world [line 300] and their life of slavery [lines 302–7]), it is renewed by means of the Song of Azarias (315–25), since the youths exhort God to keep his promise to Israel and expand their nation. The fulfillment of the theme occurs as Nebuchadnezzar returns the remnant of the Jewish captives to the youths (452–3).

39 Scholars have frequently commented on the poem's thematic attention to the sin of pride. This intense focus obviates the exploration of other themes and dynamics in the poem. For a review of this scholarship, see Bjork (221–3). Also see Caie (1978: 1–9), who reads the poem in total as an *exemplum* and warning against pride.

40 The MS reads *þe* for *þa* in line 22.

41 The MS reads *me* for *hie* in line 29.

42 The sins listed in this passage have received much commentary. Bjork (1980: 214–17) and Anderson (1987: 9) comment extensively on the patterns of feasting and drunkenness in the poem.

43 Two examples can be found in Daniel 11:35 and 12:10. The Vulgate, however, translates *eligentur* ("they shall be chosen") for the Hebrew *vayitbarru* ("they will be purified"), a change that results from a different reading of root word. Here, the Hebrew *hitbarer* ("purified") is construed in the Latin as *barar* ("chosen"). It is difficult to say which reading is definitive since the Masoretic text (the standard Hebrew texts of the bible with vowels) was not available until the seventh century CE.

44 On the order and spelling of the names of the youths in Daniel, see Remley (1996: 305, n. 194).

45 See Jerome's *Commentarii in Danielem PL* 25 col. 496D.

46 The use of the compound *godsæd* may also reflect an interpretation of which the poet could only have been aware through other biblical commentaries: the Aramaic *zerah* refers to both offspring and seeds to be eaten. In the book of Daniel, the youths shun the food of the king, and instead ask to be given "legumes/ seeds to eat and water to drink" (*min-hazroim vinochlah omayim vinishta*), so maintaining the dietary restrictions of *kashrut* (a detail otherwise omitted from the Old English). The youths are thus in multiple senses *gode in godsæd* ("good in God-seed").

47 On the poet's formulaic and repeated use of the Hebrew etymology for Daniel, see Frank (1972).

48 As Remley has pointed out (1996: 283, 319–20), Nebuchadnezzar's conversion is unusual; his role as an evangelist, however, is borne out by parts of the Septuagint, and the theme in *Daniel* may reflect its debt to this source. For a thematic reading of Nebuchadnezzar's conversion (in the context of the poem's emphases on pride and sin), see Overing (1984).

49 There are still further verbal and thematic connections between *The Dream of the Rood* and *Daniel*: for example, the phrase in Daniel 122b–3 *hwæt hine gemætte,/þenden reordberend reste wunode* which parallels *The Dream of the Rood* 2–3 *hwæt me gemætte to midre nihte,/syðþan reordberend reste wunedon*. Several further and hitherto unnoticed parallels have been cited by Orchard (2009).

50 Orchard (2009) cites these verses in order to explain the visionary experience in *The Dream of the Rood*.

51 See Barbara Neumann's essay (2005) on the difference between prophetic and medieval visionary literature. The vision experienced in *Daniel* does not quite conform to the late medieval mystical model either, for as Newmann demonstrates, such visionary experiences "involve a willfully altered state of consciousness brought on by the disciplines of memory, perception, reading, and attention" (3). See, however, my discussion of the Old English poem *Exodus* (in Chapter 1), which utilizes meditation on the covenant as a transformative devotional device.

52 Newmann (2005: 3).

53 As George Hardin Brown (1993) has demonstrated in a different context, the term *interpres* has a wide semantic range, including "middleman" and "messenger" and also "explainer, expounder, and interpreter." Although Cicero famously distinguished between the role of the *interpres*, who translated word for word, and the *orator*, who translated sense for sense, early medieval authors such as Bede and Aldhelm used the corresponding verbs to denote both types of translation, since "every *interpres*, true or false, modifies, colors, arranges, forms his matter" (48). The word *interpres* also has special currency in the context of biblical dream interpretation and prophecy. In Book X of his *De vocabulis*, Isidore of Seville writes that an "interpreter [is][so called] because he is the medium between two languages while he translates. And also he is called *interpreter* who interprets and explains the divine mysteries to men" (51).

54   Parks (1987) helpfully analyses and classifies the various formulas for "hearing" in Old English poetry.

55   Wogan-Brown *et al.* (1999: 4). In his famous essay "What is an Author," Michel Foucault argued that the advent of the author "constitutes a privileged moment of individualization in the history of ideas, knowledge, literature, philosophy, and the sciences" (Foucault 2003: 377–91). For Foucault, this moment is tied to the commodification and ownership of "discourse": "texts, books, and discourses really began to have authors (other than the mythical, sacralized and sacralizing figures) to the extent that authors became subject to punishment, that is, to the extent that discourses could be transgressive." The advent of the "real" (i.e. nonsacral) author of literary texts took place sometime in the seventeenth or eighteenth centuries, and was linked to the emergence of a system of ownership of works and ideas. However, Foucault does locate a degree of textual authority in medieval scientific texts. He writes that "those texts we now would call scientific—those sciences and geography—were accepted in the Middle Ages, and accepted as 'true' only when marked with the name of their author" (383).

56   Minnis (2010: 159).

57   Minnis (2010: 10).

58   Minnis (2010: 10). I have changed the conjugated form *auieo* to the infinitive *auiere*.

59   Minnis (2010: 10).

60   Minnis (2010: xxvii).

61   Minnis (2010: 82–3).

62   Minnis (2010: xiii).

63   Minnis (2010: xxviii).

64   It should be clear that Minnis describes a *systematic* change in emphasis that granted independence to the human *auctor* and encoded this shift within the text itself. Such clarification is important because, obviously, the fathers of the church distinguished between divine and human *auctoritas*—even in the case of the sacred bible. For them, such a division was essential for coming to terms with textual discrepancies between the versions of the bible produced in Hebrew, Greek, and Latin. Although theologians accepted the divine inspiration of the seventy translators who allegedly produced the Septuagint, they nevertheless had to allow for human scribal errors in the chain of transmission.

65 Others have sought to align the emergence of authorship with the so-called "discovery of the self" in the twelfth century. See, for example, Dronke (1970); Hanning (1977).

66 Copeland (1991: 43).

67 Copeland (1991: 43).

68 Copeland (1991: 6–7).

69 Stanton (2002: 2).

70 Stanton (2002: 5).

71 Stanton (2002: 43).

3

Judith: Holy War and Ethnic Difference

On September 1, 1689, Cotton Mather delivered a sermon entitled "Just War of New-England Against the Northern and Eastern Indians" to a group of forces armed to fight against the native inhabitants of New England.[1] Mather compared the colonists to ancient Israel, and the natives to Israel's ancient enemy, Amalek, depicting them as "murderers" and as "wolvish persecutors." The sermon had two paramount objectives: (1) to assert divine right to the territories occupied by indigenous peoples, and (2) to bring to life the biblical narrative so that the forces could imagine themselves in the role of the triumphant Israelites.[2] According to Susan Niditch, Mather's aim was to allow "the cadences of the Bible [to] speak the listeners' myth." The New Englanders are Israel in the wilderness, commissioned to subdue their enemies with God's guidance. Amalek, deserving of vengeance and total destruction, is to be (in Mather's words) " 'beat(en) small as the Dust before the Wind,' 'Cast out as the Dirt in the Streets,' (Mather 28) eliminated, exterminated." [3] For Mather, the war against the Indians of New England was twice justified: the natives are "accused of murdering Christians and therefore are worthy of death (so some biblical writers justify killing in war), but also they are Ammon, Amalek, an indigenous population who will be displaced and disinherited by divine decision to make way for the New Israel."[4]

The biblical examples that Mather cites in his homily form a series of contrasts. In addition to the assertion of "right" punishing "injustice," the sermon seeks to discriminate between the conditions of holiness and damnation, purity and impurity, belief and nonbelief, civilized life and barbarism. In each case, the former term is to displace the latter. In short, Mather's sermon calls for nothing less than total destruction of the other.

Two things stand out about this sermon in the present context. It is clear that some of these harsh views were derived directly from the bible itself: the methods of extirpation and annihilation are attested as licit strategies for war in parts of the Old Testament. Mather's focus on Amalek is an extreme adaptation of this very attitude. However, as Niditch also explains, the use of the Hebrew scriptures as a template and as a paradigm upon which to base contemporary calls to war "surely says more about [the New Englanders'] own forms of self-articulation than about ancient Israelite attitudes and traditions."[5] It is precisely the pliability and applicability of Old Testament examples for wartime purposes that has allowed their flexible appropriation and reproduction in contexts ranging from the medieval crusades to contemporary right-wing views on foreign policy.[6]

Mather's aggressive sermon provides an interesting starting point for talking about the Old English poem *Judith*, which employs a comparable list of contraries and antinomies when discussing the Hebrews and the Assyrians. Not unlike the Native Americans of Mather's speech, Holofernes, general of the Assyrians, is described as "a heathen hound" (*se hæðena hund*; 110), a man "steeped in violence" (*niða geblonden*; 34), and an "unclean one, filled with sin" (*se unsyfra, womfull*; 76–7).[7] Moreover, he is described as "the devil's kind" (*se deofulcunda*; 61), "a fiendish harmer" (*se feondsceaða*; 104), "the wicked one" (*se bealofulla*; 48, 63, 100, 248), and "the evil one" (*se inwidda*; 28). The Assyrians are also collectively demonized and are described in terms commonly reserved for God's most ancient enemy, Satan himself: they are said to be "ancient enemies" (*ealdgeniðlan*; 228), "ancient foes" (*ealdfeondas;* 315), and "ancient haters" (*eldhettende;* 320) of the Israelites. Along the same lines, the poet also establishes the difference between Holofernes and God. Whereas the former is called "the dispenser of death" (*se morðres brytta*; 90) and the lord of cities only (*se burga ealdor*), the latter, in keeping with this general pattern, is "the Dispenser of Glory" (*se tires brytta*; 93) and "the Lord of all creation" (*se frymða waldend;* 5). Judith, moreover, is uncompromisingly holy, wise, and beautiful. She is described as "a woman, resplendent like an elf" (*ides ælfscinu*; 14), a "radiant woman" (*seo beorhte idese*; 58), a "holy woman" (*seo halige meowle*; 56), and a "wise woman" (*seo snotere idese*; 55).[8] In short, Judith is "enlightened" in every sense of the word. The important point regarding these stock characterizations is that they are invented and interpolated into the biblical storyline by the poet himself. That the poet (like Mather) imagined these extreme characterizations as reflective of contemporary tensions between the Anglo-Saxons and their Viking attackers seems likely, though our inability to date the poem poses a problem in this regard. What remains clear, however, is that the story of Judith was adapted to reflect a distinctive political theology, which utilized the tropes of exceptionalism and exclusion to demarcate a boundary between "us" and "them," the Anglo-Saxons and their opponents.

Scholars of *Judith* have complained that the poet's use of such stark oppositions has the undesirable effect of flattening out the ethical complexities of the biblical text, particularly in those scenes where Judith takes an active role as a seductress, a deceiver, and a ruthless assassin. Thus, Geoffrey Shepherd laments, "of all the surviving [Old English poetic] treatments of the Bible, *Judith* is one of the most empty of theological or typological implication."[9] Anne Astell and Mark Griffith argue that the poem "literalizes" the materials extracted from patristic tradition.[10] For Griffith, the vision contained in the poem is flat and one-dimensional: "unlike the *Exodus* poet, [the *Judith*-poet] avoids explicit reference to allegorical interpretations from patristic commentary, choosing instead to handle the book as a simple exemplum of the triumph of Christian faith over the power of evil."[11] Jackson Campbell has argued that "the story as a whole is told to minimize the unique and to emphasize the typical.... Simplification, reduction and rearrangement are the hallmarks of the poet's method."[12] Yet, if Mather's sermon teaches us anything, it is that the reduplication and adaptation of biblical narratives and wartime propaganda for political, religious, and literary purposes is anything but straightforward or neutral. It is by no means a foregone conclusion that the Anglo-Saxon poet should portray Judith and the Israelites in entirely positive terms, or disparage the conquering and colonizing Assyrians. In acknowledgment of this larger theologico-political agenda, the following questions should be asked: Why choose *this* deuterocanonical text? What particular aspects of the Judith story spoke to the poet and to his audience? In order to answer these questions, it is necessary to take stock of the changes made to the biblical storyline, and to assess the impact these changes have upon the martial ethics and ideology of the text, as well as its concomitant attitudes toward Jewish and Christian identity and practice.

There has been some discussion of the political content of the Anglo-Saxon *Judith*. Most of this work has been done in the name of establishing *Judith* either as an occasional poem or as an allegory for spiritual warfare.[13] Hrabanus Maurus is cited as an important model for reading *Judith* as an occasional poem, since he dedicated his ninth-century commentary on the book of Judith to Queen Judith, wife of Louis the Pious.[14] Hrabanus's preface compares the two Judiths in order to celebrate the Queen's spiritual and physical prowess. Most patristic commentaries, however, treat the book of Judith as a spiritual allegory, in which Judith is seen as a figure for Chastity (Jerome, Aldhelm, Ælfric), Humility (Fulgentius), or the Church itself (Isidore of Seville, Prudentius, Hrabanus Maurus).[15]

Judith has also been compared to, and interpreted through the lens of, other contemporaneous Anglo-Saxon adaptations of the eponymous biblical book. Ælfric of Eynsham's homily on Judith and his letter to Sigeweard have been especially important in this respect. Ælfric dedicated his homily to a group of nuns (*myn swustor*, "my sisters"), in which he figured Judith as a *bysen ... clænysse* ("example [of] chasity"),[16] and adduced her as a correctional paradigm for *nunnan þe sceandlice libbað tellað to lytlum gylte, þæt hi hi forlicgon* ("nuns who live shamelessly and consider it a small fault that they commit fornication"). Judith in this case represents virtue and chastity. In a letter to the nobleman Sigeweard, however, Ælfric cites Judith's wartime tactics as a model for military prowess against the Vikings[17]: *þæt ge eower eard mid wæmnum bewerian wið onwinnendre here* "so that you might defend your country against the attacking army."[18] Ælfric's two Judiths attest to the flexibility of the story for political and religious purposes.

All of these treatments and rewritings are immensely interesting and help us in establishing a broad view of the uses to which Anglo-Saxon authors put the book of Judith. However, to assume that *Judith* must follow the same schematic pattern is to deny it its own specificity. The poem, in fact, cultivates a finely tuned politico-theological perspective that is quite distinct from the aforementioned patristic and Anglo-Saxon treatments.

In what follows we will explore the ways in which the Old English poet reframes two paradigms of war that are both presented in the biblical text. The first concerns guerrilla tactics and is exemplified by Judith's assassination of Holofernes. The second concerns the large-scale battle between the Israelite army and the Assyrian forces. In the Vulgate version of *Liber Iudith*, the Israelites are shown to adhere to *ius ad bellum* ("just cause for war"), since they fight to protect the temple, Jerusalem, its sacral vessels, and their people from ruin. The Anglo-Saxon poet, however, exaggerates this justification for war. He gives new emphasis to the idea of war as divine punishment of the enemies of the righteous by increasing God's role in combat and by adding an apocalyptic dimension to the eternal punishment of the heathen enemy. In doing so, the poet both acknowledges the biblical conception of holy war and revises aspects of it to bring it in line with patristic and medieval understandings of "just war."

In the process, the poet highlights the universalizing potential of the Judith story as a religious model. Although the book of Judith was accepted as canonical or deuterocanonical throughout the Middle Ages, readers and commentators from the Roman period forward were still aware of its distinctive and perhaps problematic religious, political, and social status.[19] Judith was probably composed sometime in the second half of the second century BCE (or later), during the Hasmonean period, and in the distinctive *zeitgeist* of the Maccabean revolt and the corresponding triumphalism. The book of Judith is thus commonly seen to represent "a new theology that transformed what it meant to be considered a Jew in the Hellenistic era."[20] Shaye J.D. Cohen has argued that the conversion story of Achior in the book of Judith registers a new attitude toward conversion in Judaism. The change from identification by birthright to inclusion by belief marked a decisive shift in conceptions of Jewish identity under Hellenism and in the diaspora. According to Cohen, "it was this Hasmonean redefinition of Judaism that permitted Josephus at the end of the first century CE to state that the constitution established by Moses was not only a *genus*—a nation, a 'birth'—but also a 'choice in the manner of life.'"[21] The Old English *Judith* reflects a similar understanding of *genus* and divine election: the poet systematically downplays the role of specific Jewish rituals and practices in order to place greater stress upon faith and belief, the core essentials of Pauline devotion.

Adapting Judith: From Seductress to Warrior

The biblical account of Judith begins by enumerating the "world-domination" campaigns of Nebuchadnezzar, who sought to "bring all the earth under his empire" (2:3) and to "cover the whole face of the earth" with his cavalry, foot troops, and chariots (2:7 and 19).[22] Holofernes, acting as general under Nebuchadnezzar, imposes a series of strictures and conditions on the vanquished nations: he enslaves their people; commandeers their resources; demolishes their shrines and places of worship; and requires "that all their dialects and tribes should call upon [Nebuchadnezzar] as a god" (3:8). The nation of Israel, however, refuses to submit. Judith, the unlikely heroine of the story, takes matters into her own hands (ch. 9). She removes her widow's clothing, and, dressed to kill, sets out to infiltrate the Assyrian camp with her handmaid (ch. 10). Judith is admitted to Holofernes's personal chamber because she promises to disclose strategies that will enable the Assyrians to defeat the Israelites (ch. 11). Holofernes, enraptured by her beauty, promises her protection, and even permits her to leave the camp every night so that she might pray to God for omens. On the fourth day, Holofernes invites Judith to a feast, planning to seduce her. Instead, he becomes inebriated and passes out (ch. 12).

It is roughly at this point in the narrative that the Anglo-Saxon adaptation begins. The poem, like its soon-to-be-decapitated villain, is acephalous: it begins mid sentence, picking up somewhere in the narrative just before the feast of Holofernes. The end is not authenticated either. The last six lines have been added at the bottom of the final folio of the poem by an early modern hand imitating insular script. Presumably this addition was copied from another leaf, which is now lost. For this reason, there can be no certainty that the poem's ending is genuine and complete. There has been a great deal of speculation about how much text has been lost, particularly at the beginning of the poem.[23] Opinions about the matter have guided interpretations of the poet's attitude toward *Judith*. Those who view the poem as virtually complete tend to argue that the poet has deliberately excised and sanitized those parts of the narrative that describe Judith's seduction and deceit; those who insist that the poem is merely a fragment suggest that the multiple references to Holofernes's lust and lechery were likely preceded by some kind of seduction scene. The textual evidence does not suffice to resolve the issue. The manuscript contains three numbered sections, X, XI, and XII, that appear at the end of lines 14, 121, and 235. On these grounds, it has been conjectured that the poem also contained sections I–IX, which presumably corresponded to chapters 1–11 of the book of Judith. However, it is also possible that these numbers were copied from an exemplar that also contained other materials.[24] While it is impossible to know how much text was lost, it seems very likely that the current text was preceded by at least one section that would have contained Judith's first prayer to God for help and guidance, since we are told in line 6a that God "granted her request" (*tiðe gefremede*). Moreover, lines 12–14 state that the described action takes place on the fourth day of Judith's stay in the Assyrian camp, leaving us to wonder what happened on the previous three days. If the poet followed the time sequence of the biblical narrative, then a full five days would have marked the precise number of days the Israelites agreed to wait for divine help before submitting to Holofernes. It stands to reason that the poet would have something to say about how Judith arrived at the camp.

In his edition of *Judith*, Mark Griffith provides a detailed account of the major changes in the poem as compared to the Vulgate. The most comprehensive of these is the reduction and condensation of characters. Only two characters are named in the poem, Judith and Holofernes, and the only other figure of substance is Judith's maid, who accompanies her to the Assyrian camp. There is no mention at all of Nebuchadnazzer, the king of the Assyrians, or of Achior, the heathen who converts to Judaism through circumcision. As a result, the poem contains considerably fewer speeches. Judith prays to God for strength and protection before killing Holofernes (83–94a; cf. Vulgate 13:7–9). She addresses the Israelites on three separate occasions: to communicate God's divine favor toward the Israelite forces (152–8; cf. Vulgate 13:17); to claim victory by displaying the severed head of Holofernes (177–86; cf. Vulgate 13:19–25); and to rouse the Israelite men to war and certain victory (186–98; cf. Vulgate 14:1–5). The only other speaker in the poem is the unnamed Assyrian warrior who finds Holofernes dead in his tent (285–9; cf. Vulgate 14:16) and interprets this as an omen of the impending defeat of the Assyrian troops. Judith's final psalm celebrating victory and giving thanks to God (Vulgate 16:1–17) is omitted or lost from the poem, as are all speeches by Holofernes and Achior. Such reductions obviously abbreviate the text, but they also add dramatic tension. In place of speech-making and grandstanding, the drunken Holofernes is reduced to noise-making and inebriated loutishness. The poet is at his wittiest when he expands a single verse in the Vulgate describing Holofernes's drunkenness in 12:20 ("And Holofernes was made merry on the occasion, and drank exceeding much wine, so much as he had never drunk in his life") to achieve the following scene of debauchery (17–32):

Þær wæron bollan steape
boren æfter bencum gelome,   swylce eac bunan ond orcas
fulle fletsittendum;   hie þæt fæge þegon,
rofe rondwiggende,   þeah ðæs se rica ne wende,   20
egesful eorla dryhten.   Ða wearð Holofernus,
goldwine gumena,   on gytesalum,
hloh ond hlydde,   hlynede ond dynede,
þæt mihten fira bearn   feorran gehyran
hu se stiðmoda   styrmde ond gylede,   25
modig ond medugal,   manode geneahhe
bencsittende   þæt hi gebærdon wel.
Swa se inwidda   ofer ealne dæg
dryhtguman sine   drencte mid wine,
swiðmod sinces brytta,   oðþæt hie on swiman lagon,   30
oferdrencte his duguðe ealle,   swylce hie wæron deaðe
geslegene, agotene goda gehwylces.

Deep bowls were borne with frequency to the benches, and also full goblets and pitchers to the hall-guests. The brave shield-bearers sampled it all fated to die; the powerful ruler, the terrible lord of men, did not expect it. Then Holofernes, the lord of gold and of men, became merry from drinking; he laughed and roared, he clamored and made noise, so that the sons of men were able to hear from afar how he, fierce-hearted, stormed and yelled proud and drunk with mead, and urged the bench-sitters to enjoy themselves well. So the evil one plied his men with wine the entire day, that fierce-hearted giver of treasures, until they passed out in a swoon. He over-intoxicated his entire troop, so that it seemed as though they were struck dead, drained of every drop of virtue.

The sound effects used to depict Holofernes's drunken riot echo formulas and techniques traditionally used in Old English battle poetry. Verb doublets and end-rhyme, typically used to convey the clamor of shields and the cries of the slain, here characterize the careless revelry of the Assyrians. By transposing these sounds to the feast, the poet captures the drunken impotence of Holofernes and forecasts his future demise by the sword. By plying his men with excessive drink, Holofernes ends up literally "emptied" or "poured out" (*agotene* 32a) of all "sense" (*ræd*).

 If the descriptions of Holofernes thus focus on his lack of good sense, the most dramatic changes in the poem concern the depiction of Judith. The biblical heroine has been described variously as a "gorgeous gorgon," a "femme fatale," and the quintessential "good bad woman."[25] The focus has consistently been on her sexuality: Judith is figured either as a seductress who uses feminine wiles to overcome the enemy or as a chaste and devoted widow. Following this trend, scholars have attempted to slot the Anglo-Saxon Judith into the same familiar female paradigm. This tendency has given rise to radically contradictory interpretations of her character. Some critics misleadingly describe the Anglo-Saxon Judith as a "virgin," asserting that the absence of the two scenes in which she dresses in fine clothing and plans to seduce Holofernes is proof of her chastity. However, not a single detail in the poem supports this view. Moreover, the terms *mægð* and *ides*, both meaning "young woman," are on occasion even translated erroneously as "virgin."[26] In marked contrast, other scholars highlight Judith's hypersexuality. John P. Hermann and Susan Kim employ Freudian and Lacanian psychoanalysis to reinterpret the beheading scene as a type of castration/circumcision.[27] Both scholars interpret the intriguing and strange description of Judith and the Hebrews as *wundenlocc*—meaning something like "curly-locked" or perhaps "with wound hair"—as a sexual marker. Hermann points out that the word *wundenlocc* appears only one other time in the extant Old English corpus, in the context of a riddle where, at least according to one solution, it is suggestive of pubic hair.[28] This overt sexualization of Judith is not well supported by the poet's other descriptions of either the heroine or the Israelites. It seems far more likely that the poet was familiar with the many Jewish laws concerning polling (cutting hair and shaving the head) or perhaps the less common poetic biblical trope of unbound hair (thus corresponding to the sense of "curly-locked"), which signals readiness to serve God in war.[29] Overall, the stated symbolic link between decapitation, castration, and circumcision seems less than convincing, since the poet actually omits the two biblical references to circumcision, and excises all mention of Holofernes's eunuch, Vagao. It is far more likely, as we shall see, that the predicate *wundenlocc* represents a crude attempt at the formulation of a Jewish ethnic or racial marker.

Like the head of the Gorgon, Judith's sexuality has blinded critics. Instead of providing coherent interpretations of the poem, they have simply inferred details and claims about Judith the seductress from other sources and previous commentaries. As we shall see, it is actually Judith's revised role as the handmaiden of God, and the appointed vessel of his vengeance, that is a vital feature of the rewriting of the biblical ethical and political scheme in the Anglo-Saxon *Judith*.

Holy War and Just War in Early Christian Thought

I have been using the term "holy war" to refer broadly to the warfare ideologies enshrined in the biblical text of Judith and in the Anglo-Saxon poem, and the term "just war" to refer generally to the development of Christian just war theory in the patristic and medieval periods. These are terms of convenience. In practice, it is quite difficult to distinguish between the two concepts, a phenomenon that is well attested by the later medieval crusades, which were characterized as both "holy" and "just" wars. In employing these two separate terms, I draw on the definitions provided by Frederick H. Russell in his authoritative *The Just War in the Middle Ages*:

> In Christian thought two types of war have been seen as permissible, the *holy war* and the *just war*. The *holy war* is fought for the goals or ideals of the faith and is waged by divine authority or on the authority of some religious leader. When the latter is an ecclesiastical official, the holy war becomes a *crusade*. The crusading ideal is historically bound up with a theocratic view of society, while the *just war* is usually fought on public authority for more mundane goals such as defense of territory, persons and rights (italics mine).

Russell defines the main differences between "holy war" and "just war" as follows: (1) whether the authorizing agent of war is God or some secular authority; (2) whether the cause for war is the protection of faith or the protection of freedoms; and (3) the extent to which violence is permitted in subduing the enemy (holy war justifies utter destruction, while just war advocates restrained aggression). His definition is not intended to be comprehensive or absolute, and he allows that in many cases, the differences are blurred.[30] As is clear from our own contemporary experiences of war in Afghanistan and Iraq, the difference between "defensive" and "offensive" war, and between "just" and "unjust" causes, can often hinge on clever rhetoric, popular media, and propaganda.[31]

These limitations notwithstanding, Russell's definition proves useful for an assessment and comparison of the attitudes toward war in the Old Testament Judith and the eponymous Anglo-Saxon poem. Though we cannot speak of any systematic classical or early-medieval (i.e. pre-scholastic) "just war theory," it is clear that patristic writers commented frequently and thoughtfully on the necessity of war and provided broad and varied criteria for distinguishing between just and unjust causes and methods of war.[32] Several important precursors and lines of transmission of just war thinking and theory have been identified, both from the classical to the patristic periods (by way of Cicero) and from Late Antiquity to the Anglo-Saxon period (especially by way of Ambrose, Augustine, Gregory the Great, and Isidore).[33]

In the Anglo-Saxon period, Augustine's writings on the subject were among the most influential and widely disseminated. His mature writings are especially important in this regard, since many of them were composed during the impending collapse of the Roman empire, in the throes of barbarian invasions and in the wake of threatening heresies. These crises demanded intense reflection on the causes and justifications of war. Perhaps the two most important texts in this regard are book XXII of *Contra Faustum*, and, above all, book XIX of *De Civitate Dei*—a book that, incidentally, was written between 411 and 26, after the fall of Rome to the Visigoths in 410.[34] Augustine also discusses the issue of holy war in the Old Testament in his *Quaestiones in Heptateuchum* (especially VI: 10). However, what made his writings on the subject of war both unique and historically significant was his attempt "to reconcil[e] the evangelical precepts of patience and the pacifistic tendencies of the early church with Roman legal notions."[35] As a result of this marriage of Christian and Roman ideals, Augustine emphasized the importance of the *miles Christi*, whose role it was to defend the Church from infidels and heathens, and increasingly, in the course of Augustine's lifetime, also against internal heresies such as Donatism and Pelagianism.[36]

Augustine's commentaries on war are in many ways the natural outgrowth of his evolving theological work on the origins of evil, for he viewed war as "both a consequence of sin and a remedy for it."[37] In his commentary on Joshua, Augustine provided what has been described as "the first new definition of the just war since Cicero, a theory that could be summed up by the phrase *iusta bella ulciscuntur iniurias* ('just wars avenge injuries')."[38] Cicero had viewed war as a "necessary evil," waged only to recover "lost goods"—a term that included both property *and* incorporeal rights.[39] By contrast, Augustine treated just war as a *penal sanction*. For him, "the concept of *ulcisci iniurias* rather than defense was the necessary point of departure for every *ius ad bellum*."[40] Augustine's emphasis on punishment distinguished his thought on war from subsequent Christian thinkers. Echoing Cicero's model, Isidore of Seville (seventh century) wrote that "a just war is that which is waged for the sake of recovering property seized or of driving off the enemy. An unjust war is one that is begun out of rage and not for a lawful reason" (*Etymologiae*, 18.1–3).[41]

Augustine's conception of just war could be seen as a deliberate return to the Old Testament model of holy war.[42] For him, the term *iniustus* covered both crimes against the law (as the ones that were adjudicated in Roman "justice") and sins against righteousness (as the ones that were avenged in "holy war").[43] Steeped in language that is reminiscent of the patriarchal covenants themselves, Augustine defined *ius* ("righteousness") as that which is owed to God. For Augustine, "seen in this light any violation of God's laws, and, by easy extension, any violation of Christian doctrine, could be seen as an injustice warranting unlimited violent punishment."[44] Therefore, from Augustine forward, the Old Testament provided "an exemplary tapestry of divinely-sanctioned aggressive holy wars unrestrained by any feelings of mercy or guilt."[45]

It is in this distinctly Augustinian tradition that the Anglo-Saxon poet reimagined the Israelite wars against the Assyrians in *Judith* as going beyond just retaliation and just punishment. By emphasizing "just cause" in the actions of Judith and the Hebrews, the poet deviates from the book of Judith. In the biblical text, the Assyrians offend God and Israel through the intended destruction of the temple and Jerusalem, as well as the active prevention of Jewish practice and ritual. In the Old English poem, however, the chief crimes of the Assyrians that are deserving of serious punishment and even annihilation appear to be their very status as heathens and the condition of disbelief itself. There is no mention in the poem of the temple, of Jerusalem, or of Jewish rituals. In *Judith*, the Hebrews are portrayed as being both "righteous" and "right" not because they strictly maintain Jewish law and ritual, as they do in the book of Judith, but rather because they are examples of perfect faith. To be sure, this change is entirely in keeping with the poet's emphasis on the paradigm of Christian universalism founded on Pauline doctrine.[46]

War in Judith: Toward a Pentateuchal Paradigm

In the biblical version of Judith, the issue of "holy war" is brought to the fore in the moment when Judith decides to infiltrate the

Assyrian camp and assassinate Holofernes. In Chapter 9, she prays to God for the defeat of Holofernes and for the complete destruction of the Assyrians. Her justification is twofold: she hopes to prevent Holofernes's intended ravishment and rape (even though she has not yet met him), and to forestall the future destruction and defilement of the temple, its holy vessels, its priests, and God's covenant with Israel. The events that have already unfolded in Chapters 1–8 of the biblical book suggest that Judith has good reason to fear both outcomes, for in every conquered territory Holofernes has destroyed the places of worship and enslaved the people for his use.

It is clear from the content of Judith's prayer in 9:2–14 that she is asking God to wage a "holy war" against the Assyrians—in classic Pentateuchal style. To this end, she cites two Old Testament episodes—the rape of Dinah in Genesis 34 and the crossing of the Red Sea in Exodus 14–15. In both of her retellings, Judith praises God's redemption of Israel and his total annihilation of Israel's enemies. Using these stories as justifications for her own planned attack, Judith urges God "who destroy[s] wars" to wreak his total vengeance against the Assyrians (9:11). Just as the God of Exodus crushed the Egyptians who "pursued armed after thy servants, trusting in their chariots, and in their horsemen, and in a multitude of warriors" (9:6), Judith calls on him now to crush the Assyrians who "trust in their multitude, and in their chariots, and in their pikes, and in their shields, and in their arrows, and glory in their spears" (9:9). Her citation of the Exodus miracle at the Red Sea is self-explanatory, since the book of Exodus represents the quintessential narrative of redemption and liberation for the Israelites. More puzzling, however, is the citation of the Rape of Dinah as an example of divine retribution. In verses 9:2–5, Judith prays to the God of Simeon (the brother of Dinah, who avenges her rape in Genesis 34) and extols his rightful vengeance for that rape:

2) O Lord God of my father Simeon, who gavest him a sword to execute vengeance against strangers, who had defiled by their uncleanness, and uncovered the virgin unto confusion: 3) And who gavest their wives to be made a prey, and their daughters into captivity: and all their spoils to be divided to thy servants, who were zealous with thy zeal: assist, I beseech thee, O Lord God,

me a widow. 4) For thou hast done the things of old, and hast devised one thing after another: and what thou hast designed hath been done. 5) For all thy ways are prepared, and in thy providence thou hast placed thy judgments (trans. here and throughout from the Douay-Rheims bible).

Judith presumably chooses this *exemplum* because she intends to prevent her own rape, an act that in her view deserves similar divine retribution.[47] However, closer inspection reveals that Judith revises God's role in the biblical story of Dinah's rape considerably. She claims that God *gave* Simeon a sword so that he might avenge the rape of his sister. This detail runs counter to the narrative conveyed in Genesis 34, where it is stated that the brothers used deception to subdue the men of Sichem. Simeon and Levi consent to a marriage between Dinah and Sichem, provided that all the Sichemites undergo circumcision. Dinah's brothers, however, break their promise. Just three days after the Sichemite circumcision, they slay the entire tribe (Genesis 34: 25). In Genesis, this vengeance is severely chastised when Jacob furiously berates his sons Simeon and Levi for their actions. Moreover, in Genesis 49:5–7, Jacob even denies them their birthright for this act of "violence with the sword."[48] In Judith's revisionist account, however, the Lord is praised for enabling the Israelites to capture the men of Sichem, for allowing them to enslave the women as prey and despoil all of their goods. Judith also commends God for allowing the spoils to be shared by all of God's servants "who were zealous with [his] zeal (Vulgate 9:3)." Thus, in the retelling of both stories, God is identified as the driving force behind the acts of vengeance.

Judith's revised stories entwine two major themes that run through the biblical book of Judith: the fear of defilement by the enemy and the threat of ruin through "unjust" persecution. In bringing these aspects together, Judith actually performs an expert piece of biblical exegesis. The same verb *opprimere,* "to ravish" or "to oppress," is used in the Vulgate in Exodus 3:9 to describe Israel's oppression by Pharaoh, and in Genesis 34:2 to describe the ravishment of Dinah by Sichem.[49] Naturally, this phrasing gives rich context to Judith's reverse ravishment and subsequent slaying of Holofernes, which are celebrated by rejoicing maidens at the end of the book of Judith in 16:11 in related terms: *sandalia eius rapuerunt oculos eius pulchritudo eius captivam fecit animam eius amputavit pugione cervicem eius* "Her sandals ravished his eyes, her beauty made his soul her captive, with a sword she cut off his head."

Although Judith's prayer is absent from the Old English poem, several details from her revisionist account of the Sichem story (beyond the obvious connection between sexual offense and punishment) make it into the Anglo-Saxon account. Echoing the Genesis episode, the Anglo-Saxon Judith attributes her successful sword-slaying to God's will. She, like Simeon, avenges her enemies with God's assistance. The second borrowing is adapted in a more complex fashion. At the close of the Vulgate version, a lengthy account is given of Judith's dedication of her share of the spoils of war—namely, Holofernes's personal belongings—to God. In the Old English poem, by contrast, Judith is said to keep Holofernes's armor and personal possessions, and to give thanks to God for her just reward. This new ending is well integrated into the fabric of the poem: Judith's wartime "reward" (*mede*; 334a) foreshadows her "reward in heaven" (*mede on heofonum*; 343b). But why did the poet change this detail in the first place? One explanation is that he sought to bring the description of spoliation in line with contemporary praxis.[50] In the early medieval period, it was common for "property seized during hostilities immediately [to become] the possession of the captor"—a custom that marked a definitive change from Roman law, which dictated that "moveable property" (*praeda*) had to be given over to the sovereign.[51] In this context, it is especially striking that the *Judith*-poet revises the end of the poem to mirror Judith's modified account of "just spoliation" in her retelling of the Sichem story (in Judith 9:3).

It would seem that on the basis of biblical precedent for just spoliation, the *Judith*-poet changed the Vulgate version of Judith to bring it in line with more conventional Deuteronomic formulations of Holy War. This reading is tied to an understanding of the Pentateuchal conception of *herem* (the "ban"), which specified literally that "all human beings among the defeated are 'devoted to destruction,' as a part of 'God's justice.'"[52] As we have seen, such a conception of "God's due" is connected to Augustine's understanding of holy war. In different parts of the Old Testament, the law of *herem* is interpreted according to divergent war ideologies (based, it might be supposed, on the variant political and religious ideologies of its authors and redactors). In some texts, the *herem* is understood to mean the *total* destruction of the enemy, including people, goods, and livestock. Thus, in Numbers 21:2–3, the "Israelites vow their enemies to God as a promise for his support of their successful military efforts." In Deuteronomy and Joshua, it is generally "assumed that God demands total destruction of the enemy." [53] However, in other books of the bible, it is clear that *herem* could be satisfied by allowing partial devastation, or by substituting animal sacrifices. [54] In any case, in *all* of these examples, the keeping of spoils and livestock was permitted to the captors themselves. In such cases, the spoils represented the lesser share of wartime atrocities, while the more valuable *deodand* (lit. "what is given to God") was human life itself. [55]

Read through the lens of Old Testament laws on spoliation, the conclusion of *Judith* reflects the poem's encompassing conception of just and holy war. This is an important point because it has been argued that the Anglo-Saxon poet deliberately altered the description of spoliation at the end of Judith in order to invoke a nascent "anti-Judaic" stereotype that associated Jews with avarice. [56] Yet, on the contrary, it should be clear from the thoroughly positive treatment of Judith's actions that the poet regarded her keeping of the treasure as a just reward for her part in God's holy war. In fact, this transformation brings the Anglo-Saxon rendering of the deuterocanonical story of Judith more firmly in line with the traditional canonical Pentateuchal conception of holy war.

Guerrilla Tactics: Old Testament Parallels

Although I have been referring to Judith's wartime tactics as "guerrilla warfare," the term is, of course, anachronistic—the Spanish term *guerilla* ("little war") was used in this sense only from the eighteenth century onward. The concept, however, is useful for shedding light on the beheading scene as it is scripted in the poem. Michael Walzer defines guerrilla warfare according to the following criteria: (1) guerrillas fight by means of the element of surprise, and they use concealment or camouflage as a tactic; (2) "they fight in small groups, with small arms, at close quarters" and the soldiers they fight against are identifiably soldiers, not civilians; (3) the guerrilla war is, above all, a "people's war"—"the guerilla's self image is not of a solitary fighter hiding among the people, but of a whole people mobilized for war, himself a loyal member, one among many."[57]

In the biblical narrative, Judith's assassination of Holofernes follows this paradigm in most respects: she is certainly "of the people"— neither a political nor a religious leader, but rather a mourning widow who acts on her own initiative, for the greater good of her nation. Judith, moreover, wears multiple disguises: she infiltrates the Assyrian camp as a single woman travelling together with her maid; as a civilian dressed in civilian clothing; as a seductress, who has no intention of sleeping with the enemy; and as a double agent, who pretends that she can leak the necessary information to secure the defeat of Israel. In modern "just war" theory, a fine, but important, ethical line is drawn between guerrillas who fight in camouflage and those who fight as civilians: the latter tactic is seen to be "unjust" because it destabilizes the code of war fought *by* soldiers *against* soldiers.[58] Seen from this perspective, Judith's disguise as a civilian and defector (when in fact she is an assassin) is more troubling than her getup as a beautiful seductress. The biblical author, of course, did not see things this way: his guiding paradigm was "holy war," not "just war." In the context of the Old Testament, it is clear that Judith exercises just cause.

It is important to note that Judith's guerrilla tactics follow a well-attested strategy for trenchant warfare in canonical Old Testament texts. As biblical scholars have shown, Judith's beheading of Holofernes can be compared to the story of Aod (Hebrew: Ehud), who kills King Eglon of Moab in his chamber with a concealed dagger (Judges 3:12–30), and Jael who slays general Sisera in her tent with a tent peg (Judges 4:17–22; 5:24–7).[59] This kind of comparative approach, especially linking Judith and Aod, helps us better to understand key aspects of the specific ideology of war that is expressed in the book of Judith. The Aod/Eglon narrative begins with the punishment of the Israelites, who have sinned against God, and are thus enslaved in Moab under King Eglon. During their captivity, the people repent and pray to God for deliverance. God eventually relents and sends a savior (Hebrew *moshiya*; Latin *salvator*) by the name of Aod to the people. Aod, like Judith, plans a surprise attack on the king. He hides a dagger under his cloak on his right thigh, with the intention of slaying Eglon with his left hand.[60] He then approaches the king in private, in order to relate a "secret message from God." When Eglon rises from his throne, Aod slices him through his corpulent belly. Eglon's men, who are anxiously waiting outside the king's chamber, finally enter by using a key, only to find "their lord lying dead on the ground." Aod escapes unseen, and the Moabites are left in a state of confusion (*illi turbarentur*). Returning to his people, Aod sounds the trumpet and calls the Israelites to war, saying, "Follow me: for the Lord hath delivered our enemies the Moabites into our hands" (*sequimini me tradidit enim Dominus inimicos nostros Moabitas in manus nostras*).

The parallels between the stories of Judith and Holofernes and Aod and Eglon are obvious: in both cases, a lone operative launches a surprise attack upon a tyrant in his personal quarters, and in both cases the single assassin is then able to rally the troops to a full-scale war. Jerome's Vulgate version highlights these textual parallels. In the Septuagint and Old Latin versions of Judith, the scene of the discovery of Holofernes's headless body is brief and devoid of dramatic detail. Holofernes's men go directly to the general's tent and immediately try to wake him. When the king does not answer, Vagao knocks discretely and then enters the chamber only to find his lord "cast upon the floor dead" with his "head taken from him." In the Vulgate, however, Jerome adds considerable comic relief to the episode. Like the soldiers who wait nervously outside of Eglon's chamber, Holofernes's men stand uncomfortably outside the chief's personal quarters and are reduced to making noises and clapping their hands to alert the king to their presence:

9) And they that were in the tent came, and made a noise before the door of the chamber to awake him, endeavoring by art to break his rest, that Holofernes might awake, not by their calling him, but by their noise. 10) For no man [dares to] knock, or open and go into the chamber of the general of the Assyrians.... 13) Then Vagao going into his chamber, stood before the curtain, and made a clapping with his hands: for he thought that he was sleeping with Judith.

Jerome's various expansions and additions to the Judith narrative have been well documented.[61] It may be possible to surmise that Jerome derived direct inspiration for this particular comic episode in Judith from the Aod/Eglon episode in Judges. The latter narrative would have effectively provided a canonical—and distinctively male—paradigm for Judith's unorthodox and unruly guerrilla tactics.

The Anglo-Saxon poet who followed Jerome's text expanded still further the drama of the discovery scene (267–74):

Beornas stodon

ymbe hyra þeodnes træf   þearle gebylde,
sweorcendferhðe.   Hi ða somod ealle
ongunnon cohhetan,   cirman hlude   270
ond gristbitian caesura —gode orfeorme—
mid toðon torn þoligende.   Þa wæs hyra tires æt ende,
eades ond ellendæda.   Hogedon þa eorlas aweccan
hyra winedryhten,   him wiht ne speow.

Warriors stood around the tent of their lord, fiercely emboldened, their hearts turned dark. They began to cough all at once, to cry out loudly, and to gnash their teeth, clenching their jaws and suffering miserably, entirely estranged from good. Their glory, their blessedness, and their valorous deeds had reached an end. They thought to wake their lord and friend, but their efforts were in vain.

Whereas in the Vulgate episode the officers are impatient and ashamed, in the poem *Judith* they behave almost as if they had been sentenced to eternal damnation: their hearts are darkened, they gnash their teeth, and they cry out with a *cirm*—a cry that typically appears in eschatological sequences.[62] This apocalyptic embellishment becomes all the more striking when compared with the poet's description of the fate of Holofernes's damned soul (111–21):

Læg se fula leap

gesne beæftan,   gæst ellor hwearf
under neowelne næs   ond ðær genyðerad wæs,
susle gesæled   syðða æfre,
wyrmum bewunden,   witum gebunden,   115

hearde gehæfted   in helle bryne
efter hinsiðe.   Ne ðearf he hopian no,
þystrum forðylmed,   þæt he ðonan mote
of ðam wyrmsele,   ac ðær wunian sceal
awa to aldre   butan ende forð   120
in ðam heolstran ham,   hyhtwynna leas.

The foul carcass lay behind him, devoid of life, his spirit had gone off
somewhere else under the deep cliff; thus he was subdued, fettered
with torments forever, wound with serpents, bound in torture,
severely imprisoned in a hellish burning after his [soul's] departure.
Engulfed in darkness, he had no need to hope that he might get out
of the serpent-hall; rather, he was condemned to dwell there in the
dark home forever without end, devoid of hopeful joy.

This doomsday addition has perplexed scholars, in large part because
no direct parallels have been discovered for this description in the
portions of *Judith* adapted from the bible.[63] However, it seems likely
that some details were borrowed from Judith's canticle (16:20–2),
which describes the fate of those who oppose God, and receive
permanent vengeance:

20) Woe be to the nation that riseth up against my people: for the
Lord almighty will take revenge on them, in the day of judgment
he will visit them. 21) For he will give fire, and worms into their
flesh, that they may burn, and may feel pain forever.

By transposing this foreboding description to the beheading scene,
the poet brings Judith's mission squarely in line with the Augustinian
conception of holy war as both divine vengeance and punishment.
Holofernes, the enemy of God himself, is defeated and punished for
all of eternity.

God's Vengeance: A Manifest Sign

The Augustinian conception of holy war pervades other episodes
in *Judith* as well. In two instances, the poet adduces otherworldly

marvels and signs to reveal God's will and providence, at moments when no such miraculous revelation appears in the biblical text. In the Vulgate when Judith returns to the Israelite camp, she takes Holofernes's bloody head from her food satchel (*de pera*), shows it to the people, and describes how she managed to assassinate Holofernes. Judith is concerned first and foremost with her personal integrity, for she has successfully avoided Holofernes's sexual advances. She says, "and the Lord hath not suffered me his handmaid to be defiled, but hath brought me back to you without pollution of sin, rejoicing for his victory, for my escape, and for your deliverance (Judith 13:20)." In the Old English poem, by contrast, Judith focuses on the integrity and welfare of the people, and presents Holofernes's head as a token of her success in battle (171–4 and 195–8):

> Þa seo gleawe het,   golde gefrætewod,
> hyre ðinenne   þancolmode
> þæs herewæðan   heafod onwriðan
> ond hyt to behðe   blodig ætywan
> þam burhleodum,   hu hyre æt beaduwe gespeow.   175
> Spræc ða seo æðele   to eallum þam folce:
> "Her ge magon sweotole   sigerofe hæleð,
> leoda ræswan,   on ðæs laðestan
> hæðenes heaðorinces   heafod starian,
> Holofernus unlyfigendes,   180
> þe us monna mæst   morðra gefremede,
> sarra sorga,   ond þæt swyðor gyt
> ycan wolde,   ac him ne uðe god
> lengran lifes,   þæt he mid læððum us
> eglan moste: ic him ealdor oðþrong   185
> þurh godes fultum.
> ...
>   Fynd syndon eowere   195
> gedemed to deaðe,   ond ge dom agon,
> tir æt tohtan,   swa eow gatacnod hafað
> mihtig dryhten   þurh mine hand."

Then wise Judith, adorned with gold, commanded her thoughtful maidservant to unwrap the head of the general, and to show it, all bloody, to the city-dwellers as a sign of how the battle turned out for her. The noble lady spoke to all the people: "Victorious and brave warriors, here you may openly gaze upon the head of the most hateful heathen warrior, the dead Holofernes, who wreaked upon our men the greatest number of killings and painful sorrows, and still would have done even more, except that God did not grant him a longer life, in which he might plague us with afflictions; I took away his life through God's help...."

"Your enemies are doomed to death, and you will have glory and victory in the fight, since the mighty Lord has provided a sign through my hand."

Judith attributes her victory to God himself, and appropriately uses the language of revelation and miracle to convey God's agency. She describes the head of Holofernes as a *behð*, as a divine "sign" or "token" of triumph.[64] In the poet's words, the beheading both represents Judith's personal victory and "betokens" (197) Israel's impending annihilation of the enemy. In this context, the use of the past tense *gedemed* ("doomed") in line 196 is especially powerful because it signals that the die is cast, and the victory won (as in the Aod episode). It seems likely that this entire sequence in the Old English version is loosely based on a different speech in the Vulgate in which Judith says to Achior alone: "The God of Israel, to whom thou gavest testimony, that he revengeth himself of his enemies, he hath cut off the head of all the unbelievers this night by my hand" (*quod ulciscatur de inimicis suis ipse caput omnium incredulorum incidit in hac nocte in manu mea*). This speech contains the kernel of the Anglo-Saxon poet's expansive vision of divine "revenge" (*ultio*).

The same language of signs and tokens is used again in the poem when the Assyrian officer discovers Holofernes's lifeless body. As if aware that he is already a victim of God's holy war, the officer interprets the divine "token" (*tacn*; 285) correctly:

He þa lungre gefeoll   280
freorig to foldan,   ongan his feax teran,
hreoh on mode,   ond his hrægl somod,

ond þæt word acwæð   to ðam wiggendum
þe ðær unrote   ute wæron:
"Her ys geswutelod   ure sylfra forwyrd,   285
toweard getacnod   þæt þære tide ys
mid niðum neah geðrungen,   þe we sculon nu losian,
somod æt sæcce forweorðan.   Her lið sweorde geheawen,
beheafdod healdend ure." Hi ða hreowigmode
wurpon hyra wæpen of dune,   gewitan him werigferhðe   290
on fleam sceacan.

He immediately fell as if frozen to the ground. Distraught, he
began to tear his hair and also his clothes, and spoke these
words to the unhappy warriors outside: "our own destruction is
made clear, signaled in advance. The time of tribulation has drawn
near, when we must by necessity lose and die together in battle.
Here lies our lord beheaded, cut down by the sword." They then,
distraught, threw down their weapons, and departed weary-
hearted, scattered in flight.

The phrase "here is made clear" (*her ys geswutelod*) is the
conventional language of miracle and revelation. However, the
awkward phrasing *toweard getacnod* (lit. "tokened ahead or
forwards") shows that this is a sign of doom still to come.[65]

In both the book of Judith and the poem, full-scale war waged
by the Israelites follows. However, the tactics are vastly different
in each rendering. In the biblical book, the beheading of Holofernes
sends the Assyrians into a fit of terror, weakening them into retreat.
This psychological collapse enables the Israelite army to overcome
their stronger enemy. In the Anglo-Saxon poem, by contrast, the
war waged by the Israelites is executed offensively.[66] The poet
infuses the battle scene with traditional Germanic heroic motifs
that include the conventional "beasts of battle" motif, wherein the
wolf, the raven, and the eagle are present in the fray.[67] According
to some, this change in the Anglo-Saxon *Judith* has the effect of
"diminish[ing] Judith's contribution to the Jewish cause while
magnifying the military prowess of her townspeople."[68] However,
rather than read the Anglo-Saxon rewriting as a diminution of

Judith's agency, this sequence adds another layer to the poet's Augustinian framework of holy and just war.

Judaism in *Judith*: Toward a Universalist Paradigm

More than one critic has suggested that the poet's aim is to turn Judith into a straightforward Christian example.[69] However, labeling her a "Christian woman" deprives Judith of her quintessential Jewishness and ignores the fact that the poet explicitly identifies Judith as a Hebrew (*Ebrisce meowle*), living among other Hebrews in Bethulia. In the remaining part of this chapter, I attempt to draw a distinction between national and ethnic difference, on the one hand, and religious identity, on the other hand.

To begin with, it is indeed the case that the *Judith*-poet frequently downplays and even expunges references to specific Jewish customs and rituals. In the biblical text, it is vital that the Israelites are steeped in Jewish practice, and that they are obedient to God and his covenant. Deborah Levine Gera has summarized the rich network of Jewish rituals invoked and practiced in the biblical book of Judith:

> we find many references to Jewish practices. Prayers to God are accompanied by the customary fasting, sackcloth, and ashes. The Temple in Jerusalem, with its priests, daily sacrifices, first fruits, and tithes, plays an important role as well. Judith herself is punctilious in her observance and she fasts regularly except on Sabbath and festivals and on the eve of these holidays. She eats only kosher food, even in enemy territory, where she also performs her ritual ablutions under difficult conditions.[70]

These rituals are consistent with pre-rabbinic Judaism. The only unusual detail is the reference to conversion in connection with Achior. According to Gera, it is precisely this detail that dates the biblical text to the Hasmonean period, since before this time, "Jews did not proselytize or convert non-Jews."[71]

In the Anglo-Saxon poem, most of these Jewish rituals are absent. The single exception is the reference to Judith's special food sack, which is described as follows (125–32):

> Þa seo snotere mægð   snude gebrohte   125
> þæs herewæðan   heafod swa blodig
> on ðam fætelse   þe hyre foregenga,
> blachleor ides,   hyra begea nest,
> ðeawum geðungen,   þyder on lædde,
> ond hit þa swa heolfrig   hyre on hond ageaf,   130
> higeðoncolre,   ham to berenne,
> Iudith gingran sinre.

Then the wise woman quickly put the head of the warrior, all bloodied, into that pouch which her attendant (a pale-faced woman, excellent in service) had used to carry food for both of them. Judith then placed the gory package in the hand of her own thoughtful handmaid for her to bring it home.

The verse draws many of its details from Vulgate 10:5 and 12:21, and 3:11, which mention the food satchel (Latin *pera*) and the special kosher provisions brought by Judith's handmaid. In the poem, however, no specific mention is made of *kashrut*, unless its violation may be inferred through the detail of the impure bloody head coming into contact with Judith's food bag. The only specifically Jewish ritual in the poem is the practice of praying. However, the poet revises Judith's entreaty, so that she now invokes the Trinity as she prays to the "God of Creation and Spirit of Comfort, the All-Wielder of men, The Glory of the Trinity." Thomas D. Hill has demonstrated that Judith's prayer to the Trinity resembles, and is probably based upon, a wider tradition of Germanic prayers for bodily protection, as witnessed in the tradition of the Lorica (a prophylactic prayer that is said to protect the body).[72] In altering the forms of address and the content of the prayer, the poet's twofold purpose seems to have been to adjust the forms of praying to models that were familiar to his Anglo-Saxon audience and, at the same time, to universalize its general effectiveness. This much is evident in the brief narrative interpolation that follows, the only instance when the poet breaks the narrative frame to refer to his contemporary audience (94–7):

Hi ða se hehsta dema
ædre mid elne onbryrde,   swa he deð anra gehwylcne   95
herbuendra   þe hyne him to helpe seceð
mid ræde ond mid rihte geleafan.

Then the Highest Judge quickly inspired her with courage, just as He inspires every single one of those living here who seek him for help, with counsel and right belief.

By declaring that divine "counsel" (*ræd*) and "right belief" (*riht geleafa*) are available to *all* who pray to God regardless of religion, the poet clears the way for identification of the penitential subject within the Christian world. Following the Pauline paradigm, the emphasis is on belief and faith in place of ritual and law. In fact, if we look closely at the treatment of war in the poem, it becomes clear that every victory is granted by God to the Hebrews only on the grounds of "true belief" (*soðe/trume geleafa*; 6, 89, 344).

The poet conspicuously omits all direct references to Jerusalem (Judith 4:2; 10:8; 11:19; 15:19; 16:18 and 20) and to the Temple (Judith 4:2–3, 12; 8:21, 24; 9:8, 13; 16:20). In their place we find descriptions of Bethulia, which, in the Anglo-Saxon poem, serves as the surrogate center of Israelite culture. Bethulia is depicted as "beautiful" with "shining walls" (136–8); a "spacious city" (*seo ginne byrig*; 149); a "mead-city" (*seo medobyrig*); a "bright city" (*seo beorhte byrig*; 326); and perhaps most tellingly, a "holy city" (*seo halige byrig*; 203). Through this substitution, the poet manages to extend the wonder and holiness of Jerusalem itself to all those living outside its specific geographic border. Moreover, the Hebrews are described as the rightful natives of this territory. Bethulia is their "homeland" (*eðel*; 169) and "native land" (*cyðð*), and the Hebrews are identified as "land-dwellers" or "native people" (*landbuende* 226; 314) and "protectors of their native land" (*eðelweardas*, 320). The Assyrians, by contrast, are interlopers and foreigners (*elðeodige*; 215 and 237).

Additional telltale aspects of Jewish identity and ethnicity are retained in the poem. We have already noted that the Israelites are consistently addressed as *Hebrews* (*Ebreas* 218, 253, 262, 298; *Ebrisc* 241, 305) rather than "Israelites" or "the people of Judea." However, it is clear that the poet considered the Hebrews a special "nation apart." In addition to generic terms such as *folc* and *leod* (meaning "people"), he employs specialized terms that connote distinctive ethnicity and race. Consider, for example, the following string of epithets that gloss the single Vulgate term *populus Israhel* (15:13): *seo cneoris* ("that race"); *mægða mærost* ("the most famous of nations"); and *wlanc, wundenlocc* ("proud and curly-haired"). In short, the Hebrews of *Judith* are depicted as "a people apart" in every sense of the term.

The crimes inflicted by Holofernes are also to be understood in terms of biblical law and holy war. Holofernes is described as a *wærloga* ("contract-breaker" 71) just as he passes out drunk (67–73), utterly devoid of wit (and possibly also sexual prowess, depending upon how we interpret *ræd*):

> Gefeol ða wine swa druncen
> se rica on his reste middan,   swa he nyste ræda nanne
> on gewitlocan.   Wiggend stopon
> ut of ðam inne   ofstum miclum,   70
> weras winsade,   þe ðone wærlogan,
> laðne leodhatan,   læddon to bedde
> nehstan siðe.

The warriors, sated with wine, marched quickly out of the interior, they who had led that contract-breaker, the hated lord of the people to bed for the last time.

What troth did Holofernes break? Interestingly, the most obvious definition is not easily supported in the poem. In the bible, Holofernes betrays the contract he forges with Judith. He promises her protection, agrees to let her practice *kashrut*, and allows her to go out of the camp every night to pray. But then he tries to ravish her. In the poem, however, no such promise is made. In the above passage, the word *wærloga* appears alongside other descriptions that highlight Holofernes's tyranny and his impurity. He is said to be a *lað leodhata* ("hated offender"; 72); *se atola* ("the terrible one"; 75); *se unsyfra* ("the unclean one"; 76); and *womfull* ("full of sin"; 77). Returning to

Isidore's definition of "unjust war," we might surmise that Holofernes is guilty of "breaking the compact of human society" (*humanae societatis foedus inrumpens*) because he "leads armies to destroy other lands, and to massacre or subject free peoples." His is not a war waged "for the sake of recovering property seized or of driving off the enemy," but rather for the sake of imperial expansion.[73] As the ancient enemy of Israel, Holofernes stands outside the covenant, and also outside that valorous heroic code as the Anglo-Saxon poet imagined it. The positioning of Holofernes as an "other," opposed to both systems, seals the analogy between Hebrew and Anglo-Saxon interpretations of honorable behavior and true belief.

Conclusion

It has often been said of biblical poetry composed during the Anglo-Saxon era that it is impossible to detect or recover real "political allegory," since we cannot presently determine specific dates of composition.[74] However, *Judith*'s "politics" do not rely upon the determination of a single battle or event—the poem presents, rather, a general ideology of "holy war." The *Judith*-poet looks in two directions: his gaze is fixed firmly on its biblical source, but it is also directed forward, as he seeks the active readership and participation of its contemporary audience. By maintaining this double perspective, the poet brings to the fore the universalizing potential of the Judith story. If the book of Judith (composed during the Hasmonean period) was seen to represent a new attitude toward Jewish identity as an elected rather than inherited status, the Old English *Judith* reflects a similar understanding of *genus* and divine election. By downplaying the role of specific Jewish rituals and practices, the *Judith*-poet places greater stress upon faith and belief—the core essentials of Pauline devotion.[75]

Notes

1 The full printed title is "Souldiers Counselled and Comforted, a Discourse Delivered Unto Some Part of the Forces Engaged in the

Just War of New-England Against the Northern and Eastern Indians" (Mather 1689). Quoted by Niditch (1993:3).

2   Niditch (1993: 3).

3   Niditch (1993: 3) quoting Mather (1689).

4   Niditch (1993: 3–4) Niditch cites Mather (1689).

5   Niditch (1993: 4).

6   von Rad (1991) and Walzer (2006).

7   All quotations from the Old English *Judith* are from Griffith, ed. (1997); translations are mine unless otherwise specified.

8   The adjective *ælfscinu* ("resplendent like an elf") is strange. The simplex "elf" may have positive or negative associations (see Taylor 1990). It is interesting that the same adjective is used in the poem *Genesis A* at 1827 and 2731 to describe the matriarch Sarah's overwhelming beauty.

9   Shepherd (1966: 12).

10   Astell (1989) and Griffith, ed. (1997: 79).

11   Griffith, ed. (1997: 51).

12   Campbell (1971: 155), as cited by Griffith, ed. (1997: 51–2).

13   Cook (1888: xxix–xxiii) argued that the poem might have celebrated the life of Judith, daughter of Charles the Bald, the second wife of Æthelwulf of Wessex (ca. 856). Chamberlain (1975: 158) saw the poem as an expression of the Viking crisis under Æthelred from 990 to 1010. The poem as it stands, however, makes no clear allusion to either scenario. On the poem as an allegory for spiritual warfare, see Hermann (1989: 173–98).

14   For a detailed discussion of Hrabanus's dedication to Queen Judith, see De Jong (2001).

15   For an overview of these allegorical interpretations, see Hermann (1989: 174–6). One of the key components establishing Judith as a type for the *ecclesia* is interpreting her as a figure for the Virgin Mary. As a matter of fact, the oldest extant visual program linking Judith and Mary is located in the frescoes of Sancta Maria Antiqua, in the Roman Forum.

16   "Nimað eow bysne be þyssere Iudith, hu clænlice heo leofode ær Cristes acennednysse, & ne leogað ge na Gode on ðæs godspelles timan þa halgan clænnysse þe ge Criste beheton, forðan þe he fordemð þa dyrnan forligras & þa fulan sceandas he besengð on helle, swa swa hit on Læden stent æfter Paulus lare: Fornicatores & adulteros iudicabit Deus."

17 This letter, also entitled "On the Old and New Testament," is edited and translated in Crawford (1922: 15–75).

18 Crawford (1922: 48). On Ælfric's texts, see Klein (1996), Astell (1989), and Szarmach (2012).

19 The earliest reference to the book of Judith in the Roman period was by Clement, the third bishop of Rome (see Brine 2010: 14). Although the book of Judith was never included in the Jewish biblical canon, it was accepted as a deuterocanonical text in Anglo-Saxon England, following the example of Jerome. It retained its deuterocanonical status until the period of the English reformation, when it was excised from the canon proper and treated as an apocryphal text by the Protestants.

20 Brine (2010: 11).

21 Cohen (1999: 133–4), as cited by Brine (2010: 11).

22 The main source for the poem was some version of the biblical book of Judith, Chapters 12.10–16.1, though, as I will argue, the poet also occasionally drew inspiration from Chapters 9 and 16, as well as other Old Testament writings, such as the book of Judges. The main version of the bible consulted was the Vulgate, though occasionally the poet seems to have also relied on the Old Latin version (see Griffith, ed., 1997: 47–61, for an overview). Such hybridity is not at all surprising, since the biblical texts in circulation during the period in question frequently combined readings from both versions.

23 For a summary of this debate, see Griffith, ed. (1997: 1–8).

24 Those who view *Judith* as a nearly complete poem argue that the composition contains an elaborate envelope pattern, by means of which a series of words, phrases, and formula are repeated at the beginning and end of the poem to lend circularity and closure to the poem. Lines 1–2 echo 345b–6a (*huru æt þam ende ne tweode/ þæs leanes þe heo lange gyrnde*). Put together, the pair of verses forms a balanced contrast between rewards in this life (at the beginning of the poem) and heavenly gifts in the next (at the end). These sections also strikingly contain the two longest clusters of hypermetric lines in the poem.

25 Stocker (1998: 24).

26 The association of the Anglo-Saxon Judith with virginity is common, despite the lack of textual evidence. See, for example, Cooper's interpretation of Judith (Cooper 2010: 183).

27 Hermann (1989: 173–98) and Kim (1999). Hermann argues that decapitation *is* castration, and that the central tension in *Judith* is between "being" and "having" the phallus (in the Lacanian sense).

According to Hermann, "Judith decapitates Holofernes to support the true possessor of authority, God" while "Holofernes remains a mere pretender" (196). As Hermann explains (1989), "the law of the father, which requires the child to surrender his desire to possess the mother, means he can no longer be the phallus, although he can have the phallus by submitting to paternal restrictions."

28   See Riddle 25 in the Exeter Book, whose solution is, presumably, both "onion" and "penis." In this saucy riddle, the *wif wundenlocc* ("curly-haired woman") seizes the head of the object, shaggy below, and "clamps [it] in a tight place," causing her "eye to get wet." Hermann reads the riddle as expressing castration: "if we read 'onion,' the vegetable is plucked from its bed and its greens chopped off; but if we read 'penis' the poem becomes a violent description of castration which segues into a playful description of sexual intercourse." Who would have thought?

29   An example is the Hebrew version of the militant Song of Deborah, 5:2.

30   Russell (1975: 20).

31   Walzer (2006).

32   Snook (2011: 109) explains that "'just war' theory did not exist in the Classical period; there was no 'accepted thinking' on the matter, no established canon of scholarship to consult, and no precisely defined political doctrine which authors could pick up and put down at will."

33   For excellent overviews of the longer history of "just war" theory in the classical and patristic periods, see Cross (1971) and Snook (2011).

34   See Russell (1975: 16–39) for a comprehensive treatment of Augustine's writings on war.

35   Russell (1975: 16).

36   Russell (1975: 18). Augustine develops this view of the *miles Christi* in a number of texts. For an overview, see Windass (1964).

37   Russell (1975: 16).

38   Russell (1975: 18). See Augustine, *Quaestiones in Heptateuchum* VI: 10: *Iusta autem bella ea definiri solent quae ulciscuntur iniurias, si qua gens vel civitas quae bello pretenda est, vel vindicare neglexerit quod a suis inprobe factum est, vel reddere quod per iniurias ablatum est.* See further Barnes (1982: 777–8).

39   Russell (1975: 5, n. 16, 18). He quotes Cicero, *De Officiis*, I.ii.36: *nullum bellum esse iustum nisi quod aut rebus repetitis geratur aut denunciatum ante sit et interdictum.*

40   Russell (1975: 21). See further Augustine, *Quastiones in Heptateuchum*, iv.44.

41   Quoted by Snook (2011: 113).

42   See, especially, Augustine's *De Civitate Dei*, book XIX and *Contra Faustum*, XXII. For specific references, see Russell (1975: 16, n. 3).

43   Russell (1975: 16, 19).

44   Russell (1975: 19).

45   Russell (1975: 10).

46   I want to qualify briefly what I mean by "holy war" in the context of the biblical book of Judith. I use this term to refer to the specific constellation of political, religious, and cultural war ideologies that emerge in this text. The book's late composition unquestionably shapes the biblical author's attitudes toward war. No single definition adequately encompasses the entirety of holy war thinking encapsulated in the Old Testament and related Jewish writings. The vast scholarship on this subject makes it clear that holy war ideologies changed radically as Israel transitioned from a nomadic lifestyle, to a people living under the monarchy, and finally to the conditions of the diaspora. Another important factor was the destruction of both temples. It is also important to consider the different views and ideologies expressed by different biblical authors and redactors. On the question of whether the concept of holy war was a concept that reflected reality or whether it was a late ideology read back into the text, there is much debate and little agreement. See von Rad (1991).

47   Hermann (1989) reads Judith's discussion of the rape of Dinah as a typological double for Judith's slaying of Holofernes and Achior's circumcision.

48   This passage also plays an important role in the Anglo-Saxon *Exodus* 239–61 (which I label the "tribal digression"); see Chapter 1.

49   In Genesis 34:2, it is said of Sichem that he "took her away, and lay with her, ravishing the virgin"(*rapuit et dormivit cum illa vi opprimens virginem*). In Exodus 3:9, God states, "For the cry of the children of Israel is come unto me: and I have seen their affliction, wherewith they are oppressed by the Egyptians"; *clamor ergo filiorum Israhel venit ad me vidique adflictionem eorum qua ab Aegyptiis opprimuntur.* Niditch (1993: 115) discusses these overlapping terms for oppression and rape in the Old Testament.

50   Chamberlain (1975: 155–6) makes this argument, citing examples of wartime spoliation in Anglo-Saxon England.

51 Russell (1975: 53).

52 Niditch (1993: 28).

53 Niditch (1993: 28) argues that the Deuteronomic conception of God's due comes uncomfortably close to the idea of human sacrifice to the divinity.

54 Niditch (1993: 34).

55 Niditch (1993: 35).

56 Estes (2003: 342).

57 Walzer (2006: 180).

58 Walzer (2006: 180).

59 On the use of the term "guerrilla" in the context of these biblical stories, see Niditch (1993: 117–18). There are also certain parallels with Judah's slaying of Nicanor during the Maccabean uprising (1 Mc 7:26–50; 2 Mc 15:1–36). In these instances, both Judah and Judith are "pious figures who manage to overturn the threat to the temple in Jerusalem posed by a cruel and arrogant King, and they behead the chief military commander in the process" (Gera 2010: 26).

60 While right-handed combat is conventional, and even associated with divinity, left-handed combat affords Aod the element of surprise.

61 For more detailed assessments of Jerome's textual expansions and additions, see Gera (2010: 29), Moore (1985: 94–101), and Otzen (2002: 141).

62 cf. Matthew 8:12: "But the children of the kingdom shall be cast out into the exterior darkness: there shall be weeping and gnashing of teeth."

63 Griffith, ed. (1997: 124–5), assumes that "the grim fate reserved for Holofernes's soul is an addition to the source, which makes no comment on the matter at this point. The depiction of Hell as a place beneath a cliff (113a *under neowelne næs*) filled with serpents (115a *wyrmum*, 119a *wyrmsele*) is found elsewhere in Old English poetry."

64 The *DOE* entry for *behþ* cites this as a *hapax legomenon*. From the context, it seems to mean "token, proof," and may be derived from the word *beacen*.

65 Ælfric (Ed. Lee lines 307–11) uses a similar formulation in his homily on Judith, but otherwise follows the details of the Vulgate: "A woman has now shamed us all and our lord. Here lies the nobleman, headless on the bed, sullied with his blood. They were then all wondrously afraid, and fled shamefully without any sensibility." The soldier in Ælfric's text is shocked that the perpetrator is a woman.

66 Hermann (1989: 173).

67 Hermann (1989: 174).

68 Hermann (1989: 174).

69 Estes (2003: 330); italics mine.

70 Gera (2010: 24). Most of the practices are consistent with pre-Rabbinic Judaism. As Brine explains further, the "reference to rabbinic ideology and practice—such as the institution of the synagogue, the rabbinate, and the ideology of a life of study of the Torah as described in the tractate of the Mishna, the Pirkei Avos or the Ethics of the Fathers (written hundreds of years later)—do not appear in the book" (Brine 2010: 12).

71 Gera (2010: 26–7).

72 Hill (1981).

73 Isidore, *Etymologiae* 18 (Lindsay, ed. 1957), quoted by Snook (2011: 113).

74 Scheil (2004).

75 Niditch (1993: 3).

Conclusion

The individual's limited access to physical texts of the bible in the Early Middle Ages required alternative creative means of disseminating, reinforcing, and commenting on biblical narratives in the vernacular. One complex genre that developed as a consequence was the biblical poem. *Rewriting the Old Testament* examined three Old English Old Testament poems—*Exodus*, *Daniel*, and *Judith*—with a view to exploring their idiosyncratic artistic and cultural responses to the canonical and deuterocanonical books of the Old Testament, and to the Jewish laws, practices, and beliefs they depict and invariably distort in the process. The central aim of the book was to explore how the rhetorical project of biblical adaptation maps out a variety of poetic responses toward the individual narratives they adapt, as well as toward the pervasive cultural, religious, and political traditions that inform the biblical narratives as a whole. The poems replicate and accentuate the ethnogenetic myths of the Old Testament, both in order to emphasize the exemplary status of the Hebrews as God's original chosen people and to mark that status as being transferred to the New Israel, defined rhetorically as the Anglo-Saxon Christian community. Seen from this perspective, Old English rewritings of biblical narratives are vital for constituting Anglo-Saxon religious and national identity and community.

In addition to providing readings of all three poems that closely examine the rhetorical measures and poetic resources that were brought to bear on the transfer of chosenness from the Hebrews to the Anglo-Saxons, the theoretical work in this study mainly concerns political theology and thus offers a hermeneutic approach that interrogates the ways in which theological concepts and modes of thinking underlie political, social, economic, and cultural discourses. Old English Old Testament poets unilaterally (though not uniformly) read the Old Testament as the supreme attestation of God's relationship with his "chosen people." The covenant symbolized the central contract that bound God to his people. In rewriting Old Testament narratives, Anglo-Saxon poets sought to commemorate this unique contract, and to claim the status of "chosenness" for their own *gens Anglorum* as God's newly appointed Israel. This kind of distillation and reuse of individual Old Testament narratives for theologico-political purposes was hardly unique to this period. As we saw in our various forays into sermons, poetry, and the visual arts from Late Antiquity to colonial America, politico-theological readings of the Old Testament have formed a pervasive and sufficiently elastic paradigm for self-fashioning and "nation building" in the West.

Needless to say, Anglo-Saxon poets adapted Old Testament narratives for their own unique rhetorical purposes. In their hands, the terms of chosenness were altered to reflect a broader conception of election that could include its contemporary Anglo-Saxon audience. The poets thus valorized the Israelites as the original chosen nation of God, but they also altered the conditions that might enable their full participation in, and contractual link to, the covenant. In each case, changes were made to downplay specific Jewish rituals and practices and to embrace a more universalizing Pauline ideal of election by faith and belief. Yet, despite their seemingly open and inclusive frameworks, it nevertheless became clear from a close study of the poems themselves that Anglo-Saxon England remained the chief beneficiary of this acclaim. This "nationalizing" agenda came into focus through a comparative reading of these poems within the longer history of the *populus Israhel* tradition as it was developed and changed in Anglo-Saxon England, first in the realms of the church and in the context of political sovereignty, and then later as a broader, more pliable, hermeneutic focus for reading the bible. All three Old English Old Testament poems construct a transfer of election that is specific to their own imagined textual communities.

The central concept of *translatio electionis* proved useful in generating a more precise vocabulary for assessing the mechanics of translation and adaptation utilized in individual Old Testament poems. The comparative analysis of these texts revealed that each poem marked a highly idiosyncratic mode of adaptation. The *Exodus*-poet utilized mnemonic techniques derived from the ancient and medieval *ars memoriae* in order to encourage meditation upon the concept of covenant as a personal contract. *The Daniel*-poet massively rewrote the biblical account in order to depict the Israelites as a nation fallen from God's grace—a tactic he used to transfer the status of election to his own contemporaneous Christian audiences. Finally, the *Judith*-poet rewrote and revised the biblical conception of holy war in order to bring it in line with medieval conceptions of just war. In the process, the poet emphasized faith and belief in God—not ritual and practice—as the primary conditions for election, thereby substituting a universal requirement for a specifically Jewish one.

Although *Rewriting the Old Testament* is about Anglo-Saxon poetry, it also illuminated more generally alternative modes by which medieval Christian writers encountered, interpreted, and wrote about the Old Testament. The politico-theological mode of interpretation utilized by Anglo-Saxon poets favored, overall, a literal analysis of biblical texts. Generally absent from these texts is the type of systematic allegorical and typological analysis that regarded the Old Testament as a mere precursor to the New. As such, this relatively small corpus of Old Testament poetry provides the groundwork for reconsidering and perhaps augmenting several firmly entrenched paradigms for analysing biblical analysis in the Middle Ages. Scholars such as Henri De Lubac, Jean Daniélou, and Ernst Robert Curtius have demonstrated the ubiquitous patristic and medieval practice of reading scripture through a fourfold (or fivefold) scheme of allegorical interpretation.[1] Their claims for the centrality of this hermeneutic scheme have stood the test of time and will continue to illuminate practices of reading and writing in these eras. The cultural importance of this system has, moreover, been confirmed by its lasting influence upon contemporary critical practices: the medieval exegetical mode has had a profound impact on interpretive systems from structuralism to deconstruction, and has informed the individual methodologies of theorists such as Barthes (*S/Z*) and Frye (*The Great Code* and *Anatomy of Criticism*).[2] However, this intense focus upon medieval allegorical interpretation has also had the effect of closing down or marginalizing other modes of biblical reading, inquiry, and experience. Early Christian authors and readers are sometimes treated as though they were able to interpret and comprehend scripture in just one way—through a strict program of fourfold (or fivefold) analysis. Thus, Fredric Jameson, who is generally attuned to the plurality and ubiquity of political perspectives in literature, writes as though there were only one "medieval system" of fourfold allegory.[3] He describes the "ideological mission" of medieval biblical exegesis as "a strategy for assimilating the Old Testament to the new, for rewriting Jewish textual and cultural heritage in a form usable for Gentiles."[4] For Jameson, this medieval "master narrative" represents an "archaic and cumbersome allegorical framework,"[5] and he calls for a system that will leave this way of reading—and, with it, "the medieval"—behind. Nothing, from a medievalist's perspective, could be more crippling than this reduction of medieval scriptural hermeneutics to a single method of interpretation.[6]

Looking forward, *Rewriting the Old Testament* therefore sets the stage for further reevaluation of what have become the paradigmatic models for biblical interpretation and analysis in the Middle Ages. From a material perspective, it has already been demonstrated that Old English translations of the bible, the gospels, and its glossed Psalters were transmitted and recopied in English manuscripts well into the thirteenth century, thus proving the sustained use beyond the conquest of the vernacular as an important medium for composition of biblical translations, verse, paraphrase, and sermons.[7] It is also possible that Anglo-Saxon biblical poetic texts had a long-term effect. There is anecdotal evidence to suggest that at least one prominent medieval English translator and author in the fourteenth century regarded Anglo-Saxon biblical *poetry* as an important model for biblical instruction in his own day and age. In his *Dialogus inter Dominum et Clericum* (often appended to the preface of his more famous *Polychronicon*), John of Trevisa named Cædmon, the alleged father of Old English biblical verse, in his list of celebrated biblical translators, alongside Jerome, King Alfred, and Bede.[8] In any case, it should be clear from the preceding analysis that Anglo-Saxon biblical poetry represented an important, if often neglected, stage in the history of biblical translation and adaptation.

Old English Old Testament poetry also has the potential significantly to reshape our understanding of writings about Jews in the early Middle Ages. It comes as a bit of a surprise that this small poetic corpus displays an attitude toward Old Testament Jews and their rituals and practices that was for the most part complimentary and approving. To be sure, Anglo-Saxon authors did not uniformly share this view. As Andrew P. Scheil has shown at great length, they also drew upon firmly established anti-Judaic tropes and stereotypes, inherited from earlier patristic materials. If in Old Testament poetry the Jews represented the original chosen people of God, worthy of imitation, in other contexts they were mainly seen as the killers of Christ and as obstinate and willful others. Although there is no record of actual Jews living in England at any point during the Anglo-Saxon period, it emerges that early English authors had a great deal to say about them. The extant statements run the gamut from admiration and emulation of the original chosen people, all the way to the stereotypical condemnation of them.

As this book has shown, Old Testament poetry witnessed a special dynamic that valorized the chosenness of the Old Testament Israelites and marked it as a status to be strived for and emulated. In this, Anglo-Saxon poets inherited a distinctive perspective that can be traced back to Augustine of Hippo, some six centuries earlier. In a recent and groundbreaking book, *Augustine and the Jews*, Paula Fredriksen demonstrates that it had become a central tenet of Augustine's mature writings that the Jews represented vital witnesses to the living letter of the law in Christ.[9] As Augustine himself proclaimed, "by the evidence of their own scriptures they bear witness for us that we have not fabricated the prophecies about Christ" (*De civitate Dei 18.46*).[10] In contradistinction to prevailing patristic attitudes, Augustine saw traditional Jewish practice not as an interruption or abomination of God's plan after Christ, but rather as "truly conform[ing] to divine intention."[11] Augustine's redemptive view of Jewish practice and ritual was closely tied to his writings on biblical interpretation and exegesis. The Old Testament was not to be set aside or despised, as stated in the increasingly dominant theological position in the first three centuries (since Tertullian and Marcion, to be precise), but rather to be read, studied, and cherished as an essential testament to God's comprehensive salvational plan.[12] Augustine, citing Psalm 59:12, thus memorably declared in defense of the Jews: "slay them not ... lest at some time they forget your law" (*De civitate Dei* 18.46).[13] According to Fredriksen, Augustine's revolutionary philosophy had a real-world effect—it saved the Jews from probable destruction and their testament from exclusion.[14] The readings presented in *Rewriting the Old Testament* demonstrate that Old English Old Testament poetry both channeled and reiterated Augustine's distinctive view.

Beginning with an examination of the Anglo-Saxon myth of chosenness, as it had been co-opted by Thomas Jefferson as a model for his own nationalizing program in constitutional America, *Rewriting the Old Testament in Anglo-Saxon England* has argued that the adaptation of Old Testament narratives for politico-theological purposes in Anglo-Saxon England represents a similarly compelling and fascinating story in its own right.

Notes

1   De Lubac (1998), Daniélou (1960), and Curtius (1963).

2   Holsinger (2005: ch. 5) assesses the link between structuralism and biblical exegesis. In particular, he compares Roland Barthes's "four senses" in *S/Z* (*1974*) to the four levels of medieval exegesis (182). Holsinger also discusses the impact of the two-day conference held at the University of Geneva in February 1971 on the subject of structural analysis and biblical exegesis. For the conference proceedings (with essays by Barthes, François Bovon, Jean Starobinski, Robert Martin-Achard, and Fraz-J. Leenhardt), see Barthes *et al.* (1974). On Frye and exegetical analysis, see Kraemer (1996: 3–20).

3   Jameson (1981: 17).

4   Jameson (1981: 29).

5   Jameson (1981: 29).

6   It is clear that the church fathers had very different ways of responding to, and writing about, scripture. Augustine, to cite just one example, cultivates a "literal" interpretation of Genesis (in his *De Genesi ad litteram*), which he describes as an explanation of scripture "according to the plain meaning of the historical facts, not according to future events which they foreshadow" (1.17.34). Several important studies have begun to push back on the idea of a single model of interpretation linked to allegory. See, especially, Wright (2012) and de Jong (1995).

7   See Morey's (2000) excellent guide to Middle English biblical literature.

8   See Morey (2000: 28). The corresponding quotation from Trevisa can be found in Waldron (1988: 292–3, lines 146–53).

9   Fredriksen (2008).

10 Cited by Fredriksen (2008: 290).

11 Fredriksen (2008: 244).

12 Fredriksen (2008: 316–19) summarizes Augustine's revolutionary ideas.

13 This passage is cited and analysed by Fredriksen (2008 on p. 290 and following).

14 Fredriksen (2008: 291–352).

Works Cited

Note

Since this book is meant to be accessible to both specialists and nonspecialists, I cite secondary scholarship in English translation, when available. Unless otherwise stated, all biblical quotations are from the Latin Vulgate; translations are cited from the Douay-Rheims version as revised by Challoner.

Abbreviations

ASPR	Anglo-Saxon Poetic Records
EETS	Early English Text Society
EEMF	Early English Manuscripts in Facsimile
CSASE	Cambridge Studies in Anglo-Saxon England
ASE	*Anglo-Saxon England*
CSEL	Corpus scriptorum ecclesiasticorum Latinorum
CCSL	Corpus Christianorum, Series Latina
DOE	*Dictionary of Old English*
PL	*Patrologia Latina*
MGH	Monumenta Germaniae Historica

Primary Texts, Facsimiles, and Translations

Ælfric. Homily on Judith. In *Ælfric's Homilies on Judith, Esther, and the Maccabees*. Ed. S.D. Lee. 1999. http://users.ox.ac.uk/~stuart/kings/main.htm

Alcuin. *De ratione animae*. PL 101, 369–50.

_____. "*De ratione animae*: A Text with Introduction, Critical Apparatus, and Translation." Ed. and trans. James Joseph Mark Curry. 1966. Unpublished PhD Dissertation. Cornell University.

Alcuin. *Epistulae*. In *Epistolae karolini aevi*. Ed. Dümmler Ernst. 1974. MGH 4. Berlin: Weidmann. Repr. online 2005. *Library of Latin Texts*. Turnhout, Belgium: Brepols. http://www.brepolis.net/

Alfred. *Alfred's West-Saxon Version of Gregory's Pastoral Care Gregory.*
Ed. and trans. Henry Sweet. 1871. EETS o.s. 45. London: N. Trübner &
Co.

Arator. *Aratoris subdiaconi De actibus apostolorum.* Ed. Arthur P.
McKinlay. 1951. Vienna: Hoelder-Pichler-Tempsky.

Arator. *Historia apostolica (Arator Subdiaconus).* Ed. A.P. Orbán. 2006.
CCSL 130 and 130A (glossary). Turnhout, Belgium: Brepols.

Asser. *Asser's Life of King Alfred, Together with the Annals of Saint
Neots Erroneously Ascribed to Asser.* Ed. William Henry Stevenson.
1904. Oxford: Clarendon Press.

Augustine. *Contra Faustum Manichaeum.* Ed. J. Zycha, 1891–92. CSEL
25.1. Vienna: Tempsky.

———. *Quaestiones in Heptateuchum.* Ed. J. Zycha. 1895. CSEL 28.2.
Vienna: Tempsky.

———. *The Teacher.* In *Augustine: Earlier Writings.* Trans. J.H.
S. Burleigh. 1953. Library of Christian Clasics 6. Philadelphia:
Westminister Press.

———. *De civitate Dei Libri XI–XXII.* Eds. D. Dombart and A. Kalb. 1955.
CCSL 48. Turnhout: Brepols.

———. *Confessions.* Trans. R.S. Pine-Coffin. 1961. Harmondsworth:
Penguin Books.

———. *De Magistro.* Eds. W.M. Green and K.D. Daur. 1970. CCSL 29.
Turnhout: Brepols.

———. *Confessionem Libri XIII.* Ed. L. Verheijen. 1981. CCSL 27.
Turnhout: Brepols.

———. *The Literal Meaning of Genesis (De Genesi ad litteram libri
duodecim).* Trans. John Hammond Taylor. 1982. Ancient Christian
Writers, no. 41–42. New York: Newman Press.

———. *The City of God.* Trans. Henry Bettenson. 1984.
Harmondsworth: Penguin Books.

———. *De Genesi ad litteram libri duodecim.* La génèse au sens
littéral en douze livres (I–VII). Bibliothèque Augustinienne 48. 2000.
Turnhout: Brepols.

———. *De Genesi ad litteram libri duodecim.* La génèse au sens littéral
en douze livres (VIII–XII). Bibliothèque Augustinienne 49. 2001.
Turnhout: Brepols.

———. *De Trinitate.* Eds. W.J. Mountain and F. Glorie. 2001 (1968).
CCSL 50, 50A. Turnhout: Brepols.

Avitus. *Poematum de spiritalis historiae gestis.* Ed. R. Peiper, 203–94.
MGH A A 6.2. 1883. Berlin: Weidmann. Repr. online 2005. *Library of
Latin Texts.* Turnhout, Belgium: Brepols. http://www.brepolis.net/

———. *The Poems of Alcimus Ecdicius Avitus.* Trans. George W. Shea.
1997. Tempe, AZ: Medieval & Renaissance Texts & Studies.

Bede. *Historia Abbatum. Venerabilis Baedae Opera Historica*, vol. I. Ed.
  Carolus Plummer, 364–87. 1896. Oxford: Clarendon Press.
———. *De Tabernaculo*. Ed. M.D. Hurst. 1969. CCSL 119A. Turnhout:
  Brepols.
———. *De Templo*. Ed. D. Hurst. 1969. CCSL 119A. Turnhout: Brepols.
———. *On the Tabernacle*. Trans. Arthur G. Holder. 1994. Liverpool:
  Liverpool University Press.
———. *On the Temple*. Trans. Seán Connolly. 1995. Liverpool: Liverpool
  University Press.
———. *Historia Ecclesiastica. Bede's Ecclesiastical History of the
  English People*. Eds. and trans. Bertram Colgrave and R.A.B.
  Mynors. 1969, rev. 1999. Oxford: Clarendon Press.
———. *Lives of the Abbots of Wearmouth and Jarrow*. Trans. David
  Hugh Farmer. 2011. Cambridge: Penguin Books.
Bede. *De Templo*. Ed. D. Hurst. 1969. CCSL 119A. Turnhout: Brepols.
———. *On the Temple*. Trans. Seán Connolly. 1995. Liverpool: Liverpool
  University Press.
Beowulf, digital facsimile. *The Electronic Beowulf – CD-ROM*. Eds.
  Kevin S. Kiernan and Andrew Prescott. 1999. London: British Library.
  Also now available through the British Library http://www.bl.uk/
  manuscripts/FullDisplay.aspx?ref=Cotton_MS_vitellius_a_xv
Cædmon. *Cædmon's Hymn: A Multimedia Study, Archive and Edition*
  (with CD-Rom). Ed. Daniel Paul O'Donnell. 2005. Cambridge: D.S.
  Brewer in association with SEENET and the Medieval Academy.
Daniel and Azarias. Ed. Robert T. Farrell. 1974. London: Methuen.
Exodus. Ed. Peter J. Lucas. 1994. Exeter: University of Exeter Press.
  (Reprinted from 1977. London: Methuen.)
Genesis A: A New Edition. Ed. Alger N. Doane. 1978. Madison, WI:
  University of Wisconsin Press.
*Genesis B. The Saxon Genesis: An Edition of the West Saxon Genesis
  B and the Old Saxon Vatican Genesis*. Ed. Alger N. Doane. 1991.
  Madison, WI: University of Wisconsin Press.
*Heptateuch. The Old English Version of the Heptateuch: Ælfric's Treatise
  on the Old and New Testament and His Preface to Genesis*. Ed. S.J.
  Crawford. 1922. EETS. o.s. 160. London: Oxford University Press.
Hexateuch, facsimile. *The Old English Illustrated Hexateuch: British
  Museum Cotton Claudius B. IV*. Eds. C.R. Dodwell and Peter
  Clemoes. 1974. EEMF 18. Copenhagen: Rosenkilde and Bagger.
Hrabanus Maurus. *Expositio in librum Judith*. PL 109. Cols. 541–92.
Hugh of St. Victor. *De arca Noe mystica (De pictura Arche)*. Ed. Patrice
  Sicard. 2001. CCCM 176–176A. Turnhout: Brepols.
———. "A Little Book About Constructing Noah's Ark." 2002. Trans.
  Jessica Weiss. In *The Medieval Craft of Memory: An Anthology of
  Texts and Pictures*. Eds. Mary Carruthers and Jan M. Ziolkowski,
  41–70. Philadelphia, PA: University of Pennsylvania Press.

Isidore. *Isidori Hispalensis episcopi Etymologiarvm sive Originvm: libri xx.* Ed. W.M. Lindsay. 1957 (1911). Oxonii: E Typographeo Clarendoniano.

Judith. Ed. Mark Griffith. 1997. Exeter: University of Exeter Press.

Juvencus. *Evangeliorum Libri Quattuor.* Ed. Johann Heumer. 1891. CSEL 24. Vienna: Tempsky.

Junius 11. Ed. George Philip Krapp. 1931. *ASPR 1.* New York: Columbia University Press.

Junius 11, digital facsimile. *A Digital Facsimile of Oxford, Bodleian Library, MS. Junius 11.* Bernard James Muir. 2004. Oxford: Bodleian Library.

Mather, Cotton. 1689. *Souldiers Counselled and Comforted a Discourse Delivered unto Some Part of the Forces Engaged in the Just War of New-England Against the Northern & Eastern Indians, Sept. 1, 1689.* Boston, MA: Printed by Samuel Green.

Proba. *Cento Virgilianus.* Ed. C. Schenkl. 1888. CSEL 16.1. Vienna: F. Tempsky.

Pseudo-Cyprianus. *Heptateuchos.* Ed. R. Peiper. 1891. CSEL 23.1. Vienna: Tempsky.

The Paris Psalter and the Meters of Boethius. Ed. George Philip Krapp. 1932. ASPR V. New York: Columbia University.

Sedulius. Carmen paschale, Opus paschale, Epistulae. Ed. J. Huemer 1885 repr. 2007. CSEL 10. Vienna: Österreichische Akademie der Wissenschaften.

Sedulius. *Caelii Sedulii in quinque libros distributum Carmen Paschale.* Ed. F. Arévalo. 1794. *PL* 19, 533–754.

Vulgate Bible. *The Holy Bible. Douay Version: Translated From the Latin Vulgate.* Challoner. 1956. London: Catholic Truth Society. Revised from 1749–50.

William of Malmesbury. *The Deeds of the Bishops of England (Gesta Pontificum Anglorum).* Trans. David Preest. 2002. Woodbridge, Suffolk, UK: Boydell Press.

Secondary Scholarship

Anderson, E.R. 1987. "Style and Theme in the Old English *Daniel.*" *English Studies* 68: 1–23.

Anlezark, D. 2002. "Sceaf, Japheth and the Origins of the Anglo-Saxons." *ASE* 31: 13–46.

Astell, Ann W. 1989. "Holofernes's Head: *Tacen* and Teaching in the Old English *Judith.*" *ASE* 18: 117–33.

Badiou, Alain. 2003. *Saint Paul: the Foundation of Universalism.* Trans. Ray Brassier. Stanford, CA: Stanford University Press. [Originally published 1997. *Saint-Paul: la fondation de l'universalisme*. Paris: Presses universitaires de France.]

Bale, Anthony Paul. 2006. *The Jew in the Medieval Book: English Antisemitisms, 1350–1500*. Cambridge: Cambridge University Press.

Barnhouse, Rebecca, and Benjamin C. Withers. 2000. *The Old English Hexateuch: Aspects and Approaches*. Kalamazoo, MI: Medieval Institute Publications, Western Michigan University.

Barnes, Jonathan. 1982. "The Just War." In *The Cambridge History of Later Medieval Philosophy: From the Rediscovery of Aristotle to the Disintegration of Scholasticism, 1100–1600*. Eds. Norman Kretzmann, Anthony Kenny, and Jan Pinborg. Cambridge: Cambridge University Press, 771–84.

Barthes, Roland, *et al.* 1974. *Structural Analysis and Biblical Exegesis: Interpretational Essays*. Trans. Alfred M. Johnson Jr. Pittsburgh, PA: Pickwick Press.

Bendersky, J.W. 1983. *Carl Schmitt: Theorist for the Reich*. Princeton, NJ: Princeton University Press.

Bjork, R.E. 1980. "Oppressed Hebrews and the Song of *Azarias* in the Old English Daniel." *Studies in Philology* 77: 213–26.

Bloom, Harold. 1973. *The Anxiety of Influence: A Theory of Poetry*. New York: Oxford University Press.

———. 2011. *The Anatomy of Influence: Literature as a Way of Life*. New Haven, CT: Yale University Press.

Bosworth, Joseph, and T. Northcote Toller. 1882; rev. 1998. *An Anglo-Saxon Dictionary*, based on the Manuscript Collections of the Late Joseph Bosworth. Oxford: Clarendon Press.

Bradley, S.A.J. 1982. *Anglo-Saxon Poetry: An Anthology of Old English Poems in Prose Translation*. London: Dent.

Bredehoft, Thomas A. 2009. *Authors, Audiences, and Old English Verse*. Toronto, ON: University of Toronto Press.

Brine, Kevin R., Elena Ciletti, and Henrike Lähnemann. 2010. *The Sword of Judith: Judith Studies Across the Disciplines*. Cambridge: OpenBook Publishers.

Brown, George H. 1993. "The Meanings of *Interpres* in Aldhelm and Bede." In *Interpretation, Medieval and Modern*. Eds. Piero Boitani and Anna Torti, 43–64. Woodbridge: D.S. Brewer.

Brueggemann, Walter. 2006. "Scripture: Old Testament." In *The Blackwell Companion to Political Theology*. Eds. Peter Scott and William T. Cavanaugh, 7–20. Oxford: Blackwell.

Buber, Martin. 1998 (1946). *Moses: The Revelation and the Covenant*. Amnherst NY: Humanity Books.

Bullough, Donald A. 1966. *The Age of Charlemagne*. New York: Putnam.

————. 1972. "The Educational Tradition in England from Alfred to Ælfric: Teaching *utriusque linguae*." *Settimane di studio del Centro italiano di studi sull'alto Medioevo* 19: 453–94.

Caie, G.D. 1978. "The Old English *Daniel*: A Warning against Pride." *English Studies* 59: 1–9.

Campbell, Jackson J. 1971. "Schematic Technique in *Judith*." *English Literary History* 38: 155–72.

Canning, Joseph. 1996. *A History of Medieval Political Thought, 300–1450*. London: Routledge.

Cantor, Norman F. 1993. *The Civilization of the Middle Ages: A Completely Revised and Expanded Edition of Medieval History, the Life and Death of a Civilization*. New York: HarperCollins.

Carruthers, Mary J. 1990. *The Book of Memory: A Study of Memory in Medieval Culture*. Cambridge: Cambridge University Press.

————. 1998. *The Craft of Thought: Meditation, Rhetoric, and the Making of Images, 400–1200*. New York: Cambridge University Press.

Carruthers, Mary, and Jan M. Ziolkowski. 2002. *The Medieval Craft of Memory: An Anthology of Texts and Pictures*. Philadelphia, PA: University of Pennsylvania Press.

Chamberlain, David. 1975. "*Judith*: A Fragmentary and Political Poem." In *Anglo-Saxon Poetry: Essays in Appreciation*. Eds. Lewis E. Nicholson and Dolores Warwick Frese, 135–59. Notre Dame [Ind.]: University of Notre Dame Press.

Chaney, William A. 1970. *The Cult of Kingship in Anglo-Saxon England: The Transition from Paganism to Christianity*. Berkeley, CA: University of California Press.

Cherry, Conrad. 1971. *God's New Israel: Religious Interpretations of American Destiny*. Englewood Cliffs, NJ: Prentice-Hall.

Cheyfitz, Eric. 1991. *The Poetics of Imperialism: Translation and Colonization from the Tempest to Tarzan*. New York: Oxford University Press.

Ciletti, Elena and Henrike Lähnemann. 2010. "Judith in the Christian Tradition." In *The Sword of Judith: Judith Studies Across the Disciplines*. Eds. Kevin R. Brine, Elena Ciletti, and Henrike Lähnemann, 41–65. Cambridge: OpenBook Publishers.

Clemoes, P. 1985. "Language in Context: *Her* in the 890 *Anglo-Saxon Chronicle.*" *Leeds Studies in English* n.s. 16: 27–36.

Cohen, Adam S. Forthcoming. "King Edgar Leaping and Dancing Before the Lord." In *Imagining the Jew: Jewishness in Anglo-Saxon Literature and Culture*. Ed. Samantha Zacher. Toronto, ON: University of Toronto Press.

Cohen, J. 1999. *Living Letters of the Law: Ideas of the Jew in Medieval Christianity*. Berkeley, CA: University of California Press.

Cohen, Shaye J.D. 1999. *The Beginnings of Jewishness: Boundaries, Varieties, Uncertainties*. Berkeley, CA: University of California Press.

Coogan, Michael David, Marc Zvi Brettler, Carol A. Newsom, and Pheme Perkins. 2001. *The New Oxford Annotated Bible with the Apocryphal/ Deuterocanonical Books*. Oxford: Oxford University Press.

Cook, Albert S., ed. 1888. *Judith: An Old English Epic Fragment: Edited with Introduction, Translation, Complete Glossary*. Boston, MA: D.C. Heath and Company.

Cooper, Tracey-Anne. 2010. "Judith in Late Anglo-Saxon England." In *The Sword of Judith: Judith Studies Across the Disciplines*. Eds. Kevin R. Brine, Elena Ciletti, and Henrike Lähnemann, 169–96. Cambridge: OpenBook Publishers.

Copeland, Rita. 1991. *Rhetoric, Hermeneutics, and Translation in the Middle Ages: Academic Traditions and Vernacular Texts*. Cambridge: Cambridge University Press.

Cross, James, E. 1971. "Ethic of War in Old English." In *England Before the Conquest: Studies in Primary Sources Presented to Dorothy Whitelock*. Eds. Peter Clemoes and Kathleen Hughes, 269–82. Cambridge: University Press.

Curtius, Ernst Robert. 1963; repr. 1990. *European Literature and the Latin Middle Ages*. New York: Harper & Row.

Daniélou, Jean. 1960. *From Shadows to Reality: Studies in Biblical Typology of the Fathers*. London: Burns & Oates.

Day, Virginia. 1974. "The Influence of the Catechetical *Narratio* on Old English and Some Other Medieval Literature." *ASE* 3: 51–61.

de Jong, Mayke. 1995. "Old Law and New-Found Power: Hrabanus Maurus and the Old Testament." In *Centres of Learning: Learning and Location in Pre-Modern Europe and the Near East*. Eds. Jan Willem Drijvers and A. A. MacDonald. Leiden: E.J. Brill.

———. 2001. "Exegesis for an Empress." In *Medieval Transformations: Texts, Power, and Gifts in Context*. Eds. Esther Cohen and Mayke De Jong, 69–100. Leiden: Brill.

Delany, Sheila. 2002. *Chaucer and the Jews: Sources, Contexts, Meanings*. New York: Routledge.

de Lubac, Henri. 1998. *Medieval Exegesis: The Four Senses of Scripture*. 4 vols. Trans. Mark Sebanc. Grand Rapids, MI: W.B. Eerdmans Pub. Co. [Originally published 1972, *Marges de la philosophie*. Paris: Éditions de Minuit].

Dillinger, Johannes. 2008. *Terrorismus: wissen, was stimmt*. Freiburg: Herder.

Dinkova-Bruun, G. 2007. "Biblical Versifications from Late Antiquity to the Middle of the Thirteenth Century: History or Allegory?" In *Poetry and Exegesis in Premodern Latin Christianity: The Encounter between Classical and Christian Strategies of Interpretation*. Eds. Willemien Otten and Karla Pollmann, 315–42. Leiden: Brill.

Dodwell, C.R. 1982. *Anglo-Saxon Art: A New Perspective*. Ithaca, NY: Cornell University Press.

Dodwell, C.R., and Peter Clemoes. 1974. *The Old English Illustrated Hexateuch: British Museum Cotton Claudius B. IV*. EEMF 18. Copenhagen: Rosenkilde and Bagger.

Dronke, Peter. 1970. *Poetic Individuality in the Middle Ages: New Departures in Poetry, 1000–1150*. Oxford: Clarendon Press.

Dyzenhaus, D. 1997. *Legality and Legitimacy: Carl Schmitt, Hans Kelsen and Hermann Heller in Weimar*. Oxford: Oxford University Press.

Dyzenhaus, D. 2006. *The Constitution of Law: Legality in a Time of Emergency*. Cambridge: Cambridge University Press.

Earl, James W. 2002. "Christian Tradition in the Old English Exodus." In *The Poems of MS Junius 11: Basic Readings*. Ed. R.M. Liuzza, 137–72. New York: Routledge.

Estes, Heide. 2003. "Feasting with Holofernes: Digesting *Judith* in Anglo-Saxon England." *Exemplaria* 15: 325–50.

Foot, Sarah. 2002. "The Making of *Angelcynn*: English Identity before the Norman Conquest." In *Old English Literature*. Ed. R.M. Liuzza, 51–78. New Haven, CT: Yale University Press.

———. 2006. *Monastic Life in Anglo-Saxon England, c. 600–900*. Cambridge: Cambridge University Press.

Foucault, Michel, 2003. "What is an Author?" In *The Essential Foucault: Selections from Essential Works of Foucault, 1954–1984*. Eds. Paul Rabinow and Nikolas S. Rose, 377–91. New York: New Press.

Frank, Roberta. 1972. "Some Uses of Paronomasia in Old English Scriptural Verse." *Speculum* 47: 207–26.

———. 1987. "Did Anglo-Saxon Audiences Have a Skaldic Tooth?" *Scandinavian Studies* 59(3): 338–55.

———. 1988. "What Kind of Poetry Is *Exodus*?" In *Germania: Comparative Studies in the Old Germanic Languages and Literatures*. Eds. Daniel G. Calder and T. Craig Christy, 191–205, Wolfeboro, NH: D.S. Brewer.

Frantzen, Allen J. 1990. *Desire for Origins: New Language, Old English, and Teaching the Tradition*. New Brunswick, NJ: Rutgers University Press.

Frantzen, Allen J., and John D. Niles. 1997. *Anglo-Saxonism and the Construction of Social Identity*. Gainesville, FL: University Press of Florida.

Fredriksen, Paula. 2008. *Augustine and the Jews: A Christian Defense of Jews and Judaism*. New York: Doubleday.

Gabel, John B., and Charles B. Wheeler. 1986. *The Bible as Literature: An Introduction*. New York: Oxford University Press.

Gameson, Richard. 1993. "Anglo-Saxon Inscription at St. Mary's Church, Breamore, Hampshire." *Anglo-Saxon Studies in Archaeology and History* 6: 1–10.

Garrison, Mary. 2000. "The Franks as the New Israel?: Education for an Identity From Pippin to Charlemagne." *The Uses of the Past in the Early Middle Ages.* Eds. Yitzhak Hen and Matthew Innes, 114–61. Cambridge: Cambridge University Press.

Gatch, M. McC. 1975. "Noah's Raven in *Genesis A* and the Illustrated Old English Hexateuch." *Gesta* 14(2): 3–5.

Gera, Deborah Levine. 2010. "Shorter Medieval Hebrew Tales of Judith." In *The Sword of Judith: Judith Studies Across the Disciplines.* Eds. Brine Kevin R. Ciletti, Elena, and Henrike Lähnemann, 81–96. Cambridge: OpenBook Publishers.

Gilgen, Peter. 2012. *Lektüren der Erinnerung: Lessing, Hegel, Kant.* Munich: Wilhelm Fink.

Gilson, Étienne. 1955. *Les idées et les lettres.* Paris: J. Vrin.

———. "*De translation studii.*" Unpublished lecture (Pontifical Institute Collection, Archives of the University of St Michael's College, Toronto).

———. "Alcuin and the Flowering of Carolingian Learning." Unpublished lecture (Pontifical Institute Collection, Archives of the University of St Michael's College, Toronto).

Gneuss, Helmut. 1986. "King Alfred and the History of Anglo-Saxon Libraries." In *Modes of Interpretation in Old English Literature: Essays in Honour of Stanley B. Greenfield.* Eds. Phyllis Rugg Brown Ronan Crampton, Georgia, and Fred C. Robinson, 29–49. Toronto, ON: University of Toronto Press.

———. 2001. *Handlist of Anglo-Saxon Manuscripts: A List of Manuscripts and Manuscript Fragments Written or Owned in England up to 1100.* Tempe, AZ: Arizona Center for Medieval and Renaissance Studies.

Godden, Malcolm. 1991. "Biblical Literature: The Old Testament." In *The Cambridge Companion to Old English Literature.* Eds. Malcolm Godden and Michael Lapidge, 206–26. Cambridge: Cambridge University Press.

———. 2002. "Anglo-Saxons on the Mind." In *Old English Literature: Critical Essays.* Ed. R.M. Liuzza, 284–314. New Haven, CT: Yale University Press.

Goldschmidt, Adolf. 1939. "English Influence on Medieval Art of the Continent." In *Medieval Studies in Memory of A. Kingsley Porter,* 2 Vols. Ed. Wilhelm Reinhold Walter Koehler, 709–28. Cambridge: Harvard University Press.

Gottfried, P.E. 1990. *Carl Schmitt: Politics and Theory.* Westport, CT: Greenwood Press.

Green, Roger. 2006. *Latin Epics of the New Testament: Juvencus, Sedulius, Arator.* Oxford: Oxford University Press.

Greenfield, Stanley B. 1965. *A Critical History of Old English Literature.* New York: New York University Press.

Gumbrecht, Hans Ulrich. 2011. "Introduction: The Long Shadow of Political Theology." *Modern Language Notes* 126(Suppl.): 4–11.

Gustavo Guttiérez. 1974. *Theology of Liberation: Liberation and Faith.* Eds. and trans. Sister Caridad Inda and John Eagleson. London: Concilium.

Haines, Dorothy. 1999. "Unlocking *Exodus* 11. 516–532." *Journal of English and Germanic Philology* 98(4): 481–98.

Hall, J.R. 2002a. "The Old English Epic of Redemption: The Theological Unity of MS Junius 11." In *The Poems of MS Junius 11: Basic Readings.* Ed. R.M. Liuzza, 20–52. New York: Routledge.

Hall, J.R. 2002b. "The Old English Epic of Redemption: Twenty-Five-Year Retrospective." In *The Poems of MS Junius 11: Basic Readings.* Ed. R.M. Liuzza, 53–68. New York: Routledge.

Hanning, Robert W. 1966. *The Vision of History in Early Britain: From Gildas to Geoffrey of Monmouth.* New York: Columbia University Press.

———. 1977. *The Individual in Twelfth-Century Romance.* New Haven, CT: Yale University Press.

Harbus, A. 1994. "Nebuchadnezzar's Dreams in the Old English *Daniel.*" *English Studies* 75: 489–508.

Harper, John. 1991. *The Forms and Orders of Western Liturgy from the Tenth to the Eighteenth Century: A Historical Introduction and Guide for Students and Musicians.* Oxford: Clarendon Press.

Harris, Stephen J. 2003. *Race and Ethnicity in Anglo-Saxon Literature.* New York: Routledge.

Harrison, Carol. 1999. Entry for "Senses, Spiritual." In *Augustine Through the Ages: An Encyclopedia.* Eds. Allan Fitzgerald and John C. Cavadini, 767–68. Grand Rapids, MI: W.B. Eerdmans.

Hauer, Stanley R. 1983. "Thomas Jefferson and the Anglo-Saxon Language." *PMLA* 98: 879–98.

Head, Pauline E. 1997. *Representation and Design: Tracing a Hermeneutics of Old English Poetry.* Albany, NY: State University of New York Press.

Henry, Avril. 1987. *Biblia Pauperum: A Facsimile and Edition.* Ithaca, NY: Cornell University Press.

Hermann, John P. 1989. *Allegories of War: Language and Violence in Old English Poetry.* Ann Arbor, MI: University of Michigan Press.

Herzog, Reinhart. 1975. *Die Bibelepik der lateinischen Spätantike: Formgeschichte einer erbaulichen Gattung.* München: Fink.

Hill, Thomas D. 1976. "Hebrews, Israelites, and Wicked Jews: An Onomastic Crux in *Andreas* 161–67." *Traditio* 32: 358–61.

———. 1981. "Invocation of the Trinity and the Tradition of the Lorica in Old English Poetry." *Speculum* 56: 259–67.

Hoberman, Michael. 2011. *New Israel/New England: Jews and Puritans in Early America.* Amherst, MA: University of Massachusetts Press.

Hodgkin, R.H. 1935. *A History of the Anglo-Saxons*. Oxford: Clarendon Press.

Hofer, O. 1889. "Ober die Entstehung des ags. Gedichtes Daniel." *Anglia* 12: 158–204.

Hollerich, Michael. 2006. "Carl Schmitt." In *The Blackwell Companion to Political Theology*. Eds. Peter Scott and William T. Cavanaugh, 7–20. Oxford: Blackwell.

Holsinger, Bruce W. 2005. *The Premodern Condition: Medievalism and the Making of Theory*. Chicago, IL: University of Chicago Press.

———. 2007. "The Parable of Cædmon's *Hymn*: Liturgical Invention and Literary Tradition." *Journal of English and Germanic Philology* 106: 149–75.

Holthausen, F. 1905. "Zur Quellenkunde und Textkritik der altenglische *Exodus*." *Archiv* 115: 162–63.

Howe, Nicholas. 1989. *Migration and Mythmaking in Anglo-Saxon England*. New Haven, CT: Yale University Press.

Hughes, Richard T. 2003. *Myths America Lives By*. Urbana, IL: University of Illinois Press.

Huppé, Bernard Felix. 1959. *Doctrine and Poetry: Augustine's Influence on Old English Poetry*. Albany, NY: State University of New York.

Irving, Edward B., Jr. 1972. "New Notes on the Old English *Exodus*." *Anglia—Zeitschrift Für Englische Philologie* 90: 289–324.

Jameson, Fredric. 1981; repr. 2012. *The Political Unconscious: Narrative as a Socially Symbolic Act*. Ithaca, NY: Cornell University Press.

Isaacs, Neil David. 1968. *Structural Principles in Old English Poetry*. Knoxville, TN: University of Tennessee Press.

Jeauneau, Édouard. 1995. *Translatio studii = The Transmission of Learning: A Gilsonian Theme*. Toronto, ON: Pontifical Institute of Mediaeval Studies.

Julius, Anthony. 2010. *Trials of the Diaspora: A History of Anti-Semitism in England*. Oxford: Oxford University Press.

Karkov, Catherine E. 2001. *Text and Picture in Anglo-Saxon England: Narrative Strategies in the Junius 11 Manuscript*. Cambridge: Cambridge University Press.

———. 2004. *The Ruler Portraits of Anglo-Saxon England*. Woodbridge: Boydell Press.

Kennedy, E. 2004. *Constitutional Failure: Carl Schmitt in Weimar*. Durham: Duke University Press.

Kim, Susan. 1999. "Bloody Signs: Circumcision and Pregnancy in the Old English *Judith*." *Exemplaria* 11: 285–307.

Klein, Stacey. 1996. "Ælfric's Sources and His Gendered Audiences." *Essays in Medieval Studies* 13: 111–19.

Koch, Klaus. 1982. "Spätisraelitisches Geschichtsdenken am Beispiel des Buches Daniel." In *Apokalyptik*. Eds. Klaus Koch and Johann

Michael Schmidt. Darmstadt: Wissenschaftliche Buchgesellschaft, 276–310.

Krämer, Ulrike. 1996. *Translatio imperii et studii: zum Geschichts- und Kulturverständnis in der französischen Literatur des Mittelalters und der frühen Neuzeit.* Bonn: Romanistischer Verlag.

Kraemer, David Charles. 1996. *Reading the Rabbis: The Talmud as Literature.* New York: Oxford University Press.

Kruger, Steven F. 2006. *The Spectral Jew: Conversion and Embodiment in Medieval Europe.* Minneapolis, MN: University of Minnesota Press.

Lapidge, Michael. 1993. "Schools, Learning and Literature in Tenth-Century England." In his *Anglo-Latin Literature, 900–1066,* 1–48. London: Hambledon Press.

———. 1996. "Latin Learning in Ninth-Century England." In his *Anglo-Latin Literature, 600-899,* 409–39. London: Hambledon Press.

———. 2006a. "Versifying the Bible in the Middle Ages." In *The Text in the Community: Essays on Medieval Works, Manuscripts, Authors, and Readers.* Eds. Jill Mann and Maura Nolan. Notre Dame, IN: University of Notre Dame Press, 11–40.

———. 2006b. *The Anglo-Saxon Library.* Oxford: Oxford University Press.

Lavezzo, Katherine. Forthcoming. "Building Anti-Semitism in Bede." In *Imagining the Jew: Jewishness in Anglo-Saxon Literature and Culture.* Ed. Samantha Zacher. Toronto, ON: University of Toronto Press.

Leclercq, Jean. (1961) 2009. *The Love of Learning and the Desire for God: A Study of Monastic Culture.* Trans. Catharine Misrahi. New York: Fordham University Press.

Legg, L.G. Wickham. 1901. *English Coronation Records.* Westminster: A. Constable & Co.

Liuzza, R.M. 2002. *The Poems of MS Junius 11: Basic Readings.* New York: Routledge.

Marsden, Richard. 1995. *The Text of the Old Testament in Anglo-Saxon England.* Cambridge: Cambridge University Press.

Meier, H. 1998. *The Lesson of Carl Schmitt: Four Chapters on the Distinction between Political Theology and Political Philosophy.* Chicago, IL: University of Chicago Press.

Mellinkoff, Ruth. 1970. *The Horned Moses in Medieval Art and Thought.* California Studies in the History of Art, 14. Berkeley, CA: University of California Press.

Mendelson, Michael. 2000. "*Venter animi/distentio animi:* Memory and Temporality in Augustine's *Confessions.*" *Augustinian Studies* 31(2): 137–63.

Mendenhall, George E., and Gary A. Herion. 2001. *Ancient Israel's Faith and History: An Introduction to the Bible in Context.* Louisville: Westminster John Knox Press.

Menzer, Melinda J. "The Preface as Admonition: Ælfric's Preface to Genesis." 2000. In *The Old English Hexateuch: Aspects and Approaches*. Eds. Rebecca Barnhouse and Benjamin C. Withers, 15–39. Kalamazoo, MI: Medieval Institute Publications, Western Michigan University.

Meyvaert, Dom Paul. 1979. "Bede and the Church Paintings at Wearmouth/Jarrow." *ASE* 8: 63–77.

Minnis, Alastair J. 2010. *Medieval Theory of Authorship: Scholastic Literary Attitudes in the Later Middle Ages*. 2nd edition with new preface. Pennsylvania, PA: University of Pennsylvania Press (Originally published 1984, London: Scolar Press).

Mittman, Asa. Forthcoming. " 'In those days": Giants and the Giant Moses in the Old English Illustrated Hexateuch." In *Imagining the Jew: Jewishness in Anglo-Saxon Literature and Culture*. Ed. Samantha Zacher. Toronto, ON: University of Toronto Press.

Monagle, Clare. 2010. "A Sovereign Act of Negation: Schmitt's Political Theology and Its Ideal Medievalism." *Culture, Theory and Critique*. 51 (2): 115–27.

Moore, Carey A. 1985. *Judith: A New Translation with Introduction and Commentary*. The Anchor Bible. Garden City, NY: Doubleday.

Moore, Samuel. 1911. "On the Sources of the Old-English *Exodus.*" *Modern Philology* 9(1): 83–108.

Morey, James H. 2000. *Book and Verse: A Guide to Middle English Biblical Literature*. Urbana, IL: University of Illinois Press.

Morrish, Jennifer. 1986. "King Alfred's Letter as a Source on Learning in England in the Ninth Century." In *Studies in Earlier Old English Prose: Sixteen Original Contributions*. Ed. Paul E. Szarmach, 87–107. Albany, NY: State University of New York Press.

Nelson, Janet L. 1977. "Inauguration Rituals." In *Early Medieval Kingship*. Eds. P.H. Sawyer and I.N. Wood. Leeds: University of Leeds, 50–71.

——— 1986. *Politics and Ritual in Early Medieval Europe*. London: Hambledon Press.

Newman, Barbara. 2005. "What Did It Mean to Say 'I Saw'? The Clash between Theory and Practice in Medieval Visionary Culture." *Speculum* 80(1): 1–43.

Niditch, Susan. 1993. *War in the Hebrew Bible: A Study in the Ethics of Violence*. New York: Oxford University Press.

Nodes, Daniel Joseph. 1993. *Doctrine and Exegesis in Biblical Latin Poetry*. Leeds: F. Cairns.

O'Donovan, Oliver. 1996. *The Desire of the Nations: Rediscovering the Roots of Political Theology*. Cambridge: Cambridge University Press.

Okasha, Elisabeth. 1971. *Hand-List of Anglo-Saxon Non-Runic Inscriptions*. Cambridge: University Press.

Orchard, Andy. 1994. *The Poetic Art of Aldhelm*. CSASE 8. Cambridge: Cambridge University Press.

———. 1995. *Pride and Prodigies: Studies in the Monsters of the Beowulf-Manuscript*. Cambridge: D.S. Brewer.

———. 2003. *A Critical Companion to Beowulf*. Cambridge: D.S. Brewer.

———. 2009. "The *Dream of the Rood*: Cross-References." In *New Readings in the Vercelli Book*. Eds. Samantha Zacher and Andy Orchard, 225–53. Toronto, ON: University of Toronto Press.

O'Reilly, Jennifer. 2001. "The Library of Scripture – Views from Vivarium and Wearmouth-Jarrow." In *New Offerings, Ancient Treasures: Studies in Medieval Art for George Henderson*. Eds. Paul Binski and William Noel, 3–39. Thrupp, Stroud, Gloucestershire: Sutton Publishing Ltd.

Otzen, Benedikt. 2002. *Tobit and Judith*. Guides to Apocrypha and Pseudepigrapha. London: Sheffield Academic Press.

Overing, Gillian R. 1984. "Nebuchadnezzar's Conversion in the Old English Daniel: A Psychological Portrait." *Papers on Language & Literature* 20: 3–14.

Parkes, Malcolm B. 1999. "Reading, Copying, and Interpreting a Text in the Early Middle Ages." In *A History of Reading in the West*. Eds. Guglielmo Cavallo, Roger Chartier, and Lydia G. Cochrane, 90–102. Amherst, MA: University of Massachusetts Press.

Parks, Ward. 1987. "The Traditional Narrator and the 'I heard' Formulas in Old English Poetry." *ASE* 16: 45–66.

Pfaff, Richard William. 2009. *The Liturgy in Medieval England: A History*. Cambridge: Cambridge University Press.

Pratt, David. 2007. *The Political Thought of King Alfred the Great*. Cambridge: Cambridge University Press.

Raw, Barbara C. 1978. *The Art and Background of Old English Poetry*. London: E. Arnold.

———. 1984. "The Construction of Oxford, Bodleian Library, Junius 11." *ASE* 13: 187–207.

———. 1991. "Biblical Literature: The New Testament." In *The Cambridge Companion to Old English Literature*. Eds. Malcolm Godden and Michael Lapidge, 227–42. Cambridge: Cambridge University Press.

Remley, Paul G. 1996. *Old English Biblical Verse: Studies in Genesis, Exodus and Daniel*. CSASE 16. Cambridge: Cambridge University Press.

———. 2002. "*Daniel*: The Three Youths Fragment and the Transmission of Old English Verse." *ASE* 31: 81–140.

———. 2005. "Aldhelm as Old English Poet: Exodus, Asser and the Dicta Ælfredi." In *Latin Learning and English Lore: Studies in Anglo-Saxon Literature for Michael Lapidge*. Eds. Katherine O'Brien,

O'Keeffe, and Andy Orchard, 90–108. Toronto, ON: University of Toronto Press.

Riché, Pierre. 1976. *Education and Culture in the Barbarian West, Sixth through Eighth Centuries*. Columbia, SC: University of South Carolina Press.

Rist, John M. 1994. *Augustine: Ancient Thought Baptized*. Cambridge: Cambridge University Press.

Roberts, Michael John. 1985. *Biblical Epic and Rhetorical Paraphrase in Late Antiquity*. Liverpool: F. Cairns.

Russell, Frederick H. 1975. *The Just War in the Middle Ages*. Cambridge: Cambridge University Press.

Schapiro, Meyer. 1943. "The Image of the Disappearing Christ—the Ascension in English Art Around the Year 1000." *Gazette des Beaux-Artes* XXIII: 135–52.

Scheil, Andrew P. 2004. *The Footsteps of Israel: Understanding Jews in Anglo-Saxon England*. Ann Arbor, MI: University of Michigan Press.

Scheuerman, W.E. 1996. "Legal Indeterminacy and the Origins of Nazi Legal Thought: The Case of Carl Schmitt." *History of Political Thought* 17(4): 571–90.

———. 1999. Carl Schmitt. *The End of Law*. Lanham: Rowman & Littlefield.

———. 2006. "Carl Schmitt and the Road to Abu Ghraib." *Constellations* 13(1): 108–24.

Schmitt, Carl. 1985. *Political Theology: Four Chapters on the Concept of Sovereignty*. Trans. George Schwab with an introduction by Tracy B. Strong. Cambridge, MA: MIT Press [Originally published 1922. *Politische Theologie: Vier Kapitel zur Lehre von der Souveränität*. Munich: Duncker & Humblot] .

Schwab, G., 1989. *The Challenge of the Exception. An Introduction to the Political Ideas of Carl Schmitt between 1921 and 1936*. Westport, CT: Greenwood Press.

Scott, Peter, and William T. Cavanaugh. 2006. *The Blackwell Companion to Political Theology*. Oxford: Blackwell.

Shepherd, Geoffrey. 1966. "Scriptural Poetry." In *Continuations and Beginnings: Studies in Old English Literature*. Ed. Eric Gerald Stanley, 1–36. London: Nelson.

Snook, Ben. 2011. "Just War in Anglo-Saxon England: Transmission and Reception. In *War and Peace: Critical Issues in European Societies and Literature 800–1800*. Eds. Albrecht Classen and Nadia Margolis, 99–120. Berlin: De Gruyter.

Stanton, Robert. 2002. *The Culture of Translation in Anglo-Saxon England*. Cambridge: D.S. Brewer.

Steffens, Lincoln. 1926. *Moses in Red: The Revolt of Israel as a Typical Revolution*. Philadelphia, PA: Dorrance and Co.

Stock, Brian. 1996. *Augustine the Reader: Meditation, Self-knowledge, and the Ethics of Interpretation*. Cambridge, MA: Harvard University Press.

————. 2010. *Augustine's Inner Dialogue: The Philosophical Soliloquy in Late Antiquity*. Cambridge: Cambridge University Press.

Stocker, Margarita. 1998. *Judith: Sexual Warrior, Women and Power in Western Culture*. New Haven, CT: Yale University Press.

Szarmach, "Ælfric's Judith." 2012. In *Old English Literature and the Old Testament*. Eds. Michael Fox and Manish Sharma, 64–88. Toronto, ON: University of Toronto Press.

Tanner, M. 1993. *The Last Descendant of Aeneas: The Hapsburgs and the Mythic Image of the Emperor*. New Haven, CT: Yale University Press.

Taylor, Charles. 1989. *Sources of the Self: The Making of the Modern Identity*. Cambridge, MA: Harvard University Press.

Taylor, Paul Beekman. 1990. "The Old English Poetic Vocabulary of Beauty." In *New Readings on Women in Old English Literature*. Eds. Helen Damico and Alexandra Hennessey Olsen, 211–21. Bloomington, IN: Indiana University Press.

Tolkien, J.R.R., and Christopher Tolkien. 1984. *The Monsters and the Critics, and Other Essays*. Boston, MA: Houghton Mifflin.

Tolkien, J.R.R., and Joan Turville-Petre. 1981. The Old English *Exodus*. Oxford: Clarendon Press.

Vinx, Lars. "Carl Schmitt," *The Stanford Encyclopedia of Philosophy* (Fall 2010 Edition), Ed. Edward N. Zalta. http://plato.stanford.edu/archives/fall2010/entries/schmitt/

von Rad, Gerhard. 1991. *Holy War in Ancient Israel*. Trans. Marva J. Dawn. Grand Rapids, MI: W.B. Eerdmans Pub. Co. [Originally published 1951. *Der Heilige Krieg im alten Israel*. Zürich: Zwingli-Verlag.]

Waldron, Ronald. 1988. "Trevisa's Original Prefaces on Translation." In *Medieval English Studies Presented to George Kane*. Eds. George Kane, Edward Donald Kennedy, Ronald Waldron, and Joseph S. Wittig. 285–99. Wolfeboro, NH: D.S. Brewer.

Wallace-Hadrill, J.M. 1971. *Early Germanic Kingship in England and on the Continent*. The Ford Lectures Delivered in the University of Oxford in Hilary Term 1970. Oxford: Clarendon Press.

Walzer, Michael. 1985. *Exodus and Revolution*. New York: Basic Books.

————. 2006 (1977). *Just and Unjust Wars: A Moral Argument with Historical Illustrations*. New York: Basic Books.

Westrem, Scott D. 2001. *The Hereford Map: A Transcription and Translation of the Legends with Commentary*. Turnhout: Brepols.

Windass, Stanley. 1964. *Christianity versus Violence: A Social and Historical Study of War and Christianity*. London: Sheed and Ward.

Withers, Benjamin C. 1999. "Unfulfilled Promise: The Rubrics of the Old English Prose Genesis." *ASE* 28: 111–40.

————. 2007. *The Illustrated Old English Hexateuch, Cotton Claudius B.iv: The Frontier of Seeing and Reading in Anglo-Saxon England.* Toronto, ON: The British Library and University of Toronto Press.

Wogan-Browne, Jocelyn, Nicholas Watson, Andrew Taylor, and Ruth Evans. 1999. *The Idea of the Vernacular: An Anthology of Middle English Literary Theory, 1280–1520.* University Park, PA: Pennsylvania State University Press.

Wolin, R. 1992 "The Conservative Revolutionary Habitus and the Aesthetics of Horror." *Political Theory* 20(3): 424–47.

Wormald, Patrick. 1983. "Bede, The *Bretwaldas* and the Origins of the *Gens Anglorum.*" In *Ideal and Reality in Frankish and Anglo-Saxon Society: Studies Presented to J.M. Hadrill.* Ed. P. Wormald, 99–129. Oxford: Blackwell.

————. 1992. "The Venerable Bede and the 'Church of the English'." In *The English Religious Tradition and the Genius of Anglicanism.* Ed. G. Rowell, 13–32. Wantage: Ikon.

————. 1994. "*Engla Lond*: The Making of an Allegiance." *Journal of Historical Sociology* 7: 1–24.

————. 1995. "The Making of England." *History Today* February: 26–32.

————. 1999. *The Making of English Law: King Alfred to the Twelfth Century.* Oxford: Blackwell Publishers.

Wright, Charles D. 2002. "The Lion Standard in the Old English *Exodus,* Lines 362–446." In *The Poems of MS Junius 11: Basic Readings.* Ed. R.M Liuzza, 188–202. New York: Routledge.

————. "*Genesis A ad litteram.*" 2012. In *Old English Literature and the Old Testament.* Eds. Michael Fox and Manish Sharma, 121–71. Toronto, ON: University of Toronto Press.

Zacher, Samantha. 2010. "The Chosen Peoples: Spiritual Identities." In *The Oxford Handbook of Medieval English Literature.* Eds. Elaine Treharne and Greg Walker, 457–77. Oxford: Oxford University Press.

————. 2012a. "Multilingualism at the Court of King Æthelstan: Latin Praise Poetry and *The Battle of Brunanburh.*" In *Conceptualizing Multilingualism in England, 800–1250.* Ed. Elizabeth M. Tyler, 77–104. Turnhout: Brepols.

————. 2012b. "Circumscribing the Text: Writings on Circumcision in Anglo-Saxon England." In *Old English Literature and the Old Testament.* Eds. Michael Fox and Manish Sharma, 89–118. Toronto, ON: University of Toronto Press.

Scholars Index

Note: the letter 'n' followed by locators refers to note numbers

Subject Index

Note: the letter 'n' followed by locators refers to note numbers